UNFROZEN

"Ladey has produced a heart warming blend of reflections on her personal narrative and contemporary culture. It invites thought provoking self assessment and courageous realignment with principles that transcend yet give value to individual identity."

—Dr. Adrian Holdsworth,
Vice Principal,
The Faith Mission Bible College.

"Those who broker in hope….!

'Unfrozen' flows from the heart and life experience of someone who through receiving a revelation of Grace can with understanding and confidence be a carrier and communicator of it. It has been said ' hurt people, hurt people!' So, the circle of destruction, despair, remains unbroken. But 'healed people, heal people!' Hope breaks in, breaks through and breaks out.

This book in so many ways is autobiographical. It is however full of breathed, learned and revealed wisdom, truth and compassion. It faces 'the journey' that moves us to a place called 'forward'. Not by ignoring, disregarding or by living in denial to the key issues. But by being real, open, vulnerable and intentionally determined to be transformed by unconditional Love. It's not written out of some form of post-modern optimistic psychology but it's about 'the truth that sets you free. 'Unfrozen' indeed."

—Rev Canon Chris Bowater, Order of St. Leonard,
Pastor, Teacher, Author, Songwriter, Worship Leader, Founder
Worship Academy International.

UNFROZEN

How to Melt your Heart from Life's
Disappointment, Disillusionment
and Discouragement
by Opening the Door and
Stepping into God's Warming Light.

FOREWORD BY KARY OBERBRUNNER
Author of *Day Job to Dream Job, The Deeper Path* and *Your Secret Name*

Ladey Adey

ISBN: 1943526079
ISBN 13: 9781943526079

Publisher: Author Academy Elite
Powell, Ohio.

Unless otherwise indicated, Scripture quotations are from the HOLY BIBLE, NEW INTERNATIONAL VERSION. Copyright © 1973, 1978, 1984 by International Bible Society. Used by permission.

Cover Picture by Donna Drouin

Illustrations by Abbirose Adey

Font UNFROZEN: BLACK JACK is copyright ©2002 Typadelic Fonts. All rights reserved.

To protect the privacy of those who have shared their stories with the author, some details and names have been changed.

This publication was not authorised or endorsed by The Walt Disney Company. The author does not claim any association with the Company or any member of the Walt Disney family.

Ladey Adey writing by permission Pink Parties Events Co. Ltd.

DEDICATED TO

God, Jesus and Holy Spirit

To my darling husband Denis Peter
—with one N—
My one N—One and Only

My Special Ones—You are my world
Mum—Doris Shaw,
Abbirose and Candice

For my cheerers in Heaven
Nanna—Ethel Gertrude Mayes and,
My Dad—Robert (Robbie, Robin) Shaw
Frances Marchant
Bob Young

Life is either a great adventure or nothing.
HELEN KELLER

CONTENTS

When you believe in a thing, believe in it all the way,
implicitly and unquestionable.
WALT DISNEY

HOW TO RECOGNISE AN UNFROZEN HEART?

An Unfrozen Heart:
    Beats without fear of the Past,
    Preserves and lives with Hope,
    Nurtures Plans for its full potential.
An Unfrozen Heart:
    Knows Betrayal is short lived and fleeting,
    Believes it can Heal,
    Feels God's encompassing Protection.
An Unfrozen Heart:
    Protects itself from Fear by practicing Love,
    Loves life, itself and others,
    Sacrifices and offers itself, willing and proactively.
An Unfrozen Heart:
    Searches unceasingly for God,
    Creates life and recognises God's Creation in each and every form,
    Shares a Reunion with God.
An Unfrozen Heart:
    Thanks God for its life, and
    Beats without fear of the Past …

FOREWORD

When Ladey Adey told me the premise of her book, I was immediately captivated. I knew her book blended a powerful message with an irresistible metaphor. Sometimes that's exactly what we humans need—an ancient message written with a fresh perspective so we receive it with new ears, in hopes of creating new hearts.

Life has a way of creating disappointment, disillusionment and discouragement. Left unchecked, these stresses can freeze out our potential and sidelines us spiritually.

But reversing these effects is possible.

God knocks on the door of our hearts, inviting us to step into his warming light. By melting our hurts and heartaches he promises true healing.

Ladey shows us how to make friends with the fear of our past so we can move forward into our future with confidence. She reveals how we can integrate God's plans with our own dreams to achieve true potential. And finally, she invites us to reunite with our Creator so we can ignite a fire within our hearts.

By sharing her own journey and weaving metaphors from culture, Ladey reveals how to make sense of life. *UNFROZEN* opens the door and gives us the tools to move through adversity and accept the person God created us to be.

Kary Oberbrunner
CEO of Redeem the Day and Igniting Souls. Co-creator of
Author Academy Elite.
Author of *Day Job to Dream Job, The Deeper Path*, and
Your Secret Name

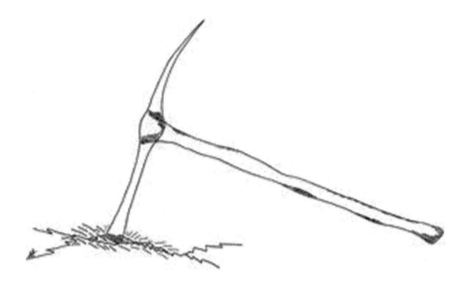

Breaking the Ice

BREAKING THE ICE

A blank piece of paper is God's way of
telling us how hard it is to be God.
SIDNEY SHELDON

Break the Ice

I hate being cold. Just thinking about being frozen gives me the 'heebie jeebies'! To avoid the cold, I dress in legions of layers. When building a snowman you will find me dressed like Sir Edmund Hillary ready for an Arctic expedition! What about you? Do you prefer warmth to chills? It is time to 'break the ice' and get to know one another. As I loathe the cold I am prepared to make any change necessary to become unfrozen, yet I had not appreciated that being frozen encompasses more than my physical body or environment. It envelops my mental, emotional and spiritual character.

How I dream of 'melting into life' and having a warm sunny personality. It has taken me years to sense the advantages of a temperate disposition rather than battle against life's experiences and the people in my life! My birth involved fighting to survive! My Mother contracted polio when she was pregnant and to this day cannot remember my birth. My human Father gave me life, twice. The first time through the obvious way and the second time by refusing to allow the doctor to perform an abortion. In 1961, medical professionals advised a termination, as they believed it would give my Mother a better chance of recovery. However, my Dad refused, he was determined that I would be born.

Another person determined that I should survive my birth was my Abba Father—God. The Psalmist says, 'For You created my inmost being; You knit me together in my mother's womb' (Psalm 139:13). The prophet Jeremiah wrote, 'that before He formed me in the womb He knew me, before I was born He set me apart' (Jeremiah 1:5). These are amazing truths. After my birth it took 8 weeks to be reunited with my Mother. She stayed in hospital while I was sent home into my Grandmother's care. My Mum, an incredible lady recovered with no obvious ill effects from polio!

Life In 3D

Life is experienced through a natural three dimensional, 3D, perspective but which dimension do you prefer to live in? Do you choose a life in 2D, constructing your life to be dulled, without risk, or limited to avoid painful experiences?

Or, do you choose a life in 4D hyped with excitement which threatens to overwhelm you? Perhaps your life appears to lurch between 2D and 4D. I offer a different 4D choice.

The cinema and DVD business has invested heavily in 3D technology. Watching films in 3D gives a deeper perspective and a more natural look and shape to the characters and their environment; this enhances the fantasy of third party experience. The cinematic industry is introducing other technologies to stimulate the senses; such as edible cinema—stimulating aroma, texture and taste—and even hot tub cinema! Yet, these sensations and colours of life are available to you each and every day. Total participation with a 3D view includes periods of learning experiences, both positive and negative. A positive 'full-on' life includes adverse times, albeit painfully enlightening. However, there is a choice to your reaction.

Do you struggle with life's challenges? You know, the 'stuff' that happens whether you like it or not? I have received my share of life's knocks, learning to recover from debilitating ill-health, heart-breaking bereavement, dissolved friendships, and painful misunderstandings. I am sure your life's journey has included distressing periods and experiences.

The majority of life challenges involve another 3D perspective, which I recognise as the 3Ds: Disappointment, Disillusionment and Discouragement. Each 'D' produces a cold war against yourself reducing you to an algid state of conflict, tension and battle. The overall effects of the 3Ds are freezing conditions in which a hardened or frozen heart needs to be restored. To have good health each 3D must be confronted for your well-being and to give you a fantastic life.

Is it helpful to consider your choices in handling the ups and downs of everyday life? I am thankful that God has shown me an open door inviting me to overcoming my own negative 3Ds. The epicentre of this offer features a change in mind-set, attitude, response to situations, by stepping into HIS warming light. God provides His love and protection—and by His Grace—heals the unhelpful 3D vision.

Enter Holy Spirit

I was christened as a baby but as an adult chose to be baptised. I was baptised on the same day as my Husband, 6th April 1996. I entered an advanced time of learning with Holy Spirit guiding me through several traumatic seasons of my life. I also learned of God's protection, Jesus' sacrifice and the love of the Trinity. It was not always an easy learning curve and I am aware of the continued work which God has to do in me (Philippians 1:6).

For me this journey starts anew every morning of my life, I wonder where you are on your journey? Are you aware of being struck by a 'frozen' attack? Do you have strategies to overcome your 3Ds? It is possible to face life challenges' with positivity, faith and trust in God, absorbing His warming power to melt your frozen heart.

Enter Disney's Frozen

What happens when a film touches and communicates with people at a deep level? Disney's film *Frozen*, has found its way into the hearts of children and adults across the globe. Do you love this film? I do! For me, its ending—the sacrifice—of one sister for another became the inspiration for writing this book. Disney's *Frozen* has become a phenomenal hit, breaking countless records including $millions at the global box office and the signature song 'Let it Go' (Lopez/Anderson-Lopez) certified 8 x Platinum. It will go down in modern history as a 'life changing' moment for thousands of people.

Do you remember what you were doing when:
- *Frozen* songs were played on the radio?
- You watched *Frozen* for the first time?
- You or your children wore the outfits and attended *Frozen* themed parties?
- Ministers and Church leaders gave sermons inspired by *Frozen*?
- You watched alternative videos on *You Tube* or commented about *Frozen* on Facebook and social media?

The list is never-ending. In 2015, according to Social Security Administration records (USA), the name Elsa entered the Top 500 for most popular girls names—the first time in 100 years. Is it any wonder that the short sequel is called *Frozen Fever*? We all need our temperatures taken!

Where was I when I watched Frozen for the first time? I was encountering all the 3Ds, consumed by disappointment, disillusionment and discouragement. My heart was in a bad shape from all perspectives: psychological, physical and emotional. My dream job had turned to ashes and I was off work for an imposed period of time. My youngest daughter, although an adult and in her 30s decided to cheer me up by playing the DVD. We laughed and cried, shared the moment and made up alternative lyrics to the song Let it Go as a tongue in cheek view of my work situation!

Becoming Unfrozen
Later the *Frozen* lyrics became mantras and the connection between the film's messages of: love, hope, self-worth, acceptance and ultimate sacrifice resonated with my beliefs. It made the Bible—containing God's

promises—meaningful to my situation. My dependence on the Bible and prayer time grew, proving God's love for me, His sacrificial covenant with me through Jesus' life, and validated God's protection on my life. As a consequence, *Unfrozen* was conceived and birthed.

This book's adventure is to explore, with you, life's frozen moments, which so readily mutate into disappointment, disillusionment and discouragement. I am mindful too of the freezing forces which trap you beneath the ice and numb your belief systems with glacial, piercing layers of lies.

I hope to thaw the deceptive, distorted and distracting lies of the 3Ds and melt your frozen heart into a deeper understanding of God.

Your heart is important to God, the heart is mentioned over 1,000 times in the Bible. One such time was when a king needed to be selected. God told Samuel, "People look at the outward appearance, but the LORD looks at the heart" (1 Samuel 16:7). He looks at your heart in the same way.

Your heart is the embodiment of mind and soul and not just a means to maintain life through pumping 7,570 litres of blood to 75 trillion cells around your body.

The Hebrew translation for heart refers to your will, feelings, intellect, understanding and awareness whereas the Greek translation for heart refers to thoughts and feelings of the mind. This makes sense of this warning, 'Above all else, guard your heart, for everything you do flows from it' (Proverbs 4:23).

This is why it is so important to guard your heart, protecting it in every way you can because your life flows from it. On this heart journey, I ask you to step into the warming light of God's love, promises and protection, to discover your life-flowing empowered heart.

Together, I would like to celebrate with you a new state of being—a natural, relaxed and life-giving reality—called UNFROZEN.

1st DIMENSION
DEFEATING DISAPPOINTMENT

1st Dimension

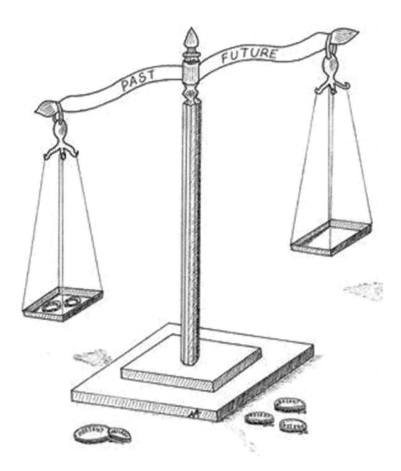

Your Persuasive Past

YOUR PERSUASIVE PAST

... for the Past is frozen and no longer flows ...
C S LEWIS

You have a Past

You have a past and I have a past. These are unique experiences yet they unite you with me, and everyone with one other. It might seem strange to start with the past and put creation of life towards the end of the book; however, your past is really the beginning. Even now, as you read this page once you put it down: to have a cup of tea, answer the phone, make a note in a journal or pray, a past memory has formed.

You were born with a past. I am not talking about reincarnation but you had nine months (give or take some weeks) in your mother's womb, growing, developing, feeling her emotions and being fed on her nutrients. You arrived into a world of expectations—your mother's, your father's, siblings', grandparents', adopted parents', foster parents'—whatever your birth story is— there were expectations from others. Perhaps this is why pregnancy is called 'expecting'!

Enter the World of Expectations

You can enter into a world of good or not so good expectations. The good expectations are for a healthy baby who will become its own person, living a full, active and happy life. Or they can be unrealistic expectations; parents wanting (expecting) a certain sex, anticipated plans for this baby to grow up and become like ... or be a ... etc. You can fill in the gaps. If the expectation is specific then there is a strong possibility of disappointment especially when the final outcome is outside your control. Disappointments are unfortunately, guaranteed in your life. A foregone conclusion when a parent attempts to enforce their expectations or their will on to a child. A vulnerable baby is expected to carry too much.

Ponder for a moment the baby born at Christmas over 2000 years ago. It is accepted that this baby was the Son of God, destined to produce miracles, change the world and bring new life—expectations given as prophecies but not enforced—Jesus chose to accept His past.

We all have expectations. The realistic ones have positive attributes when coupled with flexibility. If the plans are not realised, an alternative is accepted, appreciated and the expectation adjusted. Therefore, healthy expectations incorporate hope and excitement with a strong possibility of fulfilment. However, it necessitates guarding against expectation that robs you of joy through furtive looks into an uncertain future. As the popular idiom says, 'tomorrow never comes'—you are only allocated your 'now' or today. Tomorrow may hold your hope but do not give in to the 'lie' of tomorrow being today's total focus.

🝤   🝤   🝤

Jacky could not wait to meet the man of her dreams; he was all she could think about. She had already planned out her wedding to each exquisite detail. Who this person will be she does not know but she knows he is her future. She does not notice *Bruce*, the boy next door, who shyly watches and admires her. Jacky is too busy, looking out for 'Mr Right', wasting her 'today' moments by thinking only of her unrealistic 'rosy' future.

Unrealistic expectations have negative attributes when coupled with inflexibility. A wish or aspiration not realised within an imposed time frame produces an adverse response. Your emotions are engaged and respond first, with your behaviour exhibiting your keenly felt disappointment, regret and resentment. This internalised hurt causes further reactions within the body and spirit—which many think—spawns illness and ill health.

The Development of Disappointment

It is impossible to enjoy being disappointed with its associated feelings. It is a spirit of pain and regret, regardless of its cause. This could be over-expectation by yourself or others for a situation over which you have no control. The question is how do you cope with each disappointment and the corresponding dissenting emotions? A resilient way is to shrug it off, accept the new happening and enjoy the different result. Definitely easier said than done!

▲　　▲　　▲

Gary was a traditionalist and longed for a son. He wanted to play football with his son, teach him as his dad had taught him and his expectations for his unborn son was to see him performing in a premier league. It was all he talked about during the pregnancy. His wife gave birth to a daughter. Gary is bitterly disappointed and has to choose how he will cope with his disappointment.

Does he celebrate the birth of his daughter? Does he decide to learn to love her and give her the same teaching as he would a son? Does he decide to enjoy her feminine wiles—guaranteed to come his way—as the strong father-daughter bond naturally develops?

Or, does he choose to reject this possibility and become embittered? Choosing the latter, he will decry the fact that he has lost his family line, reject the baby, blame the mother, and lose out on joyous relationships. The 'lies' told by disappointment are triumphant as they poison Gary's mind and character. His corresponding actions fail those who love him.

Defining Disappointment

Disappointment is a sadness or displeasure caused by the non-fulfilment of your hopes, dreams, expectations or ideals. The key to overcoming disappointment is defined by your reaction—if it is allowed to 'win'—you suffer.

In Gary's story, he has some choices. He could 'miss out' on the Now by focusing dissatisfaction on the 'wrong' sex of his child. This toxic disappointment has the potential to 'take down' others as it is spread— emanating from a person like toxic rays—hurting those closest to them.

It is spread to Gary's daughter who will spend years trying to get her father's approval and try to win his love and approval. She will not realise that her father has frozen his heart against her. This is not her fault and she is not defined as a disappointment but is forced to live in the shadow of her father's unhealthy reaction to his own disappointment.

This becomes her past to carry as memories. She will remember a father who was distant and rejected her company, abilities and achievements. She will realise that she was never 'good enough' for her father as he hankered for an unachievable situation—that his daughter would be a son. Or, following the alternative choice by Gary, she will have a past featuring a father who shared his love of football with her, a father who was dependable and someone who built memories with her and who enjoyed her company. Don't forget Carl Jung's words, 'The greatest burden a child must bear is the unlived life of the parent'.

Frozen by the Past

Past hurts and wounds can inflict immense damage. Hurting people can become unwilling perpetrators. Unless healed, they carry this with them throughout their lives, passing it on to others via work scenarios, perfectionism in hobbies or within family interactions.

Devastating words are spoken out in disappointed anger or criticism with the underlying message being communicated, "I am disappointed in you". This provokes feelings of shame and powerlessness in the person receiving it. Even if it is said from a belief that the words are spoken for the other person's own good.

The reality is, it destroys the recipient's self-worth and confidence. It later produces traits in a person causing them to be over-sensitive to criticism, or quick to perceive criticism where none is intended. This produces defensiveness and stress inputting a negative trait which adversely affects a person's ability to trust, learn, explore, grow or try new things. Do you recognise these traits? Does this resonate with you? Is there a person in your life who reacts like this? Does this freeze out your healthy relationship?

Reactions to Past Hurts

Your reaction to harmful and limiting hurts from your past is motivated by self-protection. This evokes your intelligent instinct to survive and strengthen. The amazing thing about the body is its ability to memorise, recreate and re-assimilate situations. Using the imagination makes your mind a powerful collaborator or a dominant enemy.

Consequently, as you retell and remember a past incident, evoking full emotions of a past time, the body reacts as though it is happening in the now. It is a 'lie' as it is not really happening, but the mind has informed the body otherwise. Psychologically, you feel the same emotions as at the time it happened. Physiologically your muscles retain the past memory and respond accordingly, stimulating an identical response as though the actual incident is re-occurring.

This begins a cycle of continually repeating and 're-living' the past. A good memory strengthens the event, giving colour to your story. It can aid the body to produce adrenaline and skills to improve or develop expertise in an activity. You naturally want to pass good stories on, for others to learn from them, especially your children, 'tell your children about it in the years to come, and let your children tell their children. Pass the story down from generation to generation' (Joel 1:3).

A repeated unhealthy memory—without closure—causes needless hurt and revisits the damage again and again, resulting in stress and unhappiness.

The most striking example of a frozen life stemming from disappointment is shown in Charles Dickens' *Great Expectations.* Dickens' character, Miss Havisham.

▲   ▲   ▲

Miss Havisham suffers from a bitter disappointment in her past and never recovers. She chooses to remain paralysed by her past. She had fallen in love, but suffered an ultimate disappointment when she was jilted at the altar. Consequently, she chooses to live in her past including setting all the clocks in the house to 9:20, always wearing her wedding dress, leaving the wedding feast and wedding cake set out on the table. She and they decayed over the years—until her death in her mid-fifties. This formative day in her past was the filter through which Miss Havisham viewed all future relationships and incidents. She did not have the courage to move beyond her past, therefore lived out her life as a 'lie'.

'Lies' of Disappointment

Disappointment is laden with lies needing to be addressed. Another response (also a 'lie') to protect yourself against disappointment is to change high expectations into low expectations. Initially, this appears a good response but it is 'lie'. I have spoken with people who have chosen low expectations.

▲   ▲   ▲

My friend *Harry* and I were discussing expectations. Harry described how he protected himself against anticipated hurts saying, "I don't set myself high expectations as this way I can never be disappointed".

I was surprised as Harry is a very successful businessman. I responded with, "This way you can never be 'appointed' either".

My meaning here is that the appointment given by God is a designated position of trust, entrusted to you and in honour of your skills and potential. To lower expectations to a degree that stagnates or holds back experiences is a waste of opportunities. A healthier way to live life and fulfil individual potential is with large dreams, visions and positive ambition, because 'where there is no vision, the people perish' (Proverbs 29:18 NKJV). To empower His people God promises, 'He will pour out His spirit on all people. Sons and Daughters will prophesy, old men dream dreams and young men will see visions' (Joel 2:28, Acts 2:17). Is your past preventing you from having dreams and visions?

Reversing Disappointment

Are you allowing disappointments to have an adverse effect on your appointment and possible opportunities? Reversing the 'lies' of disappointment requires nurturing your mind-set regarding your confidence and values. It may mean acknowledging that your journey will contain both ups and downs—devastating though the 'downs' may be. Remember these words, 'there will also be many dark days and that most of what comes your way is smoke' (Ecclesiastes 11:8). Viewing your disappointment from a position of hindsight can be enlightening; you can see the 'smoke', situations which seemed worse at the time than they actually were. With the distance of time, it is possible to see how the past experience can be used for good and the betterment of your situation or character. Therefore, viewing your disappointment as a 'delight' is a skill to develop. It will exchange your position from belief in a frozen 'lie' to an informed and sharper unfrozen perspective.

᠕   ᠕   ᠕

My friend, *Nicola,* has a past, which includes a destroyed expectation and desperate disappointment. Her daughter-in-law endured the birth of a stillborn daughter. The grief of the family, the helplessness of a mother unable to 'make it better' for her beloved son and his wife was overwhelming. The bereavement for all the family has been painful and enduring. As she recalls the experience, she acknowledges the 'sadness' but rejoices in a child—carried for eight and a half months by her mother then carried to a small grave by her father. A child who will not be known in this world. Unfrozen, despite the disappointment, her love for her grandchildren and future grandchildren has not been diminished.

Do you live on Disappointment Island?

There are two islands in the world named *Disappointment* one an uninhabited island 180 miles south of New Zealand, home to colonies of white-capped Albatrosses. It is known as an island where survivors of shipwrecks (1866 and in 1907) waited many months to be rescued. The second is in a group of coral islands in French Polynesia, which have an arid climate and are sparsely populated.

Your body and your heart are not designed to live on a re-created island of disappointments, in isolation, without water, dusty and forever thirsty. You were created to be fertile, productive, spirited and lively. It is amazing to take on the concept that, 'long before he laid down earth's foundations, he had us in mind, had settled on us as the focus of his love, to be made whole and holy by his love' (Ephesians 1:4 The Message). I would like to discourage you from visiting these islands—figuratively speaking—or if you have done so then, like shipwrecked survivors, you need to be rescued.

Disappointed in Yourself?

A definition of self-harm is a deliberate action taken against oneself causing injury. This is usually thought of as a physical injury nevertheless it can also be psychological resulting in emotional abuse and damage. This is recognised when you speak self-deprecating 'lies' to yourself, such as, "I'm no good at ...", or "I can't do anything right", or "I must be a horrid person", or "I don't like myself".

Damaging self-talk can be from perceived failures such as a lopsided baked cake, receiving a low test or exam grades, not winning in a sport, game or competition or not obtaining a work promotion. Each one compounds a message to yourself that you are a disappointment. It is surprisingly easy to blame yourself, feel disappointed and to punish yourself.

After a while, continually reprimanding, belittling and undervaluing yourself turns into a self-fulfilling prophecy. You disallow yourself new experiences. My plea to you is to give yourself a break—accept that achieving your ambitions is a gradual progressive movement. Be gentle with your expectations.

It is necessary to discover your own workable strategies—to stop yourself in your tracks—challenging these thought patterns the moment a message of failure or self-doubt is received or spoken. Your mind is very susceptible to self-talk and, if you give yourself disparaging messages, you destroy possibilities in life. Unappreciative thoughts and actions are cruel, spiralling your thinking into failure mode. Can you recognise this 'lie'? Neuroscientists are making breakthroughs regarding your thinking affecting the chemicals and programming of your brain. It is possible to change these with some conscious effort and positively impact your mind, body and spirit.

One strategy is to listen to your stories. These are your thoughts, your words and self-talk when you are alone or how you talk about yourself to others. Your stories are very powerful; when you disrespect yourself, put yourself down or compare yourself to someone else (and in your mind they are better than you) this is perpetuating a negative spirit keeping you in your frozen past. The story you tell and repeat takes your past and present into your future. Your future—your choice—your story. To paraphrase the Proverb, 'how you think in your heart this is how you will behave' (Proverb 23:7). You can control your thoughts but it does take practice. You can be the author, internal writer of your thoughts—chapter and verse! Make it count and become your own hero or heroine.

Singer, Johnny Cash, said, 'You build on failure. You use it as a stepping-stone. Close the door on the past. You don't try to forget the mistakes, but you don't dwell on it. You don't let it have any of your energy, or any of your time, or any of your space'.

11

Johnny Cash had to learn this the hard way. What is your hard way? Are you currently in this place? Have you a strategy of hope and plans to transform your life and close the door on your disappointment? It is a good idea to make disappointment a thing of the past.

Disappointed in God?

Perhaps you feel disappointed in God? Have you prayed expecting your prayer to be answered and it has not materialised? Or perhaps you worry about world situations and ask God, "Why?" Why does God allow such dreadful things to take place?

A place where awfulness does not exist is in heaven and yet they do happen on earth. Disappointment in God can stem from many different circumstances. What are your expectations of God? Are they based upon His character and His promises or another theology?

God has his own timing; time is in His hands and not human hands. Even time itself is different for God, 'but do not forget this one thing, dear friends: With the Lord a day is like a thousand years, and a thousand years are like a day' (2 Peter 3:8). Hindsight is an element of our timing, an amazing science. It is only when you look back on your past is it possible to see patterns and perhaps be thankful that certain prayers were not granted!

We see life from a personal angle whereas God sees the bigger picture of your life. Are you setting God up for failure, with high expectations of Him? Is this the right way round or is it upside-down thinking? If God is not living up to your expectation, are you demanding or expecting Him to answer you from your limited perspective and understanding? After all, the prophet Isaiah reveals God's character, "my thoughts are nothing like your thoughts", says the Lord, and "My ways are far beyond anything you could imagine" (Isaiah 55:8 NLT).

God is your Abba Father and desires a conversation with you. If you have been disappointed—with Him—tell Him about it. Begin a discussion with Him, be open about your feelings and tell Him exactly what you think. It is a relationship He wants with you.

Closing the Door

Imagine closing a door. It puts a physical separation between two areas, provides privacy and containment. You can choose which side of door you stand and who you have on your side of the door. Activating this metaphor can serve to develop resilience towards your disappointment. There are two sides to disappointment, one which you accept and give in to, the other which you accept as part of life's learning and move on. You need to acknowledge the feelings but the step out of disappointment includes forward movement.

As humans it is natural to 'people-watch'. From birth the observations become internalised, expanding into an individual's learning. In this way you find a social-fit in the community and grow into the person you want to be. It might seem a surprise but people are watching you and wanting your success. These people are your champions—championing your happiness, achievements and God-given gifts. In times of disappointment, during the 'down-time' you are in most need of these champions in your life. They can uphold faith, healthy expectations and persistent belief in you, until the time you can receive it back and convict yourself of your own worth.

Your Champions

Who have been and are your champions? Have parents and teachers held this role for you? Children learn quickly and happily with positive coaching, encouragement and a belief that they can achieve. Through adult life, coaches and mentors, partners and friends can support, encourage and prayerfully intercede—'stand in the gap'—for you. Your minister or pastor who understands your circumstances can aid your recovery from disappointment by praying with and for you, encouraging the continuation of your dreams and aspirations. Do you find it easier to be a champion for others rather than for yourself?

The Past does not define You or Your Future

Your past can be very persuasive but being able to reassess and re-channel your past is a healthy way of moving beyond its pain. Unlike Miss

Havisham who chose to be defined by her past and consequently had no future, this does not have to be your situation. Past experiences, painful or pleasant do not define you as a person. They are circumstances which form your character as much or as little as you choose.

The contents of your present and future life are filtered through your past. How you filter or interpret this to decide on your reaction depends on numerous factors including: your personality, your relationship with people and your environment. The past is a strong influencer in your future choices but it does not mean that you need to allow what has happened in the past to limit you as a person or confine your current choice or behaviour.

Your past is important as it is your background to learn from and improve who you are as you seek to fulfil your true potential.

Victim or Victor?

It is my past experiences, good and bad, which I am bringing to the writing of this book. It has been my change of attitude, aided by Holy Spirit, which has enabled me to think through my reaction to past disappointments. I have examined my behaviour with questions such as: is this the best way for me to react? Is there another way to view this situation? Using these strategies to re-examine the truth of a situation, I can move forward, leaving behind the tyrannies of the past.

⋏　⋏　⋏

Kary Oberbrunner, author, writer of the foreword and whose encouragement and mentoring has shaped this book, has a past. Kary's past was one in which he self-harmed. Thankfully, he did not allow his past to define his future as he made new choices and no longer physically or emotionally hurts himself. Instead he used the understanding from his experience. He incorporated it positively by reviewing and renewing his self-esteem and confidence. He chose to become a victor. He built a different life by learning from his past and moving forward. Now, his ministry has reached out to thousands of people who suffer from self-harming and other low self-esteem issues. He supports them to make their own changes. He can show empathy as he has been there and got the T-shirt.

By moving from a position of victim Kary has claimed the victory God wants for him. He is now a Champion for himself and others.

Do you talk about your past? Do you call the experience 'your testimony', telling others your story with a before and after scenario? The 'after' is the story once God conversations have occurred. You have allowed God to speak to you, support you, help you and heal you. This has been true for me, working through hurtful situations, granting them permission to positively shape me has been an integral part of my past history.

My choice is to be thankful for my past and use it to grow into a healthy, enriching place, making informed decisions and reacting more slowly (with patience) to future circumstances. In George Orwell's story *1984* it is the Party who has complete political power rewriting the past to manipulate conformity of its subjects. Orwell says, 'He who controls the past controls the future. He who controls the present controls the past'.

Are you in control of your past or have you given away your control? It is time to put aside being a frozen victim with no choice or control and become a fiery victor.

Living in the Sunshine

Does your past abound with exceptional experiences? Have you enjoyed moments—highs—resulting in success and recognition? These are lovely, sunshine moments, 'oh, how sweet the light of day, And how wonderful to live in the sunshine! Even if you live a long time, don't take a single day for granted. Take delight in each light-filled hour' (Ecclesiastes 11:7 The Message).

Are you able to be thankful and stay humble in your fortunate experiences or is it too much? Does it overwhelm your present and the future? It is not possible to live constantly in the 'high'. Life contains peaks and troughs, and there comes a time when it ends, 'there is a time for everything, and a season for every activity under the heavens' (Ecclesiastes 3:1). Daniel also reminds us that it is God who is really in control, 'He changes times and seasons; He deposes kings and raises up others' (Daniel 2:21).

How do you feel about an end of a good experience? Is it a fearful place, robbing you of the joy of today's pleasure—the moment—or do you view it as the next movement forward to more prosperity and growth? Perhaps the hero worship and fêting by others which you've enjoyed ceases or someone else takes your position?

▲   ▲   ▲

Freddie was at the top of his game. He had 'made it'. He was in great demand as an actor and a comedian. Fame and fortune was at his fingertips. Overnight he was a success, welcomed on TV and the darling of every chat show host. He thought it would last forever. Overnight he was forgotten, he did not know how it happened, suddenly he was out of vogue. His agent could not get him 'gigs' or serious work. It was the days before reality TV, and game shows or advertising were not an option. From billboard face to anonymous, Freddie found the change painfully incomprehensible. He would work the Clubs but rather than be known as a 'has been' he became a recluse. He lived his remaining years alone.

Changes from high to low can give appearance of the present as dull and unexciting with the future bleak and empty by comparison. Anticipated and perceived disappointment of what is to come can precipitate a fear of the future. In the same way discontentment and refusal to move into a new season of life soon turns into a frozen stance. For some, this can even apply to a refusal to accept aging or disability, the changes which occur to the physical processes of the body.

The multi-facets of human life provide variations of past experiences and responses. It is healthy to share the good with others for these stories help you to understand your past, build bonds and develop relationships with people. These are recognised when you hear yourself saying phrases like "do you remember when?" and "let me tell you about …". This is a good and healthy approach.

Contrast these phrases with the unhealthy, unhelpful and dangerous conversations such as, "This always happens to me", or "People always let me down", or "I knew it was too good to last". These are self-deprecating 'lies'.

A Hankering for the Past

Do you want your future to be the same as your past? Allowing or predicting disappointment as inevitable is a sure way to be blinded to the possibility of a different future and keep you frozen in your past.

If your life is a heavy burden with relationships, health, work problems and difficulties, you may hanker for better times. However, no matter what is happening, to return to a past way is not the answer. Instead, talk to Jesus, bring your worries and burdens to Him, with a faith that you will survive and get through your current circumstances. In other words, to press through your dark, unhappy times and trust you will come out the other side. You may find some comfort in Psalm 23. Hold on to hope and there will be an end to this terrible period in your life—it is a temporary circumstance.

You need to keep moving forward even if it is only one a step at a time. It might be tempting to refuse to move forward, giving into the thought, 'better the devil I know'. Can you recognise this as another 'lie'? It is fear of the future and impatience to travel through your current circumstances which is at the base of these thoughts. It is God who I want to know better not the devil—who is easy to know! I know the door to recovery and letting go of the past is to move forward with Him.

Serial Slips into Past Disappointments

Serial slips into past disappointments can be evidenced in small things such as not being satisfied with a service or product, or believing that no one can do a certain job or piece of work as well as you. Granted things go wrong sometimes, a restaurant serves poor quality food or a product is faulty.

▲　　▲　　▲

> I could easily let my disappointment in various mishaps
> overcome my gratitude. I love stonework and tiles, majoring
> in mosaics, which ironically are broken tiles! However, I felt
> painfully disappointed when my floor tiles were accidently
> cracked. Each time I saw the broken tile I had a choice either
> to transport my thinking to the incident and the carelessness
> of the person who broke it, or I could choose to feel blessed
> in my possessions, and friends albeit with careless moments,
> in the knowledge that the tile could be replaced.

The danger in choosing to focus on the disappointment in your story is that you miss the other good points of the interaction. The temptation is then to repeat this complaint to all you meet for weeks or even years to come. Have you done this? I know I have. Think of the conversations you have missed because this story has taken precedence!

The good news is it can be changed as your self-awareness grows. For example, choosing to change your reaction to the person who cuts in or cuts you off while driving. Instead of raining down curses on the stupidity of their driving, send them off with blessings that they have not caused an accident and be thankful for your near miss. Notice the crash did NOT happen. Practice with the small irritants of everyday life then when a larger problem occurs you will be able to react in a more positive way. Practice today making it your life's strategy. Today, your 'Now', is the time to let it go.

Let it Go

In Disney's Frozen the feature song 'Let It Go' (Lopez/Anderson-Lopez) is sung by Idina Menzel portraying the character, Queen Elsa. The lyrics show Elsa's emotions and feelings about her childhood. It features her experience of combating the fear and shame of the power she has been born with. These negative emotions become the central focus of her life. Finally, she makes a decision to break free from living in this way.

What part of the past do you want to break free from? Your past IS in the past! This is a truism and a fact. Continually reliving the past, physically, emotionally, psychologically or spiritually harms you and hurts others. It is a wasteful use of your time and you need to find ways to think new thoughts and put the old ones behind you.

Your Helpful Healthy Past

The past is very powerful but it need not all be 'doom and gloom', it can be used for good. In therapy, stimulations of the past are encouraged, such as making memory books when working with the elderly, the bereaved, to celebrate a person or event or to pay tribute to others. Re-living history provides learning to avoid repeating the mistakes of the past. It has been used since Bible days, 'remember the days of old; consider the generations long past. Ask your father and he will tell you, your elders, and they will explain to you' (Deuteronomy 32:7).

As a country wars have been endured and it is healthy to hold memorial parades, anniversary services, celebrations and tributes. On Remembrance Day, the words "We will remember them" from Robert Laurence Binyon poem *For the Fallen* are repeated. These words are said every year across the world in memory of those who died in wars for our freedom. This past loss is revisited and commemorated to inform present and future generations. It creates events and time to give hope—moving forward, building and developing on experiences as a way of positively acknowledging the past.

Remembering the past with a healthy positive mind-set, disallowing the past from incorporating 'lies of disappointment' and persuading you otherwise, will give you a consistent, hopeful and fulfilled present and future

The one thing you cannot ask God to do is to change or rewrite your past. It is what it is and acceptance is a key element towards making peace with your past. Walter Scott said, 'Look back, and smile on perils past'. Remember the past is a backward subject and change can only occur with forward actions and motion.

Open the Door

1. **Notice** when you slip into past talk—it can feel like an unceasing stuck record. At first this can happen, unconsciously, especially when you are alone such as driving in a car, or walking for the bus, or consciously when you talk to friends, family and colleagues. Change your story by shining a light of positivity on to some part of it.

2. **Examine** when you take negative actions and question whether it is connected to a past experience.

3. **Pay attention and keep your eyes open.** Notice any change in your tone, words, mood, and tension in your body when you relive something from your past. When sharing your memories which do not produce feelings of peace and happiness to you and others— then stop repeating this story. If you are using it to show empathy to another, verbalise the recognition of your negative feelings and at the end say this is not my current reality.

4. **Jot down** in a private journal, the time of day and number of times when the negative repeating thoughts occur. Identify patterns: does this happen when you are alone or with a specific person or place etc.

5. **Consider** your feelings when anticipating events. What are your expectations or perceived disappointments? Question yourself as to the truth of such feelings.

6. **Choose** to change the way you view your past memories, be kind to yourself and take small steps at first. When you notice a repeating memory, change one word as it is repeated, add

some good things to alter the perception. Distract yourself with 'happier' memories.

7. **Let it go,** identify what you can 'let go' from your past? Which memories do not benefit your today and mire your tomorrows? Review, reflect and reshape. Choose steps, which move you forward, physically, emotionally or psychologically such as talking to God, a mentor, counsellor or a trusted friend.

8. **Celebrate** your past wins and good times, perhaps using photos and talking about happy times. Make a deal with yourself; if you retell a negative experience then retell six positive experiences to counter-balance. This will condition your mind and body with healthy memories.

9. **Acknowledge** your feelings of disappointment without turning them into an injury or becoming a victim.

10. **Listen** to your Self-Talk so that you are able to recognise your warning signs. What makes you begin to feel disappointed? Ask yourself if there is a way to move away from your unrealistic expectation/s.

11. **Write** down, as soon as you get up, names of three people, circumstances or things that you are thankful and grateful to have in your life. Make this your morning habit.

12. **Dream** with the full expectation that your ideas will be honed and fulfilled by God.

Step into God's Warming Light

Dear Lord,

Please help me to let go of my past disappointment and not allow it to rule my present. Help me to put my past behind me and to focus on today and today's 'wins'. Please make my attitude and view of life one that is thankful and buoyant despite the setbacks.

I pray that I will have good expectations for others, and myself, allowing my dreams to be uncrushable even when my expectations are not fulfilled. May I keep in balance the ups and downs of life and use the lessons of the past to improve my life and the lives of others. I want to be encouraged by You and to be able to defeat any disappointment.

Amen.

YOUR HUGGABLE HOPE

We must accept finite disappointment but never lose
infinite hope.
MARTIN LUTHER KING, JR

Claiming Your Hope

I am committed to guiding your move from the pain of your past into claiming your hope. It is not my purpose to trivialise anyone's past, especially if you have suffered through the actions of others. However, I would like to challenge you to take hold of your own healing for any emotional, psychological, physical, or spiritual wounds you may have. To gain an overflow of healing, hope is a vital element.

To claim your relief and release your appetite for life resides in hope. To unfreeze an object it is necessary to know its melting point. There has to be transference of energy for a solid to alter its structure and become a liquid. Certain objects need a high heat whilst others require a low heat for their molecule structure to change. This is the same principle in achieving a shift in your viewpoint towards a hurtful past memory.

To incorporate a melting point in a frozen heart, a hope filled charge is administered. This charge involves speed and a forward movement. Hope is like a current, a flowing energy transcending your hurts from the past. Hope is the belief in yourself and your experience functioning within a different light—His warming light. As you know nothing can travel faster than light and hope as a conductor propels you safely forward. Hope progresses you into new life by melting the coldness of your past.

Your Huggable Hope

Hope is Your Antidote

The heart carries your hope. The idiom 'he has given up all hope' is a precursor to death, as despair and hopelessness is not a sustainable state for survival. Hope is an unseen phenomenon similar to the ocean's current or an electrical current. This makes it a gargantuan task to identify or explain. How would you measure hope? Do you consider yourself a hopeful person? Does it seem that other people have more hope than you?

Hope is one of the antidotes or remedies for dealing with your problems and hurts of your past. Hope is in opposition to being frozen or encased in past memories. Whilst you remain hopeful and hope filled, the door of possibilities is opened. It is time to welcome forward movement and trust in the change for the better.

How would you explain your hope? Is it an emotion, a way of being, a thinking strategy or 'something more'? I believe it has to be the latter—this 'something more' is an innate wisdom that is inside you and me.

For instance, you may have medical knowledge or know a Doctor with training and expertise in how the body operates, but why is it that certain medical interventions or treatments work well for some people but not others? Likewise, you may have intelligence on the working of your psyche and know people who have made this subject a life-long study. Yet, it is interesting that help cannot be obtained until after an event when our psychological behaviour has manifested itself!

If you consider your emotional response to people and situations, through hindsight you can gain understanding into your reactions and if necessary, learn to control your emotions. Your knowledge of science, technology, and engineering, may vary from detailed understanding to a bare minimum. However, the latter does not prevent you from taking advantage of the phenomenal advances in everyday life. Each day, I switch on a light bulb, send emails and drive a car—I consume and use these technologies, often taking them for granted—without needing expert knowledge on how they work.

Where are you placed on your spiritual path and your all-important relationship with God? I would encourage you to feel the warmth of His light and increase your usage of His power. This climacteric relationship can grow and develop your hope in God. In this way there is 'surely a future hope for you, and your hope will not be cut off' (Proverb 23:18).

Is it possible to have 'something more' despite much remaining a mystery? Hope is our 'something more' and can be drawn upon for healing and health because 'our bodies are fearfully and wonderfully made' (Psalm 139:14). Your existence and your portion of hope are to be celebrated—albeit not fully understood.

Life without Hope

Is it possible to live without hope? Have you discovered Abraham Maslow's theory called *Hierarchy of Needs?* Maslow uses this to show what you need as a human from basic survival through to your healthiest point.

The foundation tier is the physiological level. As the tiers progress they become smaller; thus entering your advancement with choices such as free will and the ability to make choices. The pinnacle contains self-actualisation which includes love and belonging.

However, no matter how intelligent a person is, it is not possible to grow fully into the next tier unless the physiological stabilising basics (water, light, breathing, food, sleep etc) are in place. Where do you think hope would be placed? Do you see it as a one-dimensional triangle, or in deeper dimensions such as a pyramid?

This theory makes sense and life would continue even without hope if bodily functions were looked after. However, the mind's life is developed and happier as it moves up the tiers.

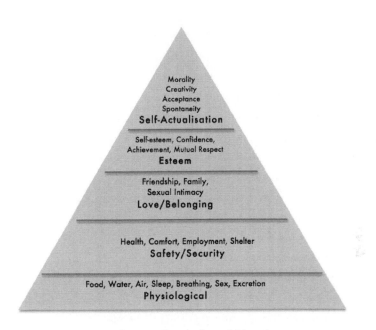

Maslow's Hierarchy of Need

The problem of life without hope is not to live having never experienced it, but the reaction that comes from knowing hope and then losing it. The loss of this hope is a death knell. This is a feature in disappointment— loss of hope. It has to be reclaimed and cultivated to sustain periods of disappointment.

▲   ▲   ▲

Lisa, who is in her 30s, has lived through a series of disappointments. Why is it that numerous bad things happen, seemingly one incident after another, to the nicest of people? Lisa felt that no sooner had she found her feet then she was pitched headfirst into another disaster. She was in a second abusive relationship, she suffered a nervous breakdown and her children were put up for adoption. When she felt that her hope had gone, despair set in and she tried to commit suicide.

Hopelessness is a recurring theme spoken by people who attempt or take their own lives. Suicide notes written describe their despair and loss of hope. The celebrated comedians *Robin Williams* and *Tony Hancock* were celebrated for bringing laughter and hope to many, yet tragically their personal lives were weighed down with disappointment and depression. Hancock's suicide note is reported to have said, 'Things just seemed to go too wrong too many times'. It would seem to me that both men lost their hope.

It is easy to understand why *Dante*, the Italian poet from the Middle Ages, in his work *Divine Comedy* inscribed on the entrance of Hell, 'All hope abandon, ye who enter in'. Despair and the inability to see past the current circumstance are symptomatic of a person without hope. However, Betsie ten Boom counteracted Dante's view. As Betsie lay dying in the Ravensbrück Concentration Camp she told her sister, Corrie, "There is no pit so deep that He (God) is not deeper still".

▲   ▲   ▲

Thomas' past included gambling, excessive debt and 'borrowing' money from his employer without permission (although he intended to pay it back). When the latter was discovered he was not charged with stealing but had to leave his job. Thomas felt hopeless. He had lost his job and felt he was now unemployable due to his poor decisions. His debts mounted up to such a point that he could not talk to anyone. The 'lies' of disappointment producing feelings of shame and stigma, overrode his hope and he contemplated what he saw as the only way out, his solution to the problem—suicide. His wife and mother of his three children were unaware of her husband's predicament, apart from thinking that her husband 'did not appear his usual self'.

I am thankful to report that both Lisa and Thomas found life-giving solutions, through supportive friends and professionals. Their testimonials include finding God in their darkest hour and hope returned to them—a teardrop at a time.

Misplaced Hope

I have experienced misplaced hope. This occurs when I will not listen or accept change as part of my life. With a perpetual glass half-full perspective, it takes me longer to realise that a situation has moved on and that I need to as well. I cling to a misplaced hope that a situation or friendship will recover, be retrieved and salvaged. At this point, I am in danger of staying stuck in an unrealistic past which perpetuates hurt.

For me, my wishful thinking tries to see things the way I am, not as they are. So I need to take the problem to God and try to see it through His eyes, then the disappointment lessens. This allows me to re-start and refocus. Renewed hope in the Lord enables me to overcome any predicament. Hope needs to be used with truth as its cornerstone. Are there any situations in which you misplace your hope?

Hope Is In Your DNA

Wikipedia cites hope as an attitude of mind, but this explanation does not satisfy me. I believe you are born with hope within your DNA as part of your unique and exclusive personality. Your DNA stores multitudes of biological information. Its biochemical structure shows that it is a nucleic acid composed of chains of nucleotides. It organises itself into long chromosome structures two of which determine whether you are male or female. According to a small DNA survey by Stanford University (Dec 2002), the Science Editor of The Telegraph (USA) the findings concluded that all human DNA is 99.9% the same as one another. This would leave a 0.1% uniqueness in making you—YOU. How incredible would it be that this minute % contains hope and the myriad unique characteristics that form you?

Where do you see hope fitting within your personality and physiological make-up? Could it sit alongside your DNA strands, with its deep characteristics incorporating your complex traits such as will power, faith, belief and confidence? Perhaps you could add more traits which you recognise and are often explored within the realms of medical science, the arts and literature. Their translucent nature is an antithesis to being 'controlled' or understood in their entirety by medical or scientific practice, yet they form your Soul. As it is written and the hope message repeated, 'Know that wisdom is sweet to your soul; if you find it, there is a future hope for you, and your hope will not be cut off' (Proverb 24:14).

God promises that you will not be separated or disconnected from Him and this can be your ultimate hope. This was told to Daniel and it still applies to you and me today, "The moment you began praying, a command was given. And now I (the angel Gabriel) am here to tell you what it was, for you are very precious to God" (Daniel 9:23 NLT). Hope is an integral part of your unparalleled personality. Hope means that you can accept and celebrate your unique individuality without listening to any unhelpful demand for change.

Measuring Hope
Hope is imperative for your soul, and manifested in the spirit, for you to grow and nourish your body. It has to be part of your relationship with others, from the deep family relationships to the intimate union between men and women, from the stirrings of friendship with strangers to contact with work colleagues and others.

Measuring the translucent nature of hope is like trying to hold water between your fingers or counting the number of crystals that form a snowflake. It might be possible to measure it by comparison, such as faith being as large as a mustard seed (one of Jesus points). Like faith, hope is impossible to see with the naked eye yet, 'for in this hope we were saved. Now hope that is seen is not hope. For who hopes for what he sees? But if we hope for what we do not see, we wait for it with patience' (Romans 8:24-25). From the perspective of this passage, hope can be viewed as a certainty—one of God's absolutes for the human condition. The writer of Hebrews aligns hope with faith "Now faith is confidence in what we hope for and assurance about what we do not see' (Hebrews 11:1).

Incredible feats can occur from the tiniest fractals of hope. When does your hope come to the fore? For me, it is when I need it most activated during extreme circumstances. In these times, my hope changes from translucent to apparent.

Hope Explored in Literature and Stories

Hope found its way into Disney's *Frozen* story through Princess Anna's persistence in believing in and searching for her Sister. The memory from her past—a happy, close relationship—anchored her and despite Elsa refusing to play or talk with her Anna continues to hope.

It was Anna's persistence which turns the story around. She believed in Elsa's loving character. She rejected doubts expressed by others. No one and nothing would persuade her to think otherwise because she knew her sister's true self. She is stalwart in her persistence hope in Elsa. Hope and persistence have an intrinsic relationship.

Disney's *Frozen* is loosely based on Han Christian Anderson's, *The Snow Queen*. In this story, it is the close friend, Gerda, who is persistent in her search for Kai. She believes in him, in his true original character—not the inflicted person he became following the piercing of his heart by a splinter of a troll's mirror. Gerda's hope is that Kai will return to being the friend she knew he was in his inner self. The story concludes with Gerda's warming tears falling on Kai and melting his frozen heart.

Hope is the heroine in Greek mythology, in the story of Prometheus and Zeus. In his anger Zeus created a box containing all manner of evil, including death, greed, hate, grief, illness, and betrayal. The metaphor for you is to see how easy it is for anger to overrule all other thoughts. In this instance, by taking revenge, a box of evil is created which brings harm to more than the one person it is aimed at!

Zeus gives Pandora the box as a wedding present but, because he loves her, he also warns against opening the box. Pandora's curiosity is so great that she ignores the instruction and opens the box. As an immediate consequence, evil is outpoured into the world. The one spirit which was not released until later was hope. I wonder why did Zeus put hope together with the other dreadful spirits?

The Roman playwright, Terence, in c159 BC coined the phrase, 'While there is life there is hope', which in turn influenced the poet Alexander Pope (1733) to write, 'Hope springs eternal in the human breast, Man never is, but always to be blest'. This shows hope to be a central part of your life and the basis of my claim for its healing power to release you from the 3Ds in your past.

The Melting Condition of Hope

Hope is a craving in your soul for change as your current situation is substandard or intolerable. What does your hope need to be encouraged and sustained? The answer is usage. To strengthen hope it can be coupled with your will. Your will to live, the will to carry on regardless of circumstance and the will to be the best you can be. The three life preservers are; faith, hope and love.

Hope is the remedy to unfreezing our hearts, guarding against the dread of the past and enabling a hope and renewed vision for the future. This can be for your own future, for your descendants, for society, or any cause close to your heart.

Living in hope is not about a false happiness—living in a protected bubble stripped from reality—but about a solid deep confidence from within. The knowledge that life is good and it will turn out okay, regardless of whatever your present day brings.

In the midst of evil, hope always remains and, where it flourishes makes an impression. The work of Dr Viktor Emil Frankl, a holocaust survivor, proves this point. Suffering all the indignities, evil and tragedies of a Jew captured and tortured in concentration camps under Hitler, he discovered insight to the meaning of life, with hope as the central figure. Upon release continued his studies in neurology and psychiatry. He later treated over 30,000 women with suicidal tendencies. Dr Frankl has brought renewed hope to many through his work. In his story, *Man's Search for Meaning* he proclaimed the final wisdom, 'Only love can endure and be man's highest aspiration'.

Has Your Hope Gone AWOL?

When hope is absent without leave (AWOL), or missing, you can expect problems to occur. It leads to negative reactions such as regret, remorse, self-reproach, bitterness, depression and despair. All of which permeate into freezing your heart.

My hope receives a dent when I cannot fix people's pain. It challenges me, as I am not meant to be a 'fixer upper' of other people's problems but a supportive witness to their life and being. I have to realise in the shock of people's stories, such as a marital breakdown or bereavement, that it is impossible to reverse their pain. My hope has to depend on God, as the healer of all things and through Him show my compassion, empathy and love. With His relationship, my hope regains its potency and true purpose.

You can establish hope through affirming conversations with people and receiving encouraging words. This can be drawn from others or with your own research.

Your spirit and mood can be lifted when you receive encouragement. This can be by a friend: contacting you, sending you a motivational quote, poem or book, texting you a Bible reference, or letting you know they are praying for you.

How gentle are you with yourself? Hope returns to your side when you put yourself into peaceful surroundings such as making use of the environment to re-energise and re-invigorate yourself. Inspire yourself by taking a trip to the seaside, countryside, mountains or forest. Engaging with nature, or watching birdlife, fish or animals boosts your hope genes as appreciation of creation's beauty and life penetrate your insular world. Natural surroundings that are 'bigger' than ourselves give opportunities for thankfulness and your soul can be filled with awe.

Are you a gregarious or an introspective person? If you have an outgoing personality then being with other people may stimulate you, whereas if you have a more reflective nature then being with one other person is often enough. Whichever is your character, you need other people to support you. Hope generation is difficult to sustain during long periods of isolation. Overall, hope is never far away, in times of stress and difficulty you might need to give it an extra boost.

Hope Shared

Hope involves practice—for keeping yourself healthy and for the prosperity of others. Consider the Disney's *Frozen* character, Olaf—who is the ultimate personification of huggable hope—he supports others and lightens the mood. Where do you find your huggable hope? If you know someone who appears full of hope speak with them and see how much can rub off on you. Conversely, when you are full of hope, share it with others who are 'down'.

Hope can be shared by your interest in another's life. You can ignite their hope by belief in their worth and it can be as little as sharing a smile to as large as financial support.

▲   ▲   ▲

Glyn and Jane Davies, live and work on the Mission field. In 1999 they set up a charity for children in Mombasa called *Education for Life*. To date they have given hope to thousands of children and families, feeding 750 children every day.

Glyn says, "I am often asked what difference does sponsoring a child make? When a child knows he or she has a meaning for someone else, his or her hope grows. It is more than just being given food to survive. Research has shown that sponsored children have 80% more chance of further education and employment, many go on to becoming Church and community leaders in their own right. Because they now have hope".

Levels of hope are being explored by academia with fascinating results from data taken from interviews with sponsored children in Third World Countries. Initial Studies by Joanna Chu and Laine Rutledge researched the impact of child sponsorship conducted studies in Uganda.

▲   ▲   ▲

A larger five-year research study was conducted with lead researcher Bruce Wydick. Bruce and his team interviewing 10,000 adults, including those who were, and were not sponsored as children and their families in six countries: Bolivia, Guatemala, India, Kenya, the Philippines and Uganda.
The Hope Hypothesis was investigated giving incredible insight in the impact of hope, its ability to change a child's prospects and potential. Hope instils aspirations in unexpected ways. It statistically proves the significant impact on educational outcomes for sponsored children. The full study appeared in the *Journal of Political Economy*, Bruce said, 'In short, it trains people to be givers instead of receivers'.

I wonder if this is a lesson from third world countries to those living in richer and more prosperous countries? Are we are in danger of losing our hope as our demands and expectations rise? Are we becoming nations of spoilt receivers—the selfish takers of the world—rather than philanthropic givers? Is this at the heart of so much disappointment? The 3Ds may be epidemic, yet I know the example Jesus gave in his Gospel message, "It is more blessed to give than to receive!"

Hope is for your survival, liberating your life and when shared this life's freedom is contagious.

The Dream Stealers

You can take encouragement from many inspiring people. *Bear Grylls* inspires me, not to go out and trek over extreme terrain but with his positivity and certainty of attitude.

▲   ▲   ▲

Bear is a modern day adventurer. He has travelled the world, survived the elements, and faced down his internal fears. He gives hope to many as he encourages others to take adventures. He pushes himself and others to live outside their comfort zones, experiencing unpredictable environments to know themselves better. He has many TV programmes depicting this.

It is no surprise, and great encouragement, that Bear is a role model for the Scout movement. He has taken on the tenure of Chief Scout giving hope of achievement to young adventurers. My favourite Bear message is his view on dream stealers. Bear says, "Life's full of lots of dream-stealers always telling you, you need to do something more sensible. I think it doesn't matter what your dream is, just fight the dream-stealers and hold onto it".

Check out who or what may be stealing your dreams. What or who is in your past which makes you withdraw rather than push forward and through? Use hope to make some change, and hold onto your dreams. Living in the past, with regret, kills your dreams.

You may have found past disappointments or regrets have robbed you of your dream? A future holding onto regret is an impossible combination as regret cancels out hope and acceptance. Whereas dreams and the hope of better things to come propel you forward and you feel alive. If you dream it you can achieve it, keep your hope alive and ask God for his help and timing—then go for it.

Finding Your Huggable Hope

Is your hope like a muscle needing regular exercise? If unused it becomes frozen, unworkable or forgotten? Treasure your hope as though it is a favourite tree; give it your time and loving attention from early sapling until it grows into maturity. It is your tree—so your choice—be an arborist and have some fun playing around with ideas. As an allegory, my tree of hope transformed from a weeping willow into a strong oak.

It is amazing how changeable your thoughts can be if you choose to let go of the damaging ones. Cognitive therapy is based on this principle. Actions follow thoughts and as the Bible says, 'for as he thinks in his heart, so is he' (Proverbs 23:7 NKJV). Where will your hopeful heart lead?

Hope, as a currency is meaningful when spent and applied to your present circumstance. Consider that using it today is like making an exchange of the past for the future. Where else can you find your huggable hope? A favourite song can stir hope and regain inspiration. A lyric resonates and reforms your thoughts, changes your attitude and propels you into positive action. I regained my positivity by listening to the beautiful lyrics written by Todd Albertson in the song 'Thank you for Today' on Phil Keaggy's album *Dream Again*. It is not only about being thankful but also about keeping in the present which is important.

When you recognise your hope, stop for a moment and acknowledge its presence within you. Be thankful for it; you may be surprised how much easier it is to cope with life's problems, challenges and issues. Cultivate a craving to furiously feel the internal affection of hope, its caress and tender kindness to yourself and others.

I am a touchy-feeling person and enjoy a timely hug. The warming light with a hug from God chases away the cold and unfreezes my heart. The Bible speaks of a hug being like honesty, 'An honest answer is like a warm hug' (Proverbs 24:26, the Message). A gorgeous metaphor is the picture of God gathering you to Him like a shepherd holding a lamb close to His heart; 'Like a shepherd, he will care for his flock, gathering the lambs in his arms, hugging them as he carries them' (Isaiah 40:11, The Message). You are God's precious lamb and He wants to hold you today. Depending on your preference of receiving either a 'bear hug' or a 'bunny hug', you can wrap a protective hug of hope around yourself or share a hug of hope with another person today.

Hope as the remedy to trauma caused by disappointment involves changing your script—decide to think about the memory in a different way—a more positive way. Give permission and allow the Spirit of hope to come out to play. Hug your hope; let it wrap itself around you. Make each of your todays matter. I can assure you, your life makes a difference in this world. Regardless of your circumstance, you have this 'now' moment—called 'today'.

Open the Door

1. **Check the size of your Seedpod**. What size of seedpod would you need to hold your portion of hope today? Pray that this can be increased and check its size each month.
2. **Identify** your dream stealers, notice what drains your hope, an activity or person, and reduce or break this interaction.
3. **Remember** a time when you were 'full of hope. How did this feel, who were you with and what were you doing at the time? Can this be repeated?
4. **Notice** how hope overcomes disappointment. How and when have you experienced these times?
5. **Choose** to inject hope into a difficult experience and see if you could render an unhelpful memory 'a thing of the past'.
6. **Note down** what hope means to you and when you are at your most hope-filled and hopeful.
7. **Ask** God what you need to do to ensure that using hope can become your strategy for positive change.
8. **Re-establish** hope in you life—list actions you can take to do this?
9. **Contact** a person you know who is 'full of hope' and ask them about their attitude and positivity.
10. **Read** a quotation or listen to a favourite song which uplifts your mood and puts you into a positive frame of mind.
11. **Share** the reason for your hope with someone else.
12. **Embrace** your hope today. Give your hope a hug and praise God for it and hug someone else (with permission).

Step into God's Warming Light

Dear Lord,

Please fill me with hope; let me see Jesus as my God of hope, and let Him determine my steps as a vital ingredient in my journey towards keeping my heart Unfrozen. May God, my Father ensure that my seed pod is filled with hope that can be used in times of need, defeating any disappointments that come my way. Protect me, Lord from the dream stealers and enable me to pursue my dreams. Father, I would like to invite your Holy Spirit into my life and may His power fill me with hope and joy so that I can be a blessing to many other people.

Amen.

Your Plans

YOUR PLANS

God does not have problems. Only plans.
CORRIE TEN BOOM

Your Number 1 Fan

Imagine having someone in your life who totally 'gets you'. A person, who sees your potential, knows your strengths and weaknesses, whose inexhaustible interest in your aptitude is profound and who are permanently on your side.

What would this person look like to you? Would he or she be a father or mother figure, or hold a privileged mentor position? This is the person who you cannot wait to tell them your ideas and news, whose advice you take immediately because their wisdom knows no bounds.

This person never criticises you but guides you intuitively, has your best interests at heart and fights for you. This person is your No 1 Fan, always on the sidelines cheering you on. They speak positivity into your heart and sometimes you wonder why they bother with you when their time could be spent somewhere else or on a more deserving person.

This is the person you gravitate towards to celebrate your successes or for comfort in moments of failure. They are the first person you reach out to for guidance or solace. Do you know this person? He is available to you—I call Him—God.

Your Unique Gifts, Abilities and Powers

Did you know that God knew you from your beginning? 'Before I formed you in the womb I knew you, before you were born I set you apart' (Jeremiah 1:5). You are special to God—He has enormous plans for you. These are 'plans to prosper you and not to harm you, plans to give you hope and a future' (Jeremiah 29:11b). The plans are not expectations because He always gives His children free will. The gift of free will provides you with a choice to go forward with these plans. Regardless of your choice, He knows you and has put in you specific capabilities—gifts. He gives these to you when you are conceived, as He does to every baby. No matter how old you are, it is time to recognise your gifts and abilities—dormant or alive—and put your trust in Him.

What powers were you born with? Were these skills, natural abilities and talents that you instinctively knew you had prior to trying them?

▲   ▲   ▲

I knew I would love typewriting, but at school in the 1970s, typewriting classes were only available to a selected few. I was not in that category. I remember standing outside the classroom door watching the other girls pounding away on their 'sit up and beg' typewriters. I had to wait until my technical college days to learn. I enjoyed all the 'drilling' lessons and was disappointed that I just missed out on learning to typing to long playing records! Achieving the highest certificate I went on to teach Typewriting Practice. This was prior to the arrival of computers and word processors.

Like most development of strengths and gifting, it was the beginning of my career in teaching and adult education. God has a way of gathering potential from an acorn of aptitude and transforming it into its maximum. I'm still waiting for flair in sewing to manifest!

Perhaps you have strengths which you are unsure of developing or your parents or teachers did not recognise? Perhaps there was a fear of following a new, untried direction and your flair was put into abeyance? It may be a simple matter that up until now the opportunity has not arisen.

What if these unique interests are your God-given gifts? He wants to see your gifts expanded, 'God has given each of you a gift from His great variety of spiritual gifts. Use them well to serve one another' (1 Peter 4:10 NLT).

Your Holy Spirit Compass

The plans He has for you to enjoy and realise your full potential arrive with an amazing advocate, friend and guide—Holy Spirit. Jesus promised, "I will ask the Father, and He will give you another advocate to help you and be with you forever, that is the Spirit of Truth" (John 14:16-17a).

Holy Spirit gives you His love as accurate as a compass, whispering directions for your safe and protected life-journey. Jesus introduces Holy Spirit as His representative who will teach you everything you need to orientate your life experiences with Him (John 14:26). As you navigate life's disappointments, Holy Spirit sees His role as your compass, indicating perfect positioning, and delineating destination to guide you into safe harbours. Holy Spirit is your consummate guide and friend.

His Plans for Your Potential

Your awesome God anticipates the unfolding of your uniqueness as you explore, develop and use your gifts and abilities He has equipped you with. To accept and acknowledge your special gifts is to enter into an 'I Can' mentality. You move into your potential although how you use them is your choice. His plans are that you use them for good. This is at the heart of His plan for you.

He also gives you permission to be adventurous in trying out these gifts and abilities until they can be honed and perfected. This can only happen with practice. You are expected to be courageous and adventurous. This explains why you often find yourself in similar testing situations—a bit like in the film *Groundhog Day* (Harold Ramis 1993)—repeating them until you understand the lesson. Experience is a great educator which includes having the confidence to make mistakes, forgive yourself and try again. Do you find that you can learn more from your mistakes than your successes? I do. However, it is having the ability to continue through the difficulties and disappointments, to advance using your God-given skills and strengths.

In the same way, it needs to be remembered that other people are also trying out their gifts—and not always getting it right! How can you encourage them? The Apostle Peter's reminder may help, 'Love covers a multitude of sins'. If you are practising your 'Love others' gift then you can spur others on, accepting their 'not quite perfected' offerings. This is an antidote to the 'lie' of criticism which the world perpetuates as constructive encouragement! I think the latter is tricky because it is dependent on the agenda of the one giving the criticism and how the one receiving it internalises any correction.

What is Your USP?

In the business world the acronym, USP stands for Unique Selling Point or Proposition. It refers to the originality of a product or service which a business needs in order to be distinctive from their competitors.

In God's world, He gives an alternative interpretation as 'He does not show favouritism' (Romans 2:11) there is no need for competitiveness with others. He does have a need for your uniqueness. This is why he has created you with your own exclusive USP—Unique Spirit-filled Personality. How are you using your uniqueness? It is with this USP that He has planned your potential, 'He knows the plans He has for you (Jeremiah 29:11a) and has given you everything you need to have a life fitting as one of His royal children.

To use or not to use your USP?

That is the question! It could be called your great commission to use your Unique Spirit-filled Personality to its full potential. The Holy Spirit assists you to implement your gifts and strengths. He teaches and reminds you how best to use your gifts. He helps you to be the person you were created to be. Like the disciples, you can receive and welcome the Holy Spirit into your life. This in turn makes your mission in life, your 'calling', and your attitude more than a little interesting. Holy Spirit as your personal friend guides you to step into God's plans for you—to fulfil your potential. In this way, you are never alone and when you incorporate the hope antidote into your life. It changes hurts of the past into a joyous journey.

God gave you free will so there is always the choice for you as to whether or not you step into your USP. It is never too late as Jesus shows in the parable of *The Workers in the Vineyard.* Jesus said: "So the last will be first, and the first will be last" (Matthew 20:1-16).

Living outside your USP seems a very uncomfortable place to be. It is hard to accept but there are people who will not accept your USP, and will attempt to change it to suit their agenda and will continue to misunderstand and misrepresent you. They simply do not 'get you' and have no intention of trying. It can be that your spirit-filled personality is at war with their non-spirit-filled personality. Have you met people like this? They have made the choice to live outside their USP, rejected God and His gifts, therefore, there is no love in them for you.

There may be people who believe themselves to be Christians but whose actions do not fit within God's USP for them. They give the appearance of believers but inside they are critical, unloving and unforgiving. They do not knowingly reject God but their actions hurt others and, in the end, they will hear the awful words from God, "Truly, I tell you, I do not know you" (Matthew 25:12). Can you imagine receiving a worst rejection?

In Disney's *Frozen* the character who exemplifies not using God's USP is *Prince Hans Westergård* of the Southern Isles. His character on first introduction appears handsome, kind, intelligent and charming. However, as the story later reveals, his ambition and greed is such that he lost any feeling of shame or remorse. Prince Hans chooses instead to use his life for his own purposes, for evil, ultimately bringing about his own downfall.

Obviously, Prince Hans is the antagonist, the villain of the film. However, it is possible that there is an adversary in your life. Is there someone, or something, which thwarts your achievements, names your disappointments and undermines your plans?

The Bible warns us of such people, 'their minds are full of darkness; they wander far from the life God gives because they have closed their minds and hardened their hearts against him' (Ephesians 4:18). This means you can expect that these people will use their lives for doing evil; they will be deliberate in hurting you and others. Further warnings against people who will harm you are: 'those who plan to deceive and trick us with lies so clever they sound like the truth, to ensure that people follow the wrong way'. Some translations call the 'tricks', this 'unprincipled cunning' (Ephesians 4:14 and John 17:11). Have you been unfortunate enough to meet people like this?

These are the kind of plans that the wicked make and are in great contrast to the plans that God has for you. Although there are times when on the surface it appears that your enemies are succeeding, God will turn it to good. This is shown in the story of Joseph, who was sold into slavery by his brothers, 'You intended to harm me, but God intended it for good to accomplish what is now being done, the saving of many lives' (Genesis 50:20). Despite the trials Joseph underwent, God was by his side and He is also by your side. His plans will use your many experiences, including any 3Ds, to benefit yourself and others

Living in His Plans

I have often been asked, "How do you (I) know His plans?" and indeed I have asked God the same question myself. I love this question and I believe God does too. It is not as mysterious or complicated as you may think. It is made problematic in that you may expect God to give you a 'blueprint' or a step-by-step manual. This is not His way.

I do not believe God is domineering but wants to see His loved ones stepping out in faith with their actions lining up with Scripture. Whilst it is unlikely you will be shown the whole of His plan, I encourage you to go forward a step at a time. If I had been shown the complete plan, I would have been faster than Jonah running in the opposite direction! Begin with one step into God's warming light; it can be a 'baby step' or a 'giant leap' towards this goal. Once more, it is your choice.

Upon occasion, God may ask you to 'wait' before He reveals the next step in the plan. My patience is as full as a pen with no ink, but I trust in Him so have to refill the pen with faith. The waiting gives further preparation time and strengthens my resolve. The art of delayed gratification enriches the journey. On any journey you need water and God is your living water. It is delightfully refreshing when tasted.

The plan begins with an invitation to you to follow Him. Do you remember how the apostles were recruited? Jesus saw them and simply said, "Come, follow me" (Matthew 4:19 and Mark 1:17). In his turn, the Apostle Peter advised, "So, friends, confirm God's invitation to you, his choice of you. Do not put it off; do it now. Do this, and you will have your life on a firm footing" (2 Peter 1:10-11). The invitation is repeated in a simpler form by the Apostle John, "Come" (Revelations 22:17). Is this invitation to follow Him of interest to you today? The invitation remains the same, "Come". I am glad that I have taken this step and coupled my plans with His. When you take this step you fill find that your plans are open to 'coincidences,' which believers term God-incidences.

Plans Warmed by His Light
God loves you so much that His warm light shines on you. This warmth is a soft penetration diffusing the heart's hard protective layers as gently as the sun brings a smile to your lips and persuades you to take off your jacket.

It might be that God demands your attention in a different way. Your dedicated plans have changed; you have suffered disappointments and in your desperation have turned towards Him.

▲ ▲ ▲

Gemma found alcohol comforting after her family and lover rejected her. To block out the lies of disappointment she began to drink a glass of vodka before going to bed. It became a regular habit and she soon needed more than one glass. It was not until she was on the hospital bed recovering from having her stomach pumped that she prayed to God for help. She found He was there at her side.

It may be that God chooses to communicate with you in a particular way. As your trust in Him develops this will become obvious, and direction from Him clear. It may be that you are unsure that you have heard from God. Keep asking Him for insight to be confident in what you think you have heard. It might have been an extreme measure but Gideon tested this by asking for a wool fleece to change its condition as a way of knowing if God's hand was true (Judges 6:36-38). Gideon did test once more but after that believed!

Clarification can come by another believer giving you a Bible reference or word, which verifies and confirms God's plan for you. It is spine tingling when this happens and they have no idea why they are giving you this message!

Other communications happen through the simple act of accepting Jesus into your life. God—your No 1 fan— knows your gifting, skills and interests and will speak to you in ways that makes the most sense to you. When Jesus invited the fishermen Simon (Peter), Andrew, James and John to follow Him it was not without a plan. He knew exactly how to use their USPs and communicate with them in terms they would understand. Their profession was in the fishing business, they were experts in fishing, boats and mending nets. Jesus used 'fishing for men' as a metaphor clearly speaking to their hearts about His plans for them. This is also an indication that nothing is wasted in God's plans.

Jesus spoke to the Samaritan women at the well. Jesus knew she understood the history of Jacob's Well and that the most refreshing water was drawn from the depth of the well rather than the surface. Consequently, in conversation He coached His message to her using her expertise, He spoke about 'thirst' and 'a well of water springing up to give eternal life' (John 4:6-42).

As a dyslexic child struggling to read, Holy Spirit guided me through a Ladybird book on *The Lord's Prayer*. Later I was guided into a deeper relationship with Him and he has spoken to me many times, via my interests in Newfoundland dogs, sign language and this writing. To answer the original question, "How do I know when God speaks to me?" I know, because a peace settles on me and life challenges are eased, I am reminded that I am not alone and He is here—in the situation or experience—with me. It can be the same for you.

Relaxing into His Plans

Are you comfortable or relaxed with His plans? Do you realise that God will not ask you to do anything unless He believes you are capable and have or will gain the skills necessary. He will provide the strength for your achievement.

🔺   🔺   🔺

I had the pleasure of working closely with the *Rev Dr Clifford Hill* for a number of years to establish the Family Matters Institute.

Clifford's past includes a mother who prayed for him, dedicating Clifford's life to the Lord and she supported him with God's plans for his life. Clifford has been an inspiration to many, serving God within his personality, finding success in academia with a communicating gift to pass this knowledge to others.

This has been done by writing numerous books, but more importantly by prophesying. God's plan for Clifford's life has been challenging. Clifford has been asked to bring pertinent but unpopular messages to Government officials and the clergy including the Archbishop of Canterbury (*Dr Rowan Williams*) regarding family life. His gifting has been to relate facts, research and truth in everyday language and he has offered it to those in authority, in terminology they can comprehend. Clifford has been faithful in stepping out in God's plans, waiting on God for finances, health and resources.

You too, can draw on Clifford's example, 'you are blessed when you are content with just who you are—no more, no less' (Matthew 5:5 The Message).

The planned journey is not without detours. The diversions include times of over-confidence or moments when prayer is not given priority. I battle in my choices whether to be guided by Holy Spirit or to decide in my own strength. Do you experience this? When the latter wins I am in trouble. I try to remember to prevents this hindrance by trusting in Him, I use this verse, 'trust in the Lord with all your heart, and do not lean on your own understanding. In all your ways acknowledge him, and he will make straight your paths' (Proverbs 3:5-6).

When Your Plans Go Awry

It is a fact of life, a 'lie' of disappointment that plans do go awry. They turn and change course without warning like the meandering bends in a river. I recently heard two stories from people whose life plans had undergone unexpected dramatic change.

Alic and Norma, are a couple who worked hard and were looking forward to retirement. They made plans to travel and see the parts of the world they had always dreamed of visiting. One night Norma suffered a stroke. Norma became ill, bedridden and need of care from a nursing home. They had to exchange their plans to visit foreign lands with the inside of a care home. Alic has used their travel money to fund her care and he visits her on a daily basis.

Karenza was a police officer who suffered a horrendous back injury forcing early retirement from the force. It has taken her 18 months to accept the disappointment in her life. She had to make significant changes and slowly began to take enjoyment in being at home. She had to reinvest her energies into new plans for a different way of life.

These are commonplace but courageous stories illustrating when life enforces change to your plans and dreams. *John Lennon* remarked, 'Life is what happens while you're making other plans'. It needs to be remembered that even when plans change, whether due to your decision or otherwise. God is good and will help you find the best—and bring out your best—in each and every situation.

You Too Can Walk on Water

There have been copious sermons and writings based on the story of Jesus and Peter walking on water (Matthew 14:22-34). I would like to view it from another perspective. What if Jesus plans for you to walk on water? Unlike Peter, it might not be a physical action but a metaphorical one.

When I picture the scene, I see Jesus with his arms outstretched towards Peter. It is rather like a baby trying

to walk for the first time, as he toddles towards his proud
Mum or Dad. The parent is facing the baby, encouraging,
calling the baby's name, with hands just out of reach but arms
ready to catch when the underdeveloped legs give way.

What would have happened if the other disciples had chosen not to be observers but to be participators? If they had been as courageous as Peter choosing to get out of the boat and walk on the water towards Jesus? That would have been a premier water-park ride! Peter was unique in that he was prepared to be the first to try. His reward was that God used him in His plans. He used Peter's skills and aptitudes to inaugurate the first church movement. Jesus said, "And I tell you that you are Peter, and on this rock I will build my church, and the gates of Hades will not overcome it" (Matthew 16:18).

Are you allowing God to show you His plans for you and then to take your first toddling steps? An acronym of PLANS could be *Personal Learning Actions Next Steps*. This frees you from making the plan itself paramount instead giving permission for its influence—like a map—to be a stepping-stone towards your growth.

Exciting Plans

Different cultures view plans and planning in different ways. In Western society, plans have become sacrosanct and immutable with any deviations warped into disrespect. A straitjacket of plans is regarded as beneficial, whereas other cultures find plans laughable, as life will happen as it is meant to happen, without attempts at controlling the unattainable. However, this can go to the extreme attitude of Mañana! God has an alternative view of plans because His way is not the same as any worldview. Take confidence, as an expression of God's steadfast love is the fulfilment of His purpose in you (Psalm 138:8).

When plans are supportive they incorporate flexibility. Plans can have the certainty of the end result whilst holding the ability to adapt to the way in which they unfold. This way you can douse disappointment putting out its harmful fire in the knowledge that it is not yet finished and the next corner needs to be turned. The exciting part is what is around that corner!

Consider your plans. Are you aware of which plans are like comforting rocks: a fortress providing safe landing places and which plans pitch you onto rocks in dangerous rushing waters? What if you were liberated from constricting opinions into believing this truth, "with man this is impossible, but with God all things are possible" (Matthew 19:26). Do you believe Jesus' words? How much more could you achieve? Where will your plans take you, if you discuss with Him what it is you want to do? You may find that He 'establishes your plans' (Proverbs 16:3).

Take a moment, do you consult with God before you make your plans or run to Him afterwards? This is Alphonsus Liguori's advice, 'Speak to Him often of your business, your plans, your troubles, your fears—of everything that concerns you'. I invite you to move forward into His plan today; trusting even when you have no clue to the end destination, and accompanied by your hope, believe in the strength of His love for you. Be brave. Take a step of faith—discard disappointment—choose instead to flourish with a warm unfrozen heart.

Open the Door

1. **Ask God** about your gifts and abilities and how He can be involved with your plans to maximise them.
2. **List your gifts**, write down in a special notebook, your gifting, strengths, powers and abilities. Can you recognise how they are being used? Do they in turn support others?
3. **Notice** the differences between your plans and the purposes of God. What are they? How are you going to bring them closer in alignment?
4. **Consider your planning.** Which areas do you like to plan in your life and why? Would you describe yourself as someone who wants a plan to be completed with no detours or as a 'free-spirit' who is hindered by planning? Can you be accepting of change? How do you keep your plans flexible, and out of reach from disappointment?

5. **Recognise** your potential and your uniqueness. How can you grow more to develop your USP—Unique Spirit-filled Potential? Is there a flair or idea, which has been in abeyance which now needs to be revealed? Is it time for this to be revealed?

6. **Respond well** to unexpected changes to your plans. How do you react when your plans have been unexpectantly changed or someone does not do what you expect or want? Does hindsight show that the change was for the better or is it too soon to say?

7. **Listen** to your communications with God. Notice the pattern of affirmation or otherwise you can receive when asking God to confirm a plan of action.

8. **Record** any messages or advice from others which you find helpful in making decisions and plans.

9. **Keep learning** using the acronym P.L.A.N.S. (Personal Learning Action Next Steps) what has been your learning and what actions will you take towards your next steps?

10. **Celebrate** your successes and achievements.

11. **Consult** your Number 1 Fan. How does it feel to know God is on your side? Has this made a difference in the way you see yourself or in what you do? Consult Him regularly on your plans.

12. **Practice walking on water**! Pray about a new approach, focus your eyes on Him and walk into His outstretched arms. Try it out today.

Step into God's Warming Light

Dear Lord,

I pray that my plans will always be heart-felt, moving forward and away from disappointment. Let my plans bring me new growth, embracing new beginnings and new developments. May I know how important my plans are to You, God and that You are my No 1 fan. You delight and bless me when my plans match Yours. May I be brave enough to walk on water towards your loving outstretched arms. Take away the fear of new experiences.

I pray that, as I journey through life, I will become immersed in your ways for my life, and I will remember to ask you for your view as I make my plans. May I lean on these words, 'may You give me the desire of my heart and make all my plans succeed' (Psalm 20:4). Please keep my heart safe and protect me from doing anything in my own strength.

Amen.

2nd DIMENSION
DISPELLING DISILLUSIONMENT

2nd Dimension

Your Betrayal

YOUR BETRAYAL, BEATEN!

"Judas, are you betraying the Son of Man with a kiss?"
JESUS CHRIST

Betrayal's Pain

If, like me, you have suffered a betrayal then you will recognise its force breathing powerlessness and bewilderment. This is due to the finality of the situation.

ᴧ   ᴧ   ᴧ

The searing pain of betrayal was released in one teardrop.
My head spun with shock as the outpouring of broken trust
was exposed. An obscure pinprick had widened into a
stinging gap. The relationship was no more and my hurting
began. The outrageous current of change carried itself along
its path nonchalant in imparting its chaos and destructive
discrimination to whoever stood in its way. Its offence
provoked a shattering of self, causing many teardrops to spill.

Betrayal arrives as a package labelled 'done-deal', consummated in secret without your input but with your name on it. There is no room to manoeuvre, no discussion, no time for defence or deliberation and it is without change.

▲   ▲   ▲

The betrayal pitched me forward into a foray of answering
accusations, reproaches and recriminations while I
was in a state of shock. It reeled me into a cycle of
self-examination, self-analysis and self-criticism. The
maxim, 'death and life are in the power of the tongue'
(Proverb 18:21) was proven—it felt like death.

The pain of betrayal bears the hallmarks of disillusionment at its most
vicious. The treachery is an acute injury—with chronic manifestations—
impossible to shrug off. It is a probability born of risking your involvement
in any relationship. You will have seen it in many scenarios such as
unfaithfulness or adultery, financial dishonesty, loss of friendship, through
deception, treason and trickery, undermining of status or position, and it
feels like a personal rejection.

Recognising Betrayal's 'Little signs'

It is easy to recognise the emblem of betrayal. A friend refuses to speak to
you. Without recourse to your defence, their perceived hurt takes revenge
by reverting to the playground actions of withdrawn communication or
without warning launches a verbal attack. The 'lies' of disillusionment
are as inconspicuous as a magician's sleight of hand. Realisation of the
situation brings on shock and then unanswerable self-questioning occurs:
"How can they believe this of me?" and "I thought they knew me?" You
are taken aback in the abrupt awareness that your perception of their
understanding of your character is false. The Psalmist had the same
experience, 'even my best friend, the one I trusted completely, the one
who shared my food, has turned against me' (Psalm 41:9 NLT).

   In each scenario, mis-communication and non-communication are
precursors to accusation. Your calls are not received, emails remain
unanswered and you are refused access to someone who hitherto had an
open door policy. The circles of influence which had been your privilege

are now cut off. You are unwelcome as an ex partner at a party. In a cherished partner relationship, love and intimacy is withheld, silence is endured and separation initiated.

Enter Disillusionment

You hold perceptions of your own reality—we all do. This comprises finding your place in the world: what is important to you, your value set, how you want to be treated and how you treat others. The wound of disillusionment is delivered in a cruel blow shattering this reality. Your state or condition changes as what you once believed as a truth now becomes obsolete. It can be slow awareness or a sudden shock—your life has changed—recovery and readjustment will take time.

A crater of disillusionment is fashioned out of the enormity of a betrayal. It may knock your core belief system or at the very least crumple the edges. How you cope with the situation depends on the readjustment to your new reality. Do you have the inner strength to rebuild, restore or rebirth your existence and authentic self?

From the school playground, the sports field, academia, work situations and relational matters at some point you will experience disillusionment. One of the first experiences can be when your mother and father cease to be mini all-knowing gods, their human frailties no longer concealed. This can be a shock but, growing up, the disillusionment can be tempered with understanding, acceptance and enjoyment of seeing your parents as individuals and in a fresh light.

More damaging betrayals may have their origins in competitiveness or may stem from jealousy or envy. These emotions gain in magnitude, sitting at the high end on the Richter scale of disillusionment.

Two Steps of Betrayal

The first step of a betrayal is a person disliking your values and actions with a desire to thwart and prevent your plans from moving forward. They are unable to share in your potential as they have an alternative vested interest, centred on themselves and their viewpoint.

The second step is a person's decision to betray you. A process follows in which they spend time:

1) Building a case against you.
2) Selecting associates to expose their information, and
3) Selecting the timing to pour out their propaganda against you.

They are cowards because they cannot operate alone, take responsibility for their own issues or communicate in an open and fair manner.

It is a hidden, furtive 'partnered' activity and they will align themselves with at least one other person with whom they can cast aspersions on your ability, actions or character. They seek to persuade them of your 'wrong-doing'. They will choose a person with influence, power and standing in order to use their assistance in bringing you down. It might well be that, 'their throat is an open grave; they use their tongues to deceive. The venom of asps is under their lips' (Romans 3:13 NLT) the Apostle Paul had also experienced it.

All of a sudden you find yourself in a situation where out of the mouths of people you have trusted comes cursing and bitterness. I am perplexed at how much effort is expended and the number of lies told in efforts to discredit and destroy another person. It is heinous when done under the semblance of friendship or as an excuse for a 'superior' purpose.

Forewarning of Betrayal

If you examine scripture, you will see that it was not a surprise to Jesus that He would be betrayed; it had been prophesied (Zechariah 11:12). Jesus shared this prediction with his disciples during the Last Supper. He had recognised the 'little signs'. Jesus knew one of His disciples would betray Him and was troubled in spirit (John 13:21). I wonder if Jesus knew who it would be because He knew Judas' character? When confronted Judas denied it although he had already put his plans into action.

Those who have gone through the agony of being betrayed by a friend or colleague can in hindsight see the 'little signs' which they had overlooked. Has this been the same in your situation?

In Disney's *Frozen* Prince Hans gives clues to his real nature. He reveals that he is the youngest of 12 brothers and speaks of his ambition to 'make his mark'. His thirst for power is such that his lies include treason as he declares the death of Princess Anna and names her sister, the Queen, as the killer. His reasoning is justified as being 'in the best interests of the Kingdom and its people'. Practising this distorted truth, he goes undercover building a nest of lies for the sisters' betrayal.

Does your 'world perception' mean you do not pick up the 'little signs'? Such as noticing small problems within a relationship, or prevent you from considering the reaction to your decision from another person's perspective? Perhaps not wanting to take off your 'rose-tinted' spectacles and therefore allowing an opening for attack that then leads to your betrayal and disillusionment?

In the Western world, instantaneity is now the expected response for all interactions. This fast pace of life involves pressure to do more, resulting in a busyness with insufficient time for reflection or the opportunity to put yourself in the other person's shoes. In general, this is acknowledged yet ignored and punished with society's quest for blame and finger pointing when things go wrong.

In a 'time-poor, cost-cutting and stress-building' culture, a lot is left to assumption. It is easy to assume that other people will automatically understand your motives and good intentions. This circumvents explaining the whys and wherefores behind your reasoned action—it is a train wreck ready to happen. It manifests itself with an email sent rather than a meeting scheduled; a text messaged rather than a telephone call made. I wonder if these are the 'little signs' which if noticed could prevent the uncertainty that allowed mistrust to prosper? The build up of these small associations can result in a person feeling that they have been taken for granted, overlooked or unimportant (despite your best efforts) leading to betrayal as that person's only recourse? Once the process is in motion, pain is as unavoidable as a gossiper being silent!

Betrayal's Chaotic Ripple Effect

Betrayal is a decision to 'kill' another person's USP, their reputation, dream, or ability to continue in a particular role. The intent is to forever change a situation for the betrayer's own elevation, personal advantage and self-agenda.

Betrayal cannot operate alone and is a beacon attracting opinion and judgement from others. It sets off a ripple effect—smaller betrayals by others follow. The knives are out and people begin to watch their own backs as they are sucked into a shocking environment beyond their control. This could be why the Apostle Peter and the other disciples denied Jesus and ran away as they found their situation untenable.

The tipping point of one person's betrayal affects many people, rather like the arcade game where one penny dropped causes many others to fall. It is as though battle lines are drawn and sides have to be taken. There is little time to think before reacting and there is pressure to take sides. It seems as though it is easier to think the worst of someone than the best. Others become fearful and seek to disassociate themselves from the situation.

▲　▲　▲

Elspeth remembered the day she was called into the meeting.
Her day had started normally enough: a day much like
any other day, chatting with a couple of colleagues about
the journey to work and the weather (they are Brits!). She
had ignored the chit-chat about her co-worker's recent
visit to a local nightclub and had got straight on to her
computer to check the email and put the finishing touches
to the papers for the scheduled meeting with her boss.

She respected and liked her boss and enjoyed working with him. They would have a laugh whilst doing the necessary work, and her role as PA was fulfilling. Lately, there had been some strain in the workplace and she had been supportive to her Boss and, as a result, had been offered more responsibility within her role.

She walked unsuspectingly into the meeting, her boss was nowhere to be seen but another director was there. She was asked all kinds of questions about her boss. Some seem strangely phrased like, "What was his emotional state?" and "How did she think he related with other staff or stakeholders"? She could not really see how her opinion was relevant but answered as best she could, aware that her own job may now be on the line. Her responses were taped and put on record, she felt uncomfortable and was now ambiguous about her boss' abilities. She doubts she would see him again.

Disassociating yourself from a situation may be necessary for reasons of survival (like Peter's denial of Christ) to keep a life or a job. It can be that in the 'lie' of disillusionment a host of minor grievances are encouraged to be aired. King David experienced this, he complained and moaned about the number of grudges which are held against him (Psalm 55). In a similar way, a century later the Apostle Paul identifies the 'gossipers who were filled with envy, greed and maliciousness' (Romans 1:29-32). You may have observed this when others add their uninvited and biased views to a situation?

In this world, deception has the opportunity to manifest itself wherever people group together. Allegations are made and bystanders become fearful thinking the worst of the accused and at first, the accuser becomes the hero! Have you witnessed this or, worse still, has this happened to you?

The Betrayer

Who is the betrayer? It is often a friend or colleague who has inside knowledge, a special closeness with you and therefore can 'twist' your words, your motivations, or your character in order for them to look good and for you to look bad.

As a conscious action, this is evil manifesting itself. As an unconscious action, it is an insidious iniquity buried in the betrayer's character as their need for recognition and approval comes to the forefront. The betrayer's ego cannot allow them to back down once they have opened this particular door. Therefore, they look for further examples and evidence to support their reasoning, allegations and to prove their argument. As they are using information gained from a privileged relationship with you—whether you are forewarned or not—it feels like a personal onslaught.

As others join in, piling on further accusations, the group or pack mentality kicks in, and you will experience suspension from the previous inner circle, being ignored or given the cold shoulder. This gives other people time to make their choice as to which side they will support! It is a time of extreme pain.

This is not unlike Princess Anna in Disney's *Frozen* who is injured and needing support when she returns to the castle. In true fairy-tale style, she believes that her true love's kiss will heal her. She seeks Prince Hans believing him to be her true love and a kiss is sought. I remember that a kiss is featured in another betrayal! She is unaware that Prince Hans has put his plans in motion—to betray her. Her request is ridiculed and he leaves her alone to die, quenching the fire so that she is left without warmth. He locks the door, confident that she cannot survive. In this moment, Princess Anna feels abandoned and alone.

If you have been betrayed this will resonate with you—there are times when you experience utter desolation. It was the same for Jesus—His Gethsemane moment—He was distressed, depressed and filled with grief. Jesus said "… I am almost dying of sorrow". Despite His request and plea to the disciples to stay awake and watch (i.e. pray) with Him, they fell asleep (Matthew 26:38-45 NLT). Jesus' friends were asleep because they did not understand His predicament. In the same way, in your own situation, friends find it incomprehensible to appreciate your predicament and may 'sleep' through it.

My Past includes Betrayal
I have been through and suffered what I believe was a major betrayal. This is my 'past' story.

▲　　▲　　▲

I was working in my dream job. One day (out of the blue) I was called to a meeting and suspended for an indefinite period. This situation lasted many months before it was resolved. It had an enormous impact on my life and I felt as though I was in the centre of a living nightmare. At the time I said, "This is the worst experience that could happened to me".

I felt that my future had been planned out without my involvement especially when information of which I was unaware came to the fore. Communication with me had ceased some time before, but I was too busy working long hours on the job to realise what was happening. On reflection, and using the qualification of hindsight, this was a 'little sign' that a difficulty had risen.

The self-examination and self-recrimination that followed was enormous. My mind went into overdrive, as I tried to comprehend the situation. In my head, I would desperately try to change what was happening, to put right what had gone wrong—without full knowledge of what had transpired. It felt like walking in the dark, never knowing when I would receive a knuckle-duster punch in the stomach. The wind had been knocked out of me. As I gulped for air another blow would be received.

It took time to realize that the situation was as unchangeable as a *Frozen* landscape: the tundra had iced over, the ship was trapped in a sea of ice, which would not release its grip. The melting point to unfreeze could only be achieved once a different scenario was enacted.

There comes a point when no matter how much you might fight against it, other minds have been set and the position becomes irretrievable without God at the centre of *all* parties.

In my case I was baffled. I believed that I was in this privileged position as part of God's plans. I now had to conclude that His plans were more far-reaching than a comfortable job until retirement. Yes, my plans were dramatic in their change, my learning intensified and my journey with God strengthened. However, it would take a couple of years before new plans would be established with God using the experience for my greater good. I can now say with hand on heart: "It was the best thing that ever happened to me!"

What about your situation? I would like to think that most readers have not and will not go through what I felt was a major life-changing betrayal. However, there can be minor hurtful treacheries: a friend who takes offence at an off-chance remark and launches into a verbal attack. The chilling silence, resulting in a change in the atmosphere when you enter a room and it becomes obvious that some discussion has taken place about you but to which you were not party.

I wonder if there has been much learning in adult interaction beyond the school playground? During school life children play off one another when they change allegiance. Any parent who has watched their child left baffled and agonised as to why their friend has swopped loyalty—preferring the company of another child and rejecting them—knows the incomprehensible pain and tears that transpire. Often in school this is short lived and the friendship returns. In adult life it may well have a more sinister and long lasting effect.

Surviving Betrayal

When my problem was acute, my energy was spent on keeping afloat, taking each day at a time and giving myself space to come to terms with my disillusionment. Acceptance of the situation can only occur once all the cards have been played out. It would end and I needed to believe that it would. In the meantime, it felt like my life was in chronic Siberian abeyance whilst everyone else's life continued as normal. It takes a period of time to pass before all the accusations are revealed and the lies untangled. This epoch can continue for months and years or beyond the betrayed person's lifetime!

Betrayal has a tendency to attract feelings of unwarranted shame. Reaching out to those who can support you can be difficult. The paradox is that this is the exact moment when your true friends emerge. It is the opportunity for your peers, family and friends to be supportive, aiding your survival and exoneration. Some friends take this opportunity with both hands, standing by your side for however long it takes, whilst others disappear into the woodwork!

Tracey was subjected to the latter when her body betrayed her to cancer. Her condition is terminal and she only has a few months left to live. She tells of her hurt when friends stop telephoning or visiting her. They are caught up with their own fears of not knowing what to say but to her it feels like further betrayal. As her body fails she wonders how many of them will attend her funeral!

Fred's business partner took out loans, wiped out the business account and disappeared overseas. As a result of this business betrayal, Fred had to choose between filing for bankruptcy or taking voluntary insolvency to pay back the debts. He described the pain of failure, his need to put his pride and shame into his back pocket in order to move forward talking with clients and staff. He had to let staff go and then sell his house and possessions to pay back all the debt over a number of years. But, with God on his side, he walked through this valley, his marriage was strengthened in this adversity and he discovered clients whose friendship transcended this difficulty.

It might take a while for friends to realise you need help. For instance, if your friends live a distance away or are not involved in your situation, it will mean you have to make a point of informing them. I found going over my story difficult and it became a milestone in my journey to recovery. Retelling brought forth conflicting emotions, masked in shame, doubt, and worry, serving only to emphasise my inability to comprehend my situation. I thought my friends would agree with the allegations! However, my friends' more objective viewpoints helped me, and their knowledge of my character was a positive reinforcement counteracting the trenchant accusations.

Sharing Your Story

When the betrayers are in a position of power they can and will use every effort to silence your story, preventing you from interaction with others or telling others. Just think how much the Enemy has tried to cover up the truth of Jesus? In today's corporate world 'confidentiality' becomes a watchword and it is necessary to be circumspect to whom and how the story is retold. There is a strong urge to tell everyone.

I researched others who were experiencing a similar 'suspension' situation and I was amazed at the openness of some people's stories. Many, in their desperate quest to be heard and believed used Internet forums as a means of support.

It is possible to receive too much advice from well-meaning friends and colleagues, which in turn becomes overwhelming. In contrast to receiving well-timed and correct succour which is like drinking at a pool in an oasis.

For me, God showed me that although I was at the centre of the situation, it was not about me! I was surprised at this, as it could not have felt more personal. God was clear, the lessons along the way would be hard and I would find them painful, but somehow I was a catalyst and it was His plan and purpose for someone else. It was not even my business to know who or why. He gave me strength in believing I would be vindicated and He had other—much better—plans for my life.

A Betrayer's Remorse

The best example of an unexpected betrayal followed by remorse is found in the Apostle Peter's story. This is in contrast to Judas who sat down for a meal with his master, having already inaugurated the betrayal (Mark 14:10). Despite his best intention, Peter swings from trying to protect Jesus to denying Him.

First, Peter attacks Malchus, the high Priest's slave sent to arrest Jesus. Peter cuts off Malchus' right ear (John 18:10). A centimetre closer and Peter could have been a murderer! Later Peter denies that he knows Jesus or was one of His disciples.

Peter's actions are significant but he is not named as a betrayer unlike Judas Iscariot, where reference is made whenever he is mentioned in the Bible. Jesus had foretold both men of their future actions and it came true. However, notice where Peter was at the time of denial. He was trying to follow Jesus perhaps seeking an opportunity to rescue Him or at the very least gain information. It could be said that Peter was in the wrong place at the wrong time. Jesus was taken to the High Priest's courtyard, which was protected with many guards.

Peter and another disciple had followed those who had arrested Jesus. The High Priest's servants recognised

the other disciple, who in turn used this influence in
gaining permission for Peter and himself to enter.

As part of the doorkeeper's duty, the servant
asked Peter a question. To enter Peter was
forced to say he did not know Jesus.

The numerous servants and guards in the courtyard lit a
fire to keep warm. This attracted others, allowing gossip and
information to flow. (Can you imagine the conversations?)
Peter joined them; once more his association with Jesus
was put to him, which he denied for a second time.

At around this time, Jesus was also being questioned with a
demand to name his disciples and his teaching. "I have spoken
openly to the world," Jesus replied. He clarified His actions,
"I always taught in synagogues or at the temple, where all the
Jews come together. I said nothing in secret" (John 18:20).

If Peter had said he was one of the disciples what would have happened
to him? No doubt he would also have been brought before the High
Priest, also beaten, and perhaps made to reveal testimony and be a
witness against Jesus. The third denial came as a result of a direct
challenge:

⋏　　⋏　　⋏

"Didn't I see you with Him in the garden?" The
question was asked by another household slave, who
happened to be a relative of Malchus—who Peter
had attacked earlier that evening (John 18:26).

What do you think would have been the reaction if Peter had confirmed
the suspicion and replied, "Yes, that was me"?

However, Peter was overcome with remorse, once he realised he had
failed to fulfil his own promise not to disown or deny Jesus (Matthew

26:35). He was incriminated by the accuracy of Jesus' word, 'Then Peter remembered the word Jesus had spoken: "Before the rooster crows, you will disown me three times". And he went outside and wept bitterly' (Matthew 26:75 and Mark 14:72).

I think that Peter's bitter tears fell at the worst point in his life but his remorse was the turning point of his life.

Perhaps you have been in a position where group dynamics came into force, peer pressure applied, the situation 'grew arms and legs' and went beyond anything you could have foreseen? Unaware of other people's hidden agendas you innocently became caught up in their perspectives and version of the truth. Once you realise, you are truly sorry. I believe that where true remorse is found then God's forgiveness will follow.

The Apostle Paul's past included persecuting innocent believers—those who followed Christ—and he had to come to terms with this. He acknowledges this point, 'for godly grief produces a repentance that leads to salvation without regret, whereas worldly grief produces death' (2 Corinthians 7:20 NLT). In this way, I pray for forgiveness for anyone who feels that I have betrayed him or her.

Beware Your Frozen Heart

A clear perspective is impossible at the time of acute pain and shock. Betrayal distributes disillusionment as part of its cargo bringing the temperature to freezing point. Your heart is at risk and forms a hardened, frozen barrier to protect itself against those who are hurting you. I found comfort in knowing that Jesus has been through the same pain—to the ultimate degree—and knew what it was like for me. Despite all, He kept His heart open and free from being frozen. This was a lesson I had to learn.

The pain of betrayal is inflicted, and the disillusionment intensified, when people who you think will always be on your side, change allegiance. The reason why is secondary, you have received a wound.

I had to counter the wounds of shock and disbelief when thoughts such as "How can they think this of me?" attacked me. This was before a defence could be mounted. Other people did have these thoughts—my self-illusion bubble was burst. I had to accept this as my 'Today'. It was not what I wanted it to be but it was what it was. There is a saying 'It is what it is', which helps to stay grounded in what is actually happening. Although this phrase implies helplessness—it can help during a transition period involving disillusionment.

Prayer was essential to coming through this experience and to be exonerated in God's, my family's, my friends' and my own eyes. I could only maintain my equilibrium with the knowledge that God had been through this all before and as my 'No 1 Fan', was there beside me. Despite feeling that I was on a physical and emotional roller coaster, I had to be wise in my defence. I worked out which battles to win and which to put aside. I found truths and facts to counter the accusations in a calm and controlled way. At times I felt isolated and alone, at other times my peers stepped forward and gave their support. However, at the end of the day it was my cross or cup to bear and carry forward, no one could take it away or carry it for me.

I had to beware of the coldness in my heart towards those against me. A frozen heart that revisited my past or decried how badly I had been treated was not a place I wanted to live. I did not intend to become a victim. I needed to heal and remember that my struggle was not against particular people, but that spiritual battles were taking place using these people as conduits. I had to digest the Apostle Paul's point, 'for our struggle is not against flesh and blood' (Ephesians 6:12). Paul continued to identify the spiritual forces of darkness and evil affecting men and I drew comfort in this, realising that I did not need to blame myself.

At the end of the day, people will believe what they want to believe. I would not be able to convince my naysayers or prevent a harassment campaign on social media. Each person had their own perspective and agenda as to whether they wanted to know my truth or facts. In the same way, you need to keep your heart unfrozen when you find yourself in unfair situations or experiencing ill treatment from others.

Why do People Hate, Hurt and Betray?

This is a universal question. Is it deliberate or unmindful action when people hate, hurt or betray others? It is as though coldness creeps through your body and drives out love, 'And because lawlessness will be increased, the love of many will grow cold' (Matthew 24:12 NLT). As part of healing it is necessary, albeit difficult, to forgive those who are hateful, spiteful and mean. It is hard to forgive those who have a complete disregard for the laws of humane interactions and the overall safety of you and others.

These traits are not confined to any one nationality or religion. All humans can demonstrate these iniquities. Hate, hurt and betrayal will happen—being as inevitable as death and taxes. Jesus said that it is to be expected, "At that time many will turn away from the faith and will betray and hate each other" (Matthew 24:10). Therefore, although you show love and kindness to your neighbours, people who do not share or uphold these qualities will still despise your efforts. Petty jealousies will form and those unfortunates who succumb to such feelings will try to depose, betray or hate you.

I draw comfort in knowing God has collected each teardrop of His opposed and wronged children (Psalm 56:8 NLT).

Is Betrayal Irreparable?

A trust betrayed is not irreparable. A folly can be healed by forgiveness and blessing where true remorse for the action is shown. *Ron* and *Julie* endured an epoch of betrayal, experiencing a long period of allegations and animosity.

ᴧ   ᴧ   ᴧ

Ron says, "I did not blame Julie for having an affair. We had allowed our relationship to slip. I had not been as kind or gentle with her as I needed to be, whether in tone of voice or in choosing the words that I spoke to her. Despite this, the levels of lying and covering up that went on during the affair hurt me. We were very acrimonious towards one another.

As the injured party, I did not feel it could get any worse. But Julie left, taking the children with her, and I could not prevent it. Suddenly I was home alone in a house we had built together, empty of love and missing our children. I was subjected to regulated visits to the kids, whereas the new man in her life had full access to them. It all felt so unfair and I felt totally betrayed.

Over a period of time, we kept communicating and talking about our problems. We continued to attend our church and our Pastor gave us counselling. Regardless of what the future held, our Pastor reminded us of Christ's love and the need to show this to one another.

Julie's affair was short-lived and she and the children moved back into the family home. Inch by inch we rebuilt trust. We forgave one another. We now have a different relationship than before, it is building into a better one with God at the centre".

This story had a happy ending, with the couple's differences resolved. God's love at the centre can repair any situation and provide forgiveness, 'for with God nothing shall be impossible' (Luke 1:37 NKJV). The past hurts were reconciled and their marriage developed into something new, despite the loss of its original sweetness. In any experience disillusionment once experienced gives way to a new reality tempered with past wisdom.

Betrayal comes clothed in many disguises. Like a volcano, it spews lies, erupting deceit and discord through the door accompanied by disillusionment, distrust and dismay. Jesus has been there too. He has the 'T-shirt', and will stand beside you in your situation.

Open the Door

1. Consider if you have been betrayed or have a friend who has been betrayed? What were the circumstances and how was this resolved?

2. Reflect on a 'betrayal' situation. Take your time to reflect and ask God to show you the way through the pain or how to help your friend through their suffering.

3. Notice and list any warning signs? Did you have any warning of your betrayal? Has hindsight given you the benefit of any signs?

4. Read the Bible passages reporting on Jesus' betrayal. Can you take comfort in knowing that He understands?

5. Believe that your betrayer will not succeed in pulling you away from God's plans for your life, and that He has amazing adventures lined up for you despite what is happening. Believe that He will use your situation for good.

6. De-personalise the situation. Consider that it is not about you! It is more about the accuser's faults than yours and you can trust that your Father God will deal with them.

7. Scrutinise the spiritual battle that is going on and how your persecutors are caught up in this. Pray for them and send blessings their way.

8. Review your past as kindly as you can. Have there been any occasions when you have betrayed someone? Are you remorseful and can you ask God for His forgiveness? Is it possible to ask the person for their forgiveness?

9. Learn from Peter's story and his remorse. What lessons can you learn?

10. Practice ways to soften your heart. How can you ensure that you do not freeze or harden your heart due to a betrayal?

11. Be thankful and praise God for the family and friends who come forward to support you in your time of need.

12. Find comfort in His arms. Understand that the situation will come to an end—you or your friend will survive and overcome.

Step into God's Warming Light

Dear Lord,

You know my situation and I pray that it will be resolved soon. Please God, let the disillusionment I feel be dispelled, changing it instead to a situation that can be used for your good. May it prove to be fruitful and that I can see the 'bigger picture' in situations so that I can learn from it.

Help me Lord to let go of betrayal's painful hurts and trust in You for any retribution. I pray for the full healing of my wounds. May I, one day, be able to say with confidence, "It was the best thing that could have happened to me!"

Amen.

YOUR HEALING: SELF-HELP AND GOD-HELP

A sad soul can kill you quicker than a germ.
JOHN STEINBECK

What is Healing?

All the riches in the world are worthless without your health—you are rich if you have your health. To be healthy is a longed for existence. A state of ill being due to disease, affliction or misfortune is not in your or God's plans. He will use you during these times yet it does not make it His plan for you to be burdened in this way. He wants you to have a healthy, happy, contented and prosperous life and where this is not evident He will give you His love, forgiveness and care in spite of adverse circumstances.

The human condition is prone to disease, infection and injury. These disabilities are external, based on adversities from outside the body. Others may be classed as internal such as the 3Ds: Disappointment, Disillusionment or Discouragement bringing sadness to your soul.

Can you imagine the magnitude of healing in this world if it was devoid of the 3Ds? It could transform your life from illness, heart-felt pain and sorrow. Perhaps it is time to call out to God, like Jabez, "Oh, that you would bless me and enlarge my territory! Let your hand be with me, and keep me from harm so that I will be free from pain" (1 Chronicles 4:10). The reference concludes with, 'And God granted his request'.

Your Healing: Self-Help and God-Help

The need to search for a cure and find healing is an intuitive response to pain and disease. To stand by and watch a loved one suffer is excruciating. The first port-of-call is to ask for help from someone with more knowledge than you. This can happen in the supernatural realm or with aid from medics, doctors and nursing staff. I believe to gain a thorough healing and recovery, you need to deploy a degree of self-responsibility and self-healing.

Give Healing a Helping Hand

For healing from betrayal and disillusionment to take place, your body, mind or soul needs a partner—You. You can hinder or expedite your healing—it is your choice—you need to know where to look to protect yourself.

⋏　⋏　⋏

Patricia and *Emma* have Diabetes Type 2 aggravated by stress of the 3Ds. Patricia is on-track for it to develop into a major insulin failure. She loves chocolate, ice cream and all foodstuffs potato-related. She turns to eating these in critical moments of stress. Her workplace involves long hours and she rarely takes a lunch break. She grabs her favourite foods and eats on the move or at her computer. She is aware that giving in to her cravings causes harm to her pancreas. She says,

"Eating makes me feel better when I feel bad or when I am stressed food is my comfort. I am not worried about my health as the advancement of medical science, all the pills and insulin will be enough to take care of my body".

⋏　⋏　⋏

Emma has similar cravings and has a job that insists on long hours and decisions affecting others. She has made a choice to change her lifestyle and diet to give her pancreas a helping hand. She says, "I will stave off the full-blown development of my diabetes for as long as possible. I take responsibility for my health, guided by my doctor; I research the subject for tips and alternative support. I use self-help and care for my body".

I can relate to both Patricia and Emma, as I have Type 2 Diabetes, accelerated by work stress. I flip-flop between the two opinions, being good to my body one week and eating well but then falling off the wagon, weakening to the call of cake the next.

My helpful hand is activated when making changes to my diet. I have found help from *Jason Vale,* the Juice-Master and have discovered that juicing fruit and vegetables has produced an impressive improvement in my blood sugar levels. Jason also understands the need to choose your health and your future. He says, "It is NOT what happens to you but what you do with what happens to you that shapes your future".

Jason has hit the nail on its proverbial head. He can give all the advice he can and suggest delicious recipes for a healthy life but it is your (and mine) choice to put any good advice into practice.

Be Gentle with Yourself

You can accept that your spirit is willing to make changes despite your body displaying overriding weaknesses. This is not a truism to 'give up'; it is an intelligence to be used for your advantage. Knowing this tendency, you can use it as a prompt to restrict the expectations you place on yourself. Delight in each and every victory when your inner voice encourages the body to do its best and follows through. Imagine your body, mind and soul expressing love, in partnership with one another, bound in strength like the 'three-stranded cord'. This would be a fulfilment of harmony, with health a natural outcome.

Your Strength as a Three-Stranded Cord

Have you noticed how difficult it is to break a cord made up of three strands? Ecclesiastes says, 'though one may be overpowered, two can defend themselves. A cord of three strands is not quickly broken' (Ecclesiastes 4:12). Rope made from a single strand is easy to pull apart; two strands are easy to unravel whereas the strand woven with three pieces is strong and difficult to break. Cables are made in this way, woven wire, which withstands changeable natural elements and malicious damage.

The Holy Trinity—the Father, the Son and the Holy Spirit—can also be viewed as a combination of three strands of manifold greatness. Each want to be part of your life, to be available for you, to draw on their combined strength, breaking the hold of illness, disease and the 3Ds by stepping into Their healing light.

You are Not Your Illness

Your story may include an illness or you may know someone whose past includes an illness. Statements such as, "I am a ..." or "I have ..." can sound like a rallying call for sympathy, used to excuse certain behaviours, or it can be a rallying call for rejuvenation.

⋏   ⋏   ⋏

Teri was upset. She cried to her husband, "You will not believe what he said to me!" The story unfolds; she had been helping her son to clean his house. For some reason she could not do anything right in his eyes. He called her stupid and generally verbally abused her until she was in tears. This was not the first time this had happened but Teri was more horrified at his reasoning behind his behaviour. It was revealed as he apologised to her, excused himself saying, "It is not my fault that I say these things to you, it is because I am bi-polar".

Do you really have little choice in your actions, behaviours and what you say to others? I believe there is a choice to move beyond hardship, or living in reduced circumstances when a chronic illness becomes part of your life. This is only possible by harvesting self-help and God-help. With this aid you will gain the strength in refusing to allow an ongoing health complaint define who you are.

God-help: Healing from the 3Ds

The next time you visit a bookshop, notice the growing categories of books dedicated to healing and self-help. Shelves are heaving with these new titles. For me, the addition to self-help is God-help fastening on to the partnership between you and the Father, Son and Holy Spirit. It takes the three Divinities to overcome all problems—helping you to recover from life's inevitable 3Ds: disappointment, disillusionment or discouragement. You can ask for God's curative help at any time.

The 3Ds direct their malfunctions towards the heart, hardening it, turning it to stone—kept frozen from feeling. The heart is perceived as more than a muscle. Whereas you can recover from an injury to the body, damage to your heart is a lifetime's trauma. Your heart stores up emotional energy; it needs to have a continuous flow, life's blood (love) moving in and out of the heart, to remain unfrozen.

Healing your heart, hurt by the 3Ds, will demand your active participation to bring unity to your mind, body and soul. Are you ready? God has already given a promise through Ezekiel— you can draw on this same promise. He says, "I will give you a new heart and put a new spirit in you; I will remove from you your heart of stone and give you a heart of flesh" (Ezekiel 36:26).

The Power of Prayer

The activity of self-help begins by talking to God, bringing your questions, appeals and requests to Him. The Apostle Paul recommended that all prayers should be accompanied with thanks and praise and without worry (Philippians 4:6). This might appear conditional and I questioned the meaning to try and understand Paul's point.

My very wise first Pastor, *Rev Geoff Larcombe* reminded me, "God is a 'God of Surprises', a God who may heal instantaneously with or without prayer, whether or not there is faith on the part of the pray-ee. He does not seem too bothered whether the one asking is a Christian or not!' It is also His sovereign choice and decision as to who He will or will not heal".

I always say be careful what you pray for, because God will answer it! I am often like a little child wanting my own way, without reflecting on the consequences. As a child, I longed for and begged my parents for a pony. It did not occur to me that since we lived in a town, on a council estate, this would have been a serious undertaking of finances and time, which was not in my parent's ability to give. They gave me what they could.

I was treated to riding lessons and my Dad would take me 'horse-spotting'. We would travel into the nearby countryside where I scoured the fields for a horse. I would bounce up and down with excitement, shouting, "Horse" whenever the jewel of my heart came into view. The car had to be reversed or turned around allowing me to get out, pet my treasure across a fence, for as long as my Dad's patience would allow!

How much more will your heavenly Father give you if you ask?

When I was baptised I asked God to show me His world. Later, I cycled through Jordan and took a trip to Bolivia,

working with a deaf school. The adventures were not
100% problem free. For instance, I did not ask God for
my husband to accompany me. The consequence was I
had to struggle with being abroad alone, dependent on
strangers, albeit with His protection. It taught me a lot about
prayer, including the need to be specific in my requests.

During my personal upsets, I relied on God's responses to my explicit appeals. I was often surprised by the answers. His answers returned to me in many forms:

- Listening to a sermon I felt that the preacher had singled me out for their message—it was so relevant,
- Reading Bible passages which highlighting my situation,
- Meeting and talking with someone and being surprised to discover they had the exact knowledge that I was searching for and,
- An awareness of 'knowing' the right response to take in the quietness of my soul.

Each prayer request would be answered with actions that I needed to complete, such as to re-assess my priorities and guard against vengeful thoughts. It was not a case of God waving a magic wand making everything hunky-dory. It was about my movement forward—I had to apply the learning if I wanted to be healed. God made it clear that I was responsible and accountable in the process of His answer to my prayers.

God's Interventions

One task God gave me was to have a serious conversation with my ego. How proud was I of my status at the pinnacle of my working life? I had found my way up the proverbial 'corporate greasy pole', I was at the top of my game. I could count God's blessings in my life. Nonetheless, I was caught up in the busyness of working, giving little time for conversations or my relationship with Him.

My days were made up with the pride of striving, fear of letting people down, and in the vicious circle of trying to please everyone. Holding an executive position involves working longer hours and a lifestyle of a very busy person. As a family the standing joke was that I had become a VIP—Very Important Person. I was influential, in demand by others, courted for my opinion, dealing daily with 101 questions, permanently on call—it felt good. It did not occur to me that my family and friends were in danger of being given second place, their needs viewed as low priority. I experienced classic symptoms: rescheduled family time, interrupted meals as demands to serve others became the norm.

Is there a cost to this? There was for me. Who is being pushed out to make way for your 'accomplishments'? Time became a commodity to be bartered in indulgent gratification.

My concentration became *all* about the job. It was the work consuming my thinking, talking and being. My typical week was upwards of 50-60 hours—hours given willingly—with my ego applauding, feeding the appetite to be needed, make a difference and be popular. I failed to heed the warning signs:

- sickness in my body,
- compromised time for God,
- reduced time to read the Bible or invest in quiet and reflection time,

- succumbing to the relentless mode of 'do more',
- captivated in the physical and mental battering of 'busy, busy, busy',
- buying into the 'lie' that busyness equals success,
- frequent rescheduling of time with my family,
- discounting friends' advice that 'burn out' was just around the corner.

I thought I would be 'fine', I was in control, and it would only be until the next project was finished. I had embraced the 'lie' that it would not happen to me.

Does this resonate with you? The only way this merry-go-round (an oxymoron as it was hurting me and was not merry at all!) could be stopped was with an intervention from God. He would not collaborate or tolerate this direction. When I was blatant in ignoring the signs, He called a halt because I had gone outside His loving plans. Have you been stopped in a brutal way as the ultimate signal to get your attention?

▲   ▲   ▲

But God is good. He said to me, "Yes I know, I know all about it ... You are not ready at this moment to understand it all, come to me, find rest and peace in me". When I questioned Him about my plans coming apart in my hands, He replied, "My timing is right, yes I put you in that place, gave you the job AND I am also taking you out of it".

Unresolved Healing at Odds with Your Faith

Healing is a process containing ups and downs, periods of tears and upset, feeling the pain of the 3D's injury. I found frustrations in my emotions, they seemed at odds with my faith in God, a constant battle for my mind, body and soul. I would have good days and bad days. Days when I could pray for those who were injuring me, other days when I felt victimised and would rage against my circumstances. This would cycle into conversations such as "I must be a 'bad' Christian to think these thoughts". Have you been in a position when how you want to behave and your actual behaviour is not in tune with one another? These cries of pain are not pleasant sounds, often triggering a response to suppress the feeling rather than acknowledging and dealing with it.

The lies of disillusionment spread confusion and doubt, breaking down your confidence alongside shrinking your hope. It is the painful path associated with injury and wounds. Like all pain it serves as a warning; to heed it, make it better, until the pain recedes. Treatment for pain release can include taking prescribed tablets though most medicines suppress your natural healing and should always be viewed as short-term measures. The opposite of the 'take a pill' solution is to wade your way through it. Acknowledge the pain and the negative thoughts: refuse to give either the room to fester in your life. This means not beating yourself up about the sound of your cry but determining to sing a new song.

To get Better not Bitter

The purpose of healing is to get better. Bitterness is not a friend of full healing; it will trip you into further hurts—hurting yourself and others. Bitterness is like a vulture circling, the opportunist looking for carrion, with the body being you! Breaking negative habits or thought patterns involve noticing when your vultures appear and chasing them away. You must refuse to become a rotting living corpse. Overcome them by saying, "There is no body here to feed upon!"

Ugly thoughts form unpleasant expressions on your face and in your body, reflecting your internal trauma.

▲   ▲   ▲

For me these are unwanted thoughts employed the 'little voice in my head' and refused to go away. The uncontrollable introspective thought would pop up

without warning, such as when I was driving. Before
I knew it, I was rehashing conversations, arguing my
point and trying to change outcomes in my head.

Does this happen to you? A person's hurtful remark can be rehearsed with the intensity of a memorised Shakespearean sonnet. The imagination puts in its effort and tries to help, putting in unconfirmed logic as the offender's reasoning; "They must hate me to say that" or "If only I had said ..." The mental track is ruthless and relentless. It drives away positive thoughts, adds in only your perspective, steering you back to the entrapment of the past, the 3Ds. It takes considerable effort to challenge the mind's constant chatter.

The challenge is replacing these thoughts with others. The brain can only contain one thought at a time therefore, it is possible to choose your thoughts and change them. A thought does not have to be true. I found the analogy that reading the word 'rain' on a piece of paper does not mean it is raining outside. The same is true with thoughts—you may be conscious of thinking negative thoughts about a particular person—this does not mean you have to act on them or that you or they are a bad person. Your thoughts do not affect the other person as he or she is blithely unaware of them!

Using phrases such as 'that is one way of thinking about it but here is another thought' provides space in your mind for alternatives to be considered without an internal argument! A shout of, "STOP" can help, a new thought needs to be exchanged with vigour before the persistent original cycle begins once again.

▲　　▲　　▲

I chose a phrase in readiness for the thought appearing. I
would recapture my mind, by reciting my maxim to change
my thought pattern. I stockpiled one liners, lyrics and
Bible verses. I memorised them, creating an arsenal to
halt my negative thoughts. These phrases could change
my victim cry into laughter or deflate the potency of a

negative thought. I would use, 'if my God is for me, who can be against me?' (Romans 8:31), or lines from favourite songs, such as, 'Let it Go' (Lopez & Anderson-Lopez) from Disney's *Frozen* (naturally) or the Proclaimer's 'It's Over and Done With' (Reid & Reid) from *Sunshine on Leith* and for a proven big hit—'The Lord's Prayer'.

The changes did not happen overnight, the old record would continue to play in my mind. I would have to remind myself that these thoughts were unhelpful and no longer wanted. However, there was huge resistance from my mind to changing negative patterns into positive thoughts.

My mind would fight my spirit by saying, "I was right— they were wrong" and my emotions would agree saying "I am justified in feeling this way", or "They have not said 'sorry', so why should I" and "It is not my fault." My body would react according to the winner of the argument. I had to choose between being right or being healed.

I was mindful of conversations where my voice was accusing, pointing the finger at others with bitter words tumbling from my mouth. During these countless inward debates, I would imagine a mirror showing my face with lines full of agitation. To smooth those ugly lines forming on my face or in my body I would take a deep breath, move my shoulders to reduce the rigidity of my body. I was desperate to get better not bitter.

There is a perverse pleasure in being a 'victim' and you need to be proactive not to fall prey to it. What can you do to get better not bitter? How do you turn your thoughts away from bitterness?

Who is Holding Your Arms Up?
Healing alone is not a good place to be—good company is needed. As humans, isolation is not tolerated well by the mind. It has a high risk for psychological and physical problems, as proved in Harlow's separation and

deprivation experiments causing profound psychological and emotional distress in monkeys. This is precisely why it is a method used for torture. Even a small level of isolation can cause distress. For young children, a few minutes on the 'naughty step' can be unbearable. Each person has an amount which is tolerable. There is a difference between choosing to distance yourself using solitude within a retreat or period of seclusion, and being forcefully banished, imprisoned, excommunicated, exiled or given the 'cold shoulder'.

There is a British idiom, 'Being sent to Coventry' when a person is deliberately ostracised as a punishment in order to be shown that their actions are unacceptable. The extreme is the enforced solitary confinement used in imprisonment and persecution. To heal from the onset of the 3Ds you need to be careful not to inflict isolation upon yourself. Take a pill of humbleness by sharing with others so that they can reach out and comfort you. You may be surprised at who God uses to aid your healing.

Ask for help from professionals and friends to support:

- your emotional stability,
- your spiritual journey,
- your practical aid such as legal or a finance expertise,
- your physical level, and
- your support, standing with you in the gap.

Standing with you in the gap involves others taking your place—momentarily—when you no longer have the strength to go on. Have your circumstances pulled you down to such an extent that even lifting your arms up to God is one thing too much? Another way of others supporting you is by holding your arms up like Aaron and Hur did for Moses (Exodus 17:12).

▲   ▲   ▲

During my time of angst, in a Church service, my wonderful Minister, *Chris Bowater* and a member of the leadership team did this for me! They held up my arms upwards to God and prayed. Through this action, they communicated their love and strength, acting as a connection to God for His power to enter me. In that moment, standing between two people lifting my arms, changed me from being alone, as a single strand—breakable at the slightest onslaught—into a three-stranded cord—unbreakable despite my circumstances.

Listen to your Body

Illness is a time when employers and society permit time away from the treadmill of work. There is broad understanding and an accepted practice that uninterrupted rest is necessary. Whereas holiday periods can be disrupted, illness is respected and undisturbed. It might be why 'duvet days' have become popular!

The body and mind is upset at any onset of the 3Ds and time is needed for recovery. The lies of the 3Ds have an insidious creep, like fermenting yeast, into your character. They manifest themselves as minor ailments— hiding the true issues.

▲   ▲   ▲

Benjamin is a model employee who does not take time off for illness. He carries on despite it, refusing to listen to his body's warning signals. His wife remarks that she can guarantee that at weekends, on holiday or at Christmas and New Year, Benjamin will go down with headaches or man 'flu. This impacts on family time and, although Benjamin is force to rest, it is only sufficient to get back to work. She thinks he is about to 'burnout' and is heading for a breakdown.

Catching the warning signs concealed in illness could be considered an art form. It takes a self-awareness that papering over the cracks is not a long-term health ticket. To live and work in your full potential the 3Ds have to be tackled. Are you listening to your body?

God's Helping Hand

Prayer is as nutritious to the soul as food is to the body. It also has the power to change your situation on physical, emotional, spiritual and psychological levels. Holy Spirit, in His gentle manner, presents His gifts for your disposal. Have you seen the list of these gifts being offered to you? There are 15 gifts listed in the Bible (found in The Apostle Paul's writings and 1 Peter 4:8-11) they include:

- understanding,
- wisdom,
- knowledge,
- serving,
- artistic skill, and
- teaching

How do you know when you have received Gifts from God and Holy Spirit ? The Bible characterises evidence of the gifts through the manner in which they are shown, attitude and action, and calls them the fruits, (Galatians 5:22-23 and 1 Peter 4:7) expressed by:

- love,
- joy,
- peace,
- patience,
- kindness,
- goodness,
- faithfulness,
- gentleness, and
- self-control

How many of these do you have? How many of these would you like to use in your daily relationships and interactions?

Your body often gives warning signs of a forthcoming illness. The warning sign is when your emotions and reactions are in opposition to the lists above and your behaviour has characteristics of:

- hate,
- unhappiness,
- impatience,
- disagreement,
- agitation,
- cruelty, and
- rashness.

All are symptoms of illness. Can you recognise these signs? Do they happen when you feel overtired or stressed? I know that when I feel upset, angry or cross because of what a person has done or not done, it means my ego is at work and I need to have 'a little chat' with myself about my unwarranted expectations. When I am tempted to criticise others, I need to be reminded that this will hurt God's heart, it is not how God wants me to look at another child of His. When I realise that a person is against me, I need to send up blessings for them (invoking help from Holy Spirit to change their mind-set to be nearer God's character) and then I need to move on leaving it in His hands.

Defending without Vengeance

The 3Ds are brought on by interaction with other people. It is tempting to defend yourself by fighting back, wanting the other person to experience the same or more pain than you. As an insult has been received to respond in kind feels natural and righteous. The opposite is true, this retaliation serves to interfere with your healing. This paradox is highlighted, 'refrain from anger and turn from wrath; do not fret—it leads only to evil' (Psalm 37:8). Exhibiting the gift of self-control puts anger in its rightful place rather than using it as a fuel for revenge.

It is God who will bring about any retribution not you or me. It is in His hands. Therefore trusting in Him is a better bedfellow than plotting to get your own back. Moses, made this clear, and quoted God, "It is mine to avenge: I will repay. In due time their foot will slip; their day of disaster is near and their doom rushes upon them" (Deuteronomy 32:35). Or, as Proverbs reminds us, 'a false witness will not go unpunished, and whoever pours out lies will not go free' (Proverb 19:5). Knowing God's heart is for your benefit, He will help you to forgive and bless your perpetrators.

Believing this release you from the responsibility of justice or finding the ultimate solution. Your healing floods in, relying on your command of goodness towards people who wish you ill. God's paradox is, as you make this your practice, it surprises your attacker. It will wound them. As the Apostle Paul writes, 'if your enemy is hungry, feed him; if he is thirsty, give him something to drink. In doing this, you will heap burning coals on his head' (Romans 12:20). I found this verse a great comfort in taking these first steps of forgiveness.

Forgiving Yourself and Others

What do you think you will say in your last moments? The standard joke is that deathbed conversations do not include, "I should have spent more time at the office". To pass on final wisdom, a blessing or final love messages would be my thought. Jesus, dying in agony spoke over His people saying, "Father, forgive them, for they do not know what they are doing" (Luke 23:34).

The Apostles had many questions about forgiveness. Peter asked Jesus how many times must he forgive a brother or sister who hurts him. He suggested seven times. Jesus replied, "Seven! Hardly. Try seventy times seven" (Matthew 18:21-22 The Message). Various Bible interpretations have put this at 77 times, others 70 x 7. If your analysis is the latter, have you done the calculation? The total is 539 times to utter a forgiveness or blessing on whoever has hurt you. Jesus explained the need to repeat forgiveness and it was a new approach. It was the reversal of the vengeance that was demonstrated in the Old Testament by Lamech (Genesis 4:24). Forgiveness involves repeated practice for your heart to be unfrozen enough to see that person in a different light—His warming light—it might be that they respond to you in a different way too.

The Apostle Paul had to forgive those who betrayed him. In his letter to Timothy, he spoke about the harm that had been done to him. He said, he was 'without defence or support as everyone had deserted him'. Once more betrayal brings isolation, although Paul knew God was with him, standing beside him and giving strength. Paul gave a blessing on his deserters asking God for their forgiveness, "May it not be held against them" (2 Timothy 4:16).

Is it time for you to forgive those who have wounded, deserted and harmed you? Is today the moment for you to forgive yourself for any mistakes or errors that you have made?

God-Help and His First Aid Kit

God will help you to forgive and bless others, as He knows they are essential ingredients in your healthy self-help and self-control. However, they involve your forethought and active participation. Practise God-help alongside self-help and turn it into a useful regular practice. A practice you can draw on as part of your healing. Forgiveness is a process involving work and practice. The habit builds up your resilience against the 3Ds. In coaching his disciples how to pray, Jesus teaches them *The Lord's Prayer*, in which forgiveness is a strong feature (Luke 11:4). Recite this prayer to change your mind-set towards others. It can become your fall back position, customised into a must-have tool as part of God's first-aid kit.

Personalising your forgiveness tool is powerful in your healing arsenal. It cures you of bearing a grudge! Your skill is in naming the person who has hurt, disappointed, disillusioned or discouraged you. By asking God to help you in showing forgiveness it takes this prayer into a heightened spiritual realm. The person you name does not need to be aware of your practice—it may well be best if they are unaware—you will be evoking a win-win benefit. You have the benefit of positive healing and they will have the benefit of not having an enemy! When I first began to practice I had a long list of people I had to offer up!

The wounds are healed inside making the scar tissue invisible! Forgiveness is the polar opposite to the world-view. You will need to practice:

- letting go of grudges,
- putting resentment aside,
- responding to hate with kindness, and
- moving away from the 'victim' status.

You have control over your responses, incorporating forgiveness as one of your values—is your considered choice. Like any decision a few people may understand, others will not. It will be noticed, though, as it affects your behaviour, speech and actions. Christ exemplified forgiveness towards you and me. He asks you and I to choose and demonstrate forgiveness in our relationships and dealings with others. It is not about forgetting the injury or staying in an abusive situation, it is about responding without anger or resentment. By holding on to these emotions you continue to hurt yourself, blocking the love of God from reaching you. Remember the words of Jesus, "For if you forgive other people when they sin against you, your heavenly Father will also forgive you" (Matthew 6:14).

It is impossible to hold hate in your heart at the same time as calling on that person to be forgiven and blessed. Whenever the person comes into your mind, in your thoughts or in the retelling of your story, add a blessing on their health, wealth and their life's journey.

Bring out the Blessings

Is forgiveness an act of blessing or does blessing flow from the act of forgiving? Which comes first? I think it is interchangeable as practising both produces healing and they can be separate activities. At first, blessing a person did not come naturally to me, I had to learn how to do this. Being asked to bless the person I disliked felt like adding insult to injury.

I had to read the words of Jesus about 'loving my enemies and doing good to those who hate me'. After all, it is easier and more fun to say blessings over loved ones! I had to make a choice and, in the privacy of my home, I insisted to myself that I would do what Jesus instructed, "Bless those who curse you, pray for those who mistreat you" (Luke 6:28) and I blessed those who were mistreating me. It made a huge difference, changing my attitudes and me. I was humbled. My heart showed mercy and it became a turning point in my healing.

Kerry Kirkwood in his book, *The Power of Blessing*, unpacks the meaning of blessings and how to speak them. Kerry explains that blessings are multi-sided and that speaking a blessing means 'to speak the intention of God', he says it encourages you 'to be happy with where you are'.

Re-read the last sentence. How powerful would you feel to be speaking the intention of God into someone's life—friend or foe? You might not like them but God loves them and your blessing would reflect His intent—not yours. My view is that blessings are my way of paying forward God's gift of salvation! Isn't it amazing that whenever I experience God I receive the benefit? Have you found the same? There is huge healing in being content with what is going on with your life right now, accepting rather than fighting the experience. This does not mean you are a push over but you have the power of God within you, to use for your own and others' healing.

Blessings are different from prayers. They are said with eyes open and are part of ministering to others. They are always positive, about another person, wanting the best for them, emphasising God's love for them—like imparting a gift. They are firmer than a hope and are guided by Holy Spirit. A blessing is made up of your words, God's word and under-written in God's name.

God taught Moses how to say a blessing. It is one of the most well known blessings, still used in Jewish synagogues and in Christian churches. It has even been found etched on a silver amulet, which archaeologists dated back to the seventh century BC. Many believers refer to it as the Lord's Prayer of the Old Testament and you can use it today.

The Lord bless you and keep you
The Lord make His face shine upon you and be gracious to you
The Lord turn His face toward you and give you Peace
(Numbers 6:24-26)

A great resource for you to use in God's first aid kit is a blessing prayer put together by my friend *Bob Oldershaw* (Your Bonus section). It helps in personalising a statement of forgiveness and aids your healing when blessings are spoken over those who you have every reason to despise. As this approach becomes your default, your heart will melt and the negative feelings towards that person will evaporate. Their power over you is lessened and this becomes part of your healing.

Blessings are a demonstration of worship and like all worship can activate change. I love the story about *King Jehoshaphat* (2 Chronicles 20) who sent the choir singing God's praises out in front of the army. They won the battle as they gave thanks to the Lord. I wonder what would happen with the terrorism in today's world if the worship leaders were sent alongside our military to the hot sandy places? In the meantime, you and I can sing praises to the Lord when in our own personal battles.

If you are struggling to give a blessing, ask a fellow believer (who understands the power of blessings) to bless your enemy on your behalf. It is best if you are there at the time of blessing as this is not a delegated request. Listen to the words that they use, later paraphrase this blessing and repeat it. Remember to include God's word and God's name as you use your own words to bless.

If it is easier for you, the blessing can be written down—perhaps as a blessing letter? This is a communication between you and God and does not have to be said or given to the named person! It is time for you to 'speak well' of the person who has brought disillusionment to your door.

Courage from Others

In the middle of your circumstance you may become aware that others in your community may also be going through similar experiences. These can be public media stories or someone coming alongside you who says, "I've been there too" and, in confidence, shares with you their past story.

Take courage from the stories of others who have been there—disillusionment affects more people than you think—they are amazing survivors. The retelling is to comfort you in knowing you are not alone and to support you in dealing with your own situation with bravery, maturity, and positivity without recrimination.

Utilise your Hope

Keep your hope alive. On days when your 3D experience seems unending, remind yourself that it will finish, there will be a conclusion and you will be exonerated. Find a point of thankfulness; be thankful for something—anything.

▲   ▲   ▲

Patrick told me, "Some days I feel so depressed that the only thing I can feel thankful for is the colour of the wallpaper!"

Where is your hope and joy? Keep a nugget in a place you can gain easy access. Question how will you feel in five years' time about this current situation? Consider the passage of time on your 'now' circumstance. As the years pass, the pain will become ineffectual, incapable of the dominating hurt you are feeling today. Is it possible to fast-forward this, so the hurt can be lessened now?

It is not Personal

It is one of life's lessons that you cannot please everyone. Are you like me and want everyone to love and agree with you? It is impossible because you and I cannot be 100% right all the time—despite me telling myself otherwise! There will always be a difference of opinion, diverse reactions and immaturity. When these come against you, it can feed into the 'lies' of self-doubt.

Disillusionment also brings a 'lie' of condemnation. You may be more comfortable in blaming yourself rather than others. Blame is not necessary for either you or them. Jesus is your defender talking to God on your behalf, 'there is now no condemnation for those who are in Christ Jesus' (Romans 8:1-2). There are numerous references to Jesus standing at the right hand of God serving as your advocate (Mark 16:19, Acts 7:55-56, Romans 8:34).

A strategy to keep you away from self-disapproval and self-censure is not to agree with the accusations that come your way. In an aggressive situation it will be necessary to 'depersonalise' it and to realise that it is not personal—though it might feel so. As someone who has been conditioned to be a 'people pleaser' I find this particularly difficult. I have to ask myself the following question. Would this betrayal be the same if it were someone else? The chances are it would be.

This is not a direct attack against you as a person it is another's view on a given situation. It does not need to deflate or destroy your whole person. Healing may call for your self-protection by clothing yourself (figuratively) with the Armour of Christ. This is God's protection for you and beautifully described by the Apostle Paul (Ephesians 6:10-18).

Five Steps for Healthy 3D Scars

The wounds of the 3Ds are stories in your past. They cannot be removed or eradicated. They will leave a scar and like scar tissue they can be healed with care and gentleness. You can assist this disfiguration into invisibility over time rather than leaving it crusty and on show.

The medical profession explains how to heal a physical wound. It involves:

1. Preventing infection (covering the wound).
2. Aiding the formation of new cells (cleansing the wound).
3. Soothing the area to minimise the scar.
4. Applying anti-itch creams (reducing the urge to scratch and irritate the wound), and
5. Applying pressure to aid its healing. Is it possible to apply these principles to your disappointment, disillusionment and discouragement wounds?

Giving yourself a helping hand to heal is hard work when you are in a fragile state. You are susceptible to interruption, resistance and failure but your body wants to help you. You have a choice to allow your mind and soul to also join in and be part of your healing. What is it that makes you feel better? What is within your control? To heal you need to love, be kind and appreciate yourself. You are worth it. Consider these five steps:

1. Preventing Infection

i) A clean wound, healed well, leaves a small scar as evidence. You may have a scar somewhere on your body from a cut or operation. It no longer hurts you and most days you forget it is there. Someone may occasionally ask you "What happened there?" But in the main, it is an old wound, a tiny reminder of the past. The same needs to happen for emotional, relational and psychological scarring. Keeping the wound clean when it first occurs is paramount for this to happen, as this will keep infection and re-infection away from the site of injury.

ii) Sleep and rest will support your healing. The body is conditioned to spend one-third of its life asleep. During this state, the body is repairing its immune and metabolic states effecting learning, repairing and growing. The interruption of sleep damages the well-being cycle and the 3D's lies can produce insomnia or disturbed sleep.

iii) Take the time to discover your best sleep pattern. Are you an early morning person or an evening person? What activities calm your thoughts to enable sleep? Christian radio and soft music were great comforts to me when I awoke in the early hours of the morning or could not settle back to sleep.

▲   ▲   ▲

My friend *Ted*, recommends the following prayer,
"Lord, into your hands I commit my spirit this night",
and inexplicably he just falls asleep. Others have
tried this and it has also worked for them. The phrase
is a version of Jesus' words, who in His last breath
on the Cross, spoke Psalm 31:5 when He committed
His spirit into His Father's hands (Luke 23:46).

iv) *Pray and Talk with God.* Use His word and draw comfort from Bible verses to lift your spirits and remind yourself of His great love for you. Ask others to pray for you as well. Consider the truth of this quote from *Loretta Young*, 'I believe that prayer is our powerful contact with the greatest force in the universe'.

v) Choose your *mantra*: a favourite saying, quote or a line from a poem or song. Chant or sing this, softly repeating it whenever awful memories overwhelm you.

vi) Create a good *ambiance* for relaxation in a number of rooms, including your bedroom. Consider the use of lighting, colour and contents.

vii) Choose nourishing *Food and Drink*. Make an effort to give yourself the best food, reducing comfort eating and the lure of sugar. Keep your meal times structured and plan them out. Give yourself a restaurant experience at home including planning menus for a week. *Hippocrates* said 'Let food be thy medicine and medicine be thy food'.

viii) Keep company with your most valuable friends—the ones who are not interested in the latest tidbit—who will listen while you 'offload'. Spend time with the friends who walk beside you without criticism during your time of hurting.

ix) Seek out *professional opinion* in all spheres and couple it with your own self-knowledge of what is right for you. Listen to your 'inner' self, the quiet voice inside.

2. Form New Cells of Thinking

The body has the natural ability to heal itself. Four phases have been identified as the intricate processes for repairing bodily wounds. These are:

i) Blood clotting (haemostasis).

ii) The onslaught of white blood cells engulfing damaged, diseased and dead tissue (inflammation).

iii) The growth of new tissue (proliferation), and

iv) Regeneration of cells (remodelling).

Wounds of the 3Ds are like a fog clamming around you, closing down your mind and soul with their slow 'lies' of sadness and lethargic-ness!

Discover your own phases and processes; engage with them and partner with your body to combat the destructive effects.

v) *Writing* reduces and releases stress, emptying your head of toxic thoughts by committing them to paper or in the computer. This can take many forms: Journal, Diary Writing or Poetry to name a few. Make a note of your feelings as you write including your emotional stage. Creating a time-line will give you an insight on how your circumstances have got you to this point and this can be used later if needed to prepare a defence. Keep it private. Later it might be useful for a blog or an article, though at the time of pain keep it to yourself.

vi) Take up a *Virtual Advisor Role* and consider what advice you would give someone else in this difficulty. The advice may surprise you as being the counsel you need to take!

vii) Insist that you are *Mindful* by exercising your mind to dispel the fog of disillusionment. Expand your mind with quizzes, cross words, Sudoku and mind teasers so that your thinking and logical muscles are exercised. Watching TV quiz shows do not count as you are in a passive mode—whereas making an application to be on a programme would involve full participation!

viii) Take a *volunteer role*. This can be informal and a short-term arrangement, simply giving someone else a helping hand. It can keep your mind off your problems. It is good to be reminded that others are suffering too, or are less fortunate than yourself and you have an opportunity to help whilst experiencing your own pain.

ix) *Focus* on other people for a while and your problems may reduce in comparison. By focusing on other people's hurts and actively seeking to help them you can transform your thoughts away from your own hurts—bringing your own healing is rather like a backward compliment!

3. Soothe your 3Ds wound

Choose some soothing activities to act as natural tranquilisers. The calmness from soothing actions mitigates your 3D wound encouraging anti-bacterial properties to form. Soothe yourself with creams or sounds as part of your first aid kit to dispel and distil disillusionment.

i) Give yourself a *Massage* and engage your body with touch. Flowing movements with the aid of a sweet smelling cream or oil quietens down the mind and sends self-affirming messages.

ii) Allow *Music, Books, Film, Dance and Art* to transport you to another place. Concentrate on the meaning of the lyrics, the rhythms of the music, and the characterisations in the book or film. Overall, take a break from your present mood. Choose uplifting melodies and inspirational books and film. Looking at your preferred art, look at the intent behind the artist's work and what it communicates to you. Let it motivate you away from dark thoughts. Make time for artistic inputs to influence the soothing of your soul. Try creating some art yourself.

iii) *Visit a place of natural beauty.* For me this is the seaside; the sound of waves swishing or crashing on the shore fills my soul with goodness. The salty air and smell can keep me going for months. For you it might be mountains or the countryside. Walk in it and let your mind relax in creation's beauty. Find an outside place where you can visit and 'take in the air'.

iv) *Tears* contain healing as they release hormones acting as a natural painkiller. Allow yourself to express yourself by crying—accepting its healing properties.

v) Allow yourself occasional *'Wallow Moments'* as it is tiring always trying to be upbeat, constantly trying to motivate yourself, or forcing yourself into a lighter mood.

▲   ▲   ▲

Marion explains her strategy, "I give myself a 15 minute session in which to re-live all the 'badness' of my betrayal and permission to feel very sorry for myself. My deal is that after this 'wallow moment' I had to counteract it with at least 2-3 hours of worry-free activity". Marion told me that by the time 15 minutes was up she did not want to sustain her own suffering and could not wait for an alternative exercise. She says, "Later I could laugh at how 'bad' I could make it". The extreme retelling of her story gave way to a more balanced mind-set.

4. Anti Itch

How many times can you revisit your wound, scratch it until it re-bleeds, picking at and pulling the scab off irritating yourself in your misery? It could be a person who is your irritant, or that it is the resurfacing memory itself. It is impossible to live a good life in constant pain. Continually 're-opening old wounds' rebounds you into the past and reverses present healing. It is unhealthy. Find a way to apply anti-itch techniques:

i) There is something very therapeutic about *Decluttering.* Sort out collections and keep only a few special items. Tidy up a desk or cupboard and throw away needless memorabilia or a clear out the garage cluttered with those piles of wood, screws and objects coming under the category 'might come in handy one day'.

ii) *Regulate* the amount of time you:
- watch television,
- sit at the computer,
- use social media,
- sit alone, or
- talk on the phone/email or text to someone who is negative.

Do not give in to your particular 'itch' as it re-scars or interferes with your healing.

iii) There are three ways to *Lighten UP.*
a. Firstly, ensure that you have enough light in your life. A sunshine moment, particularly on your skin, pouring in essential vitamins is a healing time. Good light and the sun can heighten the impact on your mood and energy levels. As part of your biological clock, light is an enormous healing factor. It transmits wellbeing to the emotional brain, relieving depression, anxiety and stress.
b. Secondly, comes through your humour. Is it time for you to *Lighten UP?* I know when one of the 3Ds has hit me as my humour leaves home. My laughter dries up and life appears to be a series of serious interventions. Humour has been shown to improve immune-cell functions and boost brainpower. You will know that laughter is not only contagious it is attractive. It is a natural relaxant, apparently when you laugh the lining in your blood vessel walls relax and expand! Even watching a funny movie allows 20% more blood to flow through your heart!

Laughter connects you with others and is a resource against insurmountable problems. The amazing work of

Dr Hunter Doherty 'Patch' Adams and his *Gesundheit! Institute* is testimony to the healing power of laughter.

It might be necessary to force a smile or help yourself by watching or listening to a comedian, read a joke book, plan events for Red-Nose Day (British comic fund-raiser), play with a young animal or join in with a child playing at his or her level. There has to be a movement towards reclaiming the birth right of your laughter. Encourage your innate and inborn lighter side of life. Think what has been the funniest event that has happened to you ever or just this week, share this with friends and ask them for their anecdotes.

c. Thirdly, engage with the *Light of the World*—your spiritual light—Jesus. He is a great way to *Lighten UP*, "I am the light of the world. Whoever follows me will never walk in darkness, but will have the light of life" (John 8:12). His light, chases away every shadow which threaten to engulf your heart in darkness, transforms your emotions, feelings and upsets. Do you need more of Jesus in your life?

5. Positive Pressure

On a wound, pressure helps the tissues to knit together and supports the energy levels of the body. Pressure implies exertion of force. Dealing with the 3Ds you need to make the choice to move forward. Apply active force to chase away the negative impacts. When suffering from the 3Ds it is worth the effort to administer pressure and self-help.

i) Stimulate your endorphins by *exercise*. There is a lot of evidence about the change on your mood and well being by encouraging endorphins to be released. The moving of your body and deliberate exercise sets off this group of peptides and helps the brain to raise your pain threshold. The benefits of exercise occur when you enjoy the moment and afterwards the body gives pleasurable vibes back. Stimulated endorphins flow through your body giving a feeling of happiness. There is a limitless variety of exercise to choose from: gardening, swimming, sex, golf, dance, visiting a gym, taking the dog for a jog. What exercise do you enjoy doing?

ii) *Be loving* to your significant other. Although they will take a lot from you during your hurting, be fair about how much you 'dump' on them. Think loving thoughts towards them and enjoy lovemaking and sex together. Sex is a huge body defender against germs and virus. It supports your immune system, keeping you happy with an improved libido. Research suggests there is a link between sex and lower blood pressure and a reduction in the likelihood of heart attack or stroke. Bearing in mind the old joke, "Not tonight dear, I've got a headache", the hormones released during an orgasm can block pain. So here is an alternative to an aspirin!

iii) *Face your Fear* and go there anyway. It took me a while to realise that I was avoiding places where I might 'bump into' someone who I knew was against me. I had to be careful that I was not changing my habits to accommodate my pain. By coincidence, I met one opponent at the cinema and had to put on my 'smiley polite mask' and tuck my 'what I'd really like to say', together with the desire to bolt and run away, into my popcorn!

Helping Hands: Self-Help and God-Help

To heal from the mutiny of the 3Ds you will need to nurture yourself. Look for the helping hands; practise some self-help, self-love, self-respect and self-regard. Consider replacing the 'self' words with the prefix God, and introduce God-help, God-love, God-respect and God-regard etc into your life. He views you as a special child of His and together you will exponent your healing. To entertain thought patterns such as, "I do not like myself at the moment" is a huge 3D 'lie' warped by depression. You are, and can only be, yourself and you are loveable, special and unique. It might take time to realise this but you must.

I believe it is love, rather than time that is the great healer. Love can heal all wounds and render scars to minuscule lines. I am in agreement with *Rose Kennedy*, 'It has been said, "time heals all wounds". I do not agree. The wounds remain. In time, the mind, protecting its sanity, covers them with scar tissue and the pain lessens. But it is never gone'.

Every great story features ups and downs, valleys and mountains, peaks and troughs. Could you be grateful and thankful for the brilliant experiences if that was all you ever had? Without the downs would you appreciate the ups? Appreciate moments of disillusionment as a shining light on your story—they give your story meaning. Take hold of them and do not settle for a second-best, placid, or mediocre life.

Open the Door

1. **Decide** to use your Self-help and God-help. Your healing comes in many ways and styles. What is your preferred choice for your current situation? How can you implement it?
2. **Memorise** a number of motivational phrases and Bible verses. Repeat these out loud when a negative thought pops into your head to replace the negative with a positive thought.
3. **Acknowledge** your disillusionment and track where it has come from. Give yourself a time-line and check to see if it has got caught up with insecurity from your past.
4. **Change** any bitter feelings and thoughts. What do you need to do to change your thought patterns to become better not bitter?

5. **Partner** with your body, mind and soul not stopping until they are in agreement. What can you do to ensure they are working together for your healing with the strength of a 3-strand cord?

6. **Choose** to forgive making this an important decision and part of your first aid kit. Think of a situation when you have been hurt and choose to forgive the person who hurt you. If you have forgiven them, how do you know? If you are stepping out on this journey, for the first time, notice any differences. Do you think God has or is using this situation?

7. **Say a Blessing.** Use the Lord's Prayer or Blessing Prayer from Your Bonus Section or write your own blessing. As you say it, name the person with whom you have had the difficulty with and bless them through God working in their lives.

8. **Write down** any issues whenever you are stressed or feel under pressure. List 3-5 alternative actions to counteract your reaction. Celebrate and reward yourself whenever you take a positive step.

9. **Give the Disillusionment a Number.** On a scale of 1-10, what do you think your intensity of feeling will be towards your disillusionment in 5 years time?

10. **Who is holding your arms up**? Ask two people to read Exodus 17:8-15 with you and then to stand in the gap with you, lifting your arms as they pray into your situation.

11. **Communicate with God** about your priorities as a check on your stress levels. Ask whether you need to rest, take a break or readjust what is taking precedence in your life.

12. **Compile** a first aid kit filling it with God-help remedies. Use self-help and self-love to heal your visible and invisible scars until you have a full recovery.

Step into God's Warming Light

Dear Lord,

I pray for my healing, that I may find the right support to recover from my disillusionment and suffering. I pray that I can subscribe the best self-help and Your-help for my circumstances and place in my first aid kit. Please send Your Spirit to dispel all disillusionment and prevent further harm.

I pray that I will be healed from my wounds, be stronger in my resolve and kinder to myself. May my situation be used to help others and aid their healing. Meanwhile, Lord, come into my life and take away all my pain, burdens and discomforts. Thank you God for your healing power.

Amen.

YOUR PROTECTION

People protect what they love.
JACQUES YVES COUSTEAU

Picture of Protection

A perfect picture of protection is one of a mother guarding her young. To make sure youngsters are safe, parents will do whatever is necessary for the health and well being of their offspring. This works both in the animal and the human world making protection a natural instinct. It is the instinct to keep the defenceless and vulnerable safe and sound. You are protective of those you cherish and love and you show this in your actions to keep them from risk, to shelter and shield them from harm.

Life does not come with a guarantee against danger; in fact, the opposite is true. There is only so much you can do to guard yourself and your loved ones. It is impossible to put up an impregnable wall of safety against all eventualities. Protection based on a cosseted lifestyle—wrapping yourself in cotton wool—precludes enjoyment of a full life. The best you can do is to be taught and teach self-preservation, taking actions in certain circumstances to reduce the probability of injury.

An obvious form of protection is vaccinations against disease. You probably had some as a baby and as you grew up. Protection includes wearing appropriate clothing according to the circumstance; for example, protection against weather, protective sporting equipment or armour, and later protecting ourselves by assessing risks. It might also include taking relevant precautions such as warranties on cars, taking a driving test, insurances and so on.

Your Protection

Society is structured in such a way that the dangers of living near wild creatures is minimised. Houses are built to keep out wildlife and unless you have a personality like *Bear Grylls*, pitting yourself against natural elements is done in a conservative manner.

There are natural disasters offering no protection for people, creatures or plant life who are in the path of a hurricane, tsunami or earthquake. The empathetic response from others is to send aid to those who suffer such catastrophes. Overall, it seems to me that one of the main cause of hazards, misadventures and those calamities from which protection is needed, is Man himself.

Protection in Your World

Protection in this world comes from many sources, though each has its limitations. Parents will do their best in their individual ways, sometimes in spite of their own past and experiences, but overall, their protection is inconsistent. Government and insurances have to be paid for and have their own agendas and 'exclusion clauses'. Insurance is a paid protection which can only be collected after the event. It may prevent financial hardship but it cannot protect against the event happening in the first place.

Reliance on another person to protect you is not sustainable as it can only last for the lifetime of that partnership. Work situations, no longer protected by a liege, such as a lord and servant relationship have transformed into employer and employee relationships. Each has to safeguard themselves against each other via solicitors or unions. Self-protection carries you only as far as your learning goes. So, whom can you turn to?

The Psalmist answers this question, 'my help comes from the LORD, the maker of heaven and earth' (Psalm 121:2). I believe this understanding of God's protection has not changed for thousands of years. In 1491 Saint Ignatius of Loyola spoke this prayer of protection, "May the perfect grace and eternal love of Christ our Lord be our never-failing protection and help".

God protects you—yet you are often unaware and ignorant of how much protection He provides. He does this because He loves you. He protects what He loves. Jesus spoke about the outpouring of God's love, "He knows the number of hairs on your heads" (Luke 12:7, 21:18 and Matthew 10:30) or, if you are bald, consider it the number of hair follicles on your head!

▲　　▲　　▲

Anita felt as though she was wrapped in a coat of God's protection when she was delayed from catching a train to work. The train would later de-rail with many deaths and injuries. She thanked God for her escape and His protection.

There are many similar testimonies of a situation out of control, where inexplicable protection was given. This can only be reasoned as God's protection or God-help.

Evidence of God's Protection

We know God as a provider, from daily bread to fulfilling all needs, now it is time to explore your perception of God as a protector. Ask Him how He does this? See His arm outstretched towards you, protecting you from fatal danger. In American football, the quarterback who plays in offensive lines needs to be protected and defended from the opposition. He needs a member of the team to protect him from the onslaught of the opposing player, especially when he cannot see danger coming. They call this the Blind Side. This is illustrated in the film *The Blind Side* (John Lee Hancock, 2009); the true story of Michael Oher is featured. One scene involved Michael and his younger brother, SJ Tuohy, in a car collision where Michael's protective instincts were revealed. He used his arm to shield SJ, later these protective instincts were maximised in his American football career becoming a renowned American football offensive tackle.

How many natural protective instincts do you have and how aware are you of God's protective nature towards you?

The Psalms speak of God being like an eagle carrying you, covering you with his feathers, and as a place of refuge like a fortress guarding you. They remind you to wait in hope as He is your help, promising that He will deliver you from all your troubles (Psalms 91:1, 91:4, 34:17). These are passages to meditate on and memorise. God proves His care in remarkable ways, including sending His angels to look after you, 'He will command His angels concerning you to guard you in all your ways' (Psalm 91:11).

⋏   ⋏   ⋏

Frank waited for his friend *Lee* to arrive—it was an accustomed wait. Frank would arrive ten minutes earlier than the scheduled time and stand at a prearranged spot. He would pray and sing to God preparing himself for Lee's arrival and they would then travel on to the band rehearsal. Tonight was a usual night with an unusual outcome. As Lee's car drew up to the kerb, the lorry (truck) behind him continued to bear down on him.

For Frank the next moments appeared in slow motion. The juggernaut rammed into Lee's car, appearing to go over the top of it and sliced off the roof in its efforts to continue its trajectory. After the noise of the crash, metal on metal, came a silence. A stillness broken by the sirens of emergency vehicles as they rushed to the scene. To everyone's surprise, Lee got out of the car unscathed. It was a miracle and both men got down on their knees and thanked God.

Have you had any accidents or near misses? Can you give God the credit? Can you feel His protective arm around you or in front of you? Perhaps, you have experienced a smaller incident when you knew your safety was assured despite everything around you being in crisis. Have you been aware of one of God's angel's looking after you? Consider your answers.

Will your answers reveal how much God is protecting you in your life where previously you may have been unaware?

The Apostle Peter warns that you may be distressed or grieved by various trials in this world. Once more, you are told that life will contain difficulties. Peter explains that it is your faith which assures you of your place in Heaven as you claim His promises in faith (1 Peter 1:3-7). This is God's protection for you. Would it be irreverent to suggest that it is like God putting a towel over a chair to reserve a place in Heaven—with your name on it!

God's Withdrawn Protection

The alternative to receiving the blessing of God's protection is to be without it. This could be the doorway to Hell! God promises to avenge your enemies; He will remove His protection over them. God will not protect those who live in such a way as to hurt or harm others: withholding love, being spiteful or acting in a way that grieves Holy Spirit. The people who inflict disaster are those who are caught up in wickedness, ignorance, abuse, self-indulgence and spiritual warfare. These people will be cast into outer darkness experiencing the finality of isolation from Him, unless they truly repent, like the flawed *King David*. David did not go unpunished by God for his sin of sending *Uriah* to his death in order that he could have Uriah's wife, *Bathsheba* for himself, (2 Samuel 11-27). Coming under God's displeasure and the fear of being without God (Psalm 51:11) must have featured in David's repentance.

A person who understood God's withdrawn protection and was terrified of this retribution was *Job.* God was ready to punish *Job's* friends, *Eliphaz, Bildad* and *Zophar* because they had spoken untruths (lied) about the Lord. Job prayed for his friends asking God for His mercy. Can you imagine how desperate Job must have been for his friends to be forgiven? God answered Job's prayer, forgiving them as well as blessing Job with health and riches (Job 42:7-17).

▲   ▲   ▲

Billy is at his son's bedside praying for his recovery,
he had been involved in a motorbike accident on his
way to church. Billy sets up a prayer chain for his son,
prayers that the brain damage would be minimal. He
reached out to God even in his questioning.

▲   ▲   ▲

Gillian heard that the overseas ministry she prayed for daily
was attacked in a 'church-cleansing' bombing. Atrocities
were committed: the school was burnt to the ground. She
asked God where was His protection when her loved one
needed it most? Gillian kept her faith though she could
not understand the circumstances. While her teardrops
fell, she blessed the unknown and unnamed perpetrators.
The blessing was for their souls, not for their actions.

Protection, like healing is in God's gifting—given by God or not. It is a mystery
as to who and what will be protected. It is God's prerogative. There are times
when, despite prayer covering, His protection appears to be absent—the
enemy is allowed to win. It is for you and I to trust that God has His timing,
His way and for His purposes. We cannot understand senseless genocides.

▲   ▲   ▲

Recently in Libya, 21 Egyptian Coptic Christians (February
2015) and 30 Ethiopian Christians (April 2015) were
beheaded or shot in the head by Islamic State militants for
refusing to abandon their faith in Jesus Christ. They went
to their deaths with the name of Jesus on their lips.

Could it be that their witness of unshakable love for God is for other people's salvation? He will use it for good. At times, it seems that God has lifted His protection because you cannot see it or you are in the middle of a miserable or life-threatening situation. If this is your circumstance, consider that God is protecting you from falling away from Him and is in and through the situation with you. He is not, for mysterious reasons that cannot be revealed right now, protecting you from the experience itself. Unfortunately, this still needs to be endured.

Protection Against Your Sin

When was the last time you used the word 'sin' in a general conversation? It is more likely it was a chat with a believer who still has sin in their vocabulary. Yet, sin is a choice tempting you, others and me around us!

Acting out sin stunts our spiritual growth, harming your and my relationship with God. It even happened for Jesus. When Jesus died on the cross, He took on the sins of the entire world. For a brief moment in time—it must have seemed forever for Jesus—the Father turned His face away. Jesus cried out to His father, "My God, My God, why have you forsaken me?" (Matthew 27:46). The reason for this apparent rejection comes from the minor prophet Habakkuk who tells us about God's character, 'Your eyes are too pure to look on evil; You cannot tolerate wrongdoing' (Habakkuk 1:3). This was demonstrated by God—even for His own son.

Feeling guilty is uncomfortable. Acknowledging that you choose to sin may be equated with weakness and wrongdoing. Who wants to admit to these? Yet, it matters to God that sin is acknowledged and dealt with. He can heal, correct and make right your shortcoming. It does not matter to God whether the sin you undertake is a mild offence or a malignant misdemeanour, it is still wrong in His eyes. He wants this to change. He does not condemn you for it but accepts it as in the past and I believe asks, "What are we (you and He) going to do about it?"

What is your sin? Perhaps an over-indulgence, or a bad habit, moving you off-balance with God? You live in a world where everything is permissible, with the caveat, 'If it is not hurting anyone then it is OK', this employs an attitude which permeates the beginning of sin. It starts with small offences, insidiously running along a continuum—like a meandering river— until it reaches a crisis or tipping point—entering the door of evil. This door has numerous signs on it:

Sex:	from mild lustful thoughts to malignant pornography.
Food:	from mild overeating to malignant obesity.
Conversations:	from mild criticism to malignant judgment.
Lies:	from mild white lies to malignant lying.
Wanting:	from mild wishing for more to malignant stealing.
'Bigging':	from mild belief that you are better than other people by bigging yourself up to malignant arrogance.
Swearing:	from mild expletives to malignant blasphemy.
Hurting:	from mild attack to malignant murder.
Conspiring:	from mild plans for bad things to happen to malignant schemes for a person's downfall.
Gossip:	from mild interest for titillation to malignant repeating of perceived knowledge.
Accusation:	from mild blaming to malignant false witnessing.
Instigating:	from mild meddling to malignant stirring up of conflict.
Hate:	from mild hostility to malignant enmity.
Disbelief:	from mild denouncing to malignant incitement of Godlessness.

Do you recognize yourself on any of these ranges? I recognize myself. I pray for protection to avoid the temptations and for help to change my habits. These are all sins disguised as wilful habits (and many more could be listed) creating a hurting sickness in ourselves. This in turns forms a separation from God, Jesus and Holy Spirit.

If you are unsure whether your sin is a problem, or even a sin at all, check out Proverbs 6:16-22, asking yourself the following question, 'Does the action hurt myself in anyway or hurt another person?' If the answer is, 'Yes'—be honest—then it is a violation of your potential that causes offence to God.

Ask God for a 'Hedge' of Protection
Your sin does not need to be a permanent feature. You can pray for help and ask Holy Spirit to support you. Pray for a 'hedge' of protection around you—like a thorn bush with sharp defences—to stop you when you are tempted in your habit. It stops undesirables from getting to you.

▲　　▲　　▲

Joe is a loving husband and a great father. His work takes him away from home and he spends a lot of time in hotels. His temptation is to watch the soft porn channels available through the TV offering the pay-to-view videos. His colleague says, "It is just for a laugh" and recommends the latest titles also suggesting that they attend local strip clubs.

Joe prays before he leaves home that he will not look at the porn programmes, and that he can leave his colleague's room when the films are playing as he knows it is disrespectful to his marriage. Even watching these films at home with his wife does not honour God or their relationship. Joe and his wife pray for God's protection against this temptation in times of separation. They say *The Lord's Prayer.*

They receive protection by highlighting a verse in *The Lord's Prayer.* The ask is within the verse, 'do not lead us into temptation' (Matthew 6:9-18 and Luke 11:2-4). To counteract the temptations Joe uses You Tube to watch uplifting programmes. This replaces the sinful activity with a God-loving one.

Seven Deadly Sins

Can you remember the seven deadly sins? They are called deadly for a reason—they kill the relationship between you, others and God. Holy Spirit cannot support you or live in you when sin is present. Sin is abhorrent to Him. It is not the example that Jesus set, so why do it?

The deadly sins are identified and commented on throughout history, including in the writings of Pope Gregory in the 6th Century, and Thomas Aquinas and Geoffrey Chaucer in the middle ages.

The seven deadly sins are:

- Pride,
- Envy,
- Gluttony,
- Lust,
- Anger,
- Greed, and
- Sloth

They are just as prevalent today albeit described with other names. To say, "I cannot help it" or "It's not my fault", or "It does not hurt anyone" are hopeless cries. These are 'lies' of disillusionment which further your sin habit, escalating in severity as each one is practiced. They become uncontrollable, feeding a ceaseless appetite. Sin develops into an addiction that destroys both you and others. It does not care about anything apart from itself. Like a parasite, it feeds on your person-hood, eventually making you unrecognisable. God cannot abide this, He sent Jesus to help you and He, in turn sent Holy Spirit to be available for you.

Your Gifts versus Your Sin

I like to view protection as a present from Holy Spirit; 'gift' or 'gifting are presents involving action and 'fruits' or 'fruits of the Spirit' are presents involving your attitude. I love receiving presents and God's presents are the best! They are a marvellous protection for you and me. Accepting His presents is your insurance against your sin. They keep you out of reach of the seven deadly ones. It is impossible to exhibit a gift or fruit and a sin at the same time. This gives you reassurance that you are not being sinful—as the two cannot breathe the same space.

A sin is only a sin when it is put into action or committed. Jesus was tempted to sin but chose not to take up the offer (Matthew 4:10). You can do the same.

How to Recognise the Seven Deadly Sins	*How to Recognise Holy Spirit's Presents* (Gifts and Fruits)
But your iniquities have separated you from your God; your sins have hidden His face from you, so that He will not hear. (Isaiah 59:2)	A spiritual gift is given to each of us so we can help each other. (1 Corinthians 12:7)

A sinful *Gordon* is full of *pride* he is successful in work and at sport. He knows he can beat his competitors any day of the week. He has forgotten his mentors who helped him to win. He says, "I do not need to listen to others, they have got nothing to teach me. They need to learn from me." He is condescending and arrogant in his manner and sneers at his peers behind their back.

A saved *Gordon* shows *gentleness, meekness and humbleness.* He appreciates his achievements, is gracious when he wins at sport, praising God for his success. He knows that with God in his life he has been blessed and is thankful for those who helped him along his journey. He shares his skills and strengths with others, ready to listen and be there for his peers.

A sinful *Grace* is *envious* of her friends. She puts herself down as she thinks her friends as better than her.

A saved *Grace* is *generous* in her praise for her friends. She builds up her self-confidence with *patience*

She is discontented with her life. She wants to be the same as *Betty* who is popular and has more money than her. She says, "Life is unfair, other people are more intelligent than me, she makes me feel stupid."

She wants what her friends have but without having to do anything to change.

A sinful *Paul* is a *glutton*. He eats and drinks more than he should, always going back for seconds or thirds! He likes to go out on the 'razz' at the weekends. A good night out is to 'have a skinful' and get drunk. He believes that drink makes him popular and funny.

A sinful *Mark* looks at women with *lust* in his eyes. He assesses each one by collecting statistics on their bodies. He dreams of having sex with as many women as possible. Under the cloak of social media, he is able to make suggestive comments to women without revealing himself.

knowing her friends have had to work hard for their successes.

She is content with her life and *cheerful* despite not having everything she would like. She *serves* her friends whenever she can.

A saved *Paul* is *hospitable*. He welcomes visitors, sharing the food that he grows in his garden and the home brewed beer that he makes as a hobby. He thanks God that he always has more than enough. Paul is a recovering alcoholic who knows God's grace and protection from bad decisions when under the influence of drink.

A saved *Mark* practices *self-control* waiting many years to meet the girl of his dreams. His *self-control* is shown in his *faith*. He enjoys being a loving husband.

▲ ▲ ▲

A sinful Penelope has a quick temper and she lets anger get the better of her. She is a Head Teacher. She says, "I sometimes behave unprofessionally, I do not seem to be able to stop flying off the handle at the least provocation." She regrets her outbursts knowing that her tongue injures others.

▲ ▲ ▲

A saved *Penelope* prays that she can be *clear minded* and *peaceful* to offset her quick temper. She is *mindful* how she speaks. She reserves her rage for *righteous anger* towards those who harm children.

▲ ▲ ▲

A sinful Timothy is greedy for material wealth. He wants to have a lot of money and a lifestyle of the rich and famous. He does not mind what he has to do to make this happen. He loves technology and is the first to get the latest toy or gadget. He is in debt with maxed out credit cards.

▲ ▲ ▲

A saved Timothy is exuberant about life and full of joy. He is patient, sticking at things until he can afford them within his budget. He uses delayed gratification to his advantage and is satisfied with his life.

▲ ▲ ▲

A sinful Brian is lazy and falls into slothful habits. He lives his life on the couch watching TV and expecting his friends to do things for him. He squanders his time and feels tired and sad all the time.

▲ ▲ ▲

A saved Brian is always on the go. He is busy and likes to do works of service. He studies and tells other people about God. He is cheerful and is studying for the lay ministry.

It is your choice to be sinful or saved. God is ready with His Spirit to fulfil your preference. Jesus said, "I have come that they may have life, and have it to the full" (John 10:10).

Protective Prayers

Even in fiction, prayers are used as protection. In *The Snow Queen*, (Anderson) Gerda, our heroine, reaches her enemy's dominion—the Snow Queen's palace. Gigantic ugly snowflakes guard the palace. They are formed into formidable, terrifying shapes to repel intruders. Gerda prays, using the *Lord's Prayer* to protect herself and giving her courage to move forward. God answers the prayer, 'causes her breath to take the shape of angels'. In true protective angelic style, the discouraging snowflakes cannot resist God's inspired breath providing Gerda with her opportunity to enter.

Which prayers do you use when you need courage to face down disappointment, disillusionment or discouragement? You can choose from many prayers. *The Lord's Prayer* is an exemplary protective prayer as it encompasses all the promises of God.

God's Promises

His promises are unchangeable as God himself does not change (Malachi 3:6). Once a promise is given then He will keep it. Unlike my capricious opinions, God is the same today as He was yesterday and will be tomorrow. This means you can rely on Him. He promises never to leave or forsake you (Genesis 28:15) and His love for you will last forever (Jeremiah 31:3).

At the last supper, Jesus gave His final live teach-in (John 14:1-32). His speech featured instruction, prophecy, insights, promises, 'Heaven 101', a Q & A session with the disciples, revelation plus a gift. An extraordinary after-dinner speech! The largest promise was His gift of Holy Spirit, "And I will ask the Father, and he will give you another advocate to help you and be with you forever—the Spirit of Truth" (John 14:16-17).

This supernatural presence is available to you as the most protective covering you could ever receive. He is your helper, advocate, and counsellor. He is the reminder of God's words, Jesus' work and Their promises.

Access to God's Promises

You can access God's promises by thinking of a crossroads with four choices:

1. Talking to God.
2. Seeking Jesus who said, "I am the way, the truth and the life" (John 14:6).
3. Asking Holy Spirit for reminders, and
4. Reading your Bible.

The Bible is filled with the promises made to you by God. This precious package of Truths explains in part why it has not been possible to knock the Bible from the best seller's list. It is the most distributed book EVER. Current records say global sales have exceeded 17.75 million copies and it has been translated into 349 languages (*Guinness World Records*). Other books by believers support your faith as testimonies of God's promises.

A quick look at a major online store under a search for 'Christian books' gave the number available as 983,357—an amazing selection. Access to God's word is made simpler now using TV, Radio and the Internet: Blogs, articles, and testimonials are all aids to remind you of God's promises. And yet, there is so much that is unknown, as it was not recorded 'Jesus did many other things as well. If every one of them were written down, I suppose that even the whole world would not have room for the books that would be written' (John 21:25). This is still the case, even with the Kindle and eBooks!

A Proper Dressing

In Disney's *Frozen*, Princess Anna leaves to search for her sister without any protection. She has inadequate clothing and footwear for wintry elements, does not have a map to give her direction and does not have a weapon to ward off attacks from the wolves. She has not taken any guards with her; she loses her horse and is lost. She is forced to seek the protection of a stranger, *Kristoff*, providing him with supplies, yet she is still unprepared for her journey.

Living in God's plans can mean that you may also set off on your journey without a map. The letter to the Hebrews recalls *Abraham's* journey: God told him to go without knowing where he was going (Hebrews 11:8). This is called stepping out in faith.

You need to be properly dressed in preparation to protect yourself against the 3Ds. This means seeking help from God who is involved and interested in your plans. He has given you equipment for your protection— His armour—for you to wear (Ephesians 6:13-18). Read the passage and apply it to your situation. I recommend that you put this spiritual armour on as part of your daily dressing.

God's Protective Armour

The Apostle Paul took the analogy of a soldier's armour and a soldier's state of mind—you can use the seven articles in a similar way.

1. Take up Your Armour

This begins with the battle for your mind-set—your choice to accept the challenge and take up your armour as you enter the battle. In Unfrozen your battle means fighting against and resisting the 3Ds disappointment, disillusionment and discouragement. An advantage you have is that the betrayer, or adversary, is so confident in his or her own beliefs, buoyed up in their moment of 'power', that they have not considered the truth of the situation. This is your strength; you know the landscape, so be prepared to take a stand in your own defence. In this way you can 'stand your ground', fighting against danger and evil like a heavily armed soldier in God's army. The armour, as part of a uniform, gives a soldier his status and bearing. For your protection, God has supplied your armour.

▲   ▲   ▲

George and Hannah were forced to change their mind-set and enter a court battle when they realised that a fellow Christian was embezzling their money in a property deal. They put on the armour of God to prepare themselves for entering a foreign territory of legal language. They were one of many in this person's scam portfolio, however they were the only ones prepared to take action. Although they lost money, they went forward under God's protection. Their strong faith did not let this disillusionment deter them from trusting others in this field.

2. The Belt of Truth

A belt goes round the middle of the body keeping everything together—not just your tummy! Like all belts it goes all round you, encircling you with His Truth.

Think of the belt like a tradesman's belt, made of strong leather with pockets, pouches, quick fastening buckles and loops to attach tools. In this, you will place your Truth: evidence, your first aid kit, prayers, blessings and God's promises. This protection is for your safety and it is worth repeating, 'if God is for me who can be against me?' (Romans 8:31).

▲   ▲   ▲

Francis goes to work each day knowing he will receive jokes and jeers about his faith. He will be challenged as colleagues make assumptions about his beliefs baiting him with verbal traps based on their perception of how a Christian should or should not behave. Francis can bear this as he put on the Belt of Truth, using the many tools attached to show his love for his job and his fellow workmates.

3. Breastplate of Righteousness

The breastplate protects the heart and other vital organs. For you the breastplate will protect your heart, keeping it warm, safe and unfrozen by the 3Ds. Righteousness is how you speak about God, use His words, live in the fruits of His spirit and obey His commandments. The breastplate demonstrates a protective layer of love and faith, shining bright with your integrity, values and morals.

▲   ▲   ▲

Matthew suffers from depression. He needs to put on the breastplate of righteousness to fight against the negative thoughts that tell him that he is not good enough, does not have anything to contribute, and cannot make friends. He draws on some of the gifts given by Holy Spirit. He tries to be gentle with himself and, using self-control, has taken up a sport. Exercise is a pro-active process and protects him from feeling 'too low'. He can engage with others interested in his sport and is considering a sponsored event to raise money for a charity.

4. Shoes of Peace

Your footwear dictates your circumstance. Roller boots are useless if you want to go deep sea diving, whereas boots needed for scaling rocky mountains differ from those wanting to put their footsteps across the Antarctic. A soldier can move with speed when the right covering is on the feet. God's armour provides shoes of the Gospel of peace, to give you firm-footed stability. A person who approaches in peace and reconciliation is welcomed when a fight can be avoided. God views your feet as beautiful when peace and goodness underline your approach.

▲　　▲　　▲

Martha's friends tell her that she is a peaceful person. When arguments arise in the family, she is able to deflect the 'poison' in the attacks and, by neutral questioning, gets to the bottom of the problem, offering solutions to both sides. She is taking a course in mediation, although in the secular world she believes that Jesus gives the best examples of peaceful living in a frustrated discordant world. As part of her quiet time, she puts on the shoes of the gospel of peace each day. Her heroes are *Mother Teresa* and *Mahatma Gandhi.*

5. Shield of Faith
A shield can be decorated with your coat of arms, proclaiming your values. It is an object you have to lift, positioning it to keep out pointed darts or objects being thrown at you. A shield can be very large and shaped to cover you. It symbolises your faith covering you, deflecting disillusionment 'lies' and accusations. When the shield of faith is lifted, worry and doubt bounce off you. Faith will not allow negative emotions to attach or make contact with any part of your body.

Joining your shield with other people's shields, in the way riot police protect themselves, stops the rain of insults from penetrating your mind. Ground can be gained by physically moving forward in a group. Figuratively, you can link your shield of faith with other believers so that the 3Ds do not freeze you into one position.

▲   ▲   ▲

Betty and Fred hold up their shields of faith together as they live on an estate with a poor and violent reputation. Then as they venture out they protect each other with God's promises and truths. Their neighbours respect them and, although their neighbours do not believe in God, they turn to Betty and Fred for prayer when a family member is ill or they have a problem.

6. Helmet of Salvation

Helmets protect the brain against elements such as the sun and wind as well as accidental or deliberate damage sustained by impact. The 3Ds mess with your head! Your helmet of salvation is your protection and reminder that Jesus died for you. It can also be seen as a ceremonial helmet as it denotes your standing with Christ. A bit like nailing your colours to a mast, your helmet declares that you are His, a believer in Jesus as the Son of God. Or as the Apostle Paul puts it, 'for it is by grace you have been saved, through faith—and this is not from yourselves, it is the gift of God' (Ephesians 2:8).

Salvation is given to you as a mark of His great love. It is not given because of your good works, efforts or by making the 'grade', nor can it be bought. God chooses to rescue you from darkness and save you from sin and its consequences— the backstory to sending Jesus to die for you. God only gives this gift to people who are genuine in wanting it. This is why people say the 'Sinner's' or 'Salvation 'Prayer (see Your Bonuses) to start their first conversation with God. When we finally meet Him face-to-face, this is when God will replace the helmet with a crown!

▲   ▲   ▲

Patricia is a nurse. She laughingly describes her uniform as God's armour, "I put on the helmet of salvation when I put on my uniform and don my cap". She knows her cap proves her worth as its colour denotes her rank in the hospital. She thanks God that she has been saved by Jesus dying for her. She is able to pray unobtrusively for her patients and for the medical assistance she can bring in her work.

7. Sword of the Spirit
The sword is your weapon to wield, to be on the offensive when all else fails against your enemies. It is for face-to-face spiritual warfare when battles or combat are fought with words. This sword will defeat any enemy. You need to have knowledge of His Word. Ask Holy Spirit to help you find the correct words for your protection. It is your prayers, filled with all kinds of requests and petitions, based on His character and promises that 'makes you ready' to take on the Enemy. Jesus used this sword when He was tempted in the desert. Remember 'the word of God is living and powerful, and sharper than any two-edged sword, piercing even to the division of soul and spirit, and of joints and marrow, and is a discerner of the thoughts and intents of the heart' (Hebrews 4:12).

▲ ▲ ▲

Arthur is a military man and in charge of several
squadrons. He has been taught how to fight. As part of
the armour he is provided with a gun rather than a sword.
He views the bayonet as his sword. He talks with Holy
Spirit asking to be shown His Word as his sword. Arthur
clarifies, "I ask Holy Spirit for help and guidance in many
difficult situations, including: separation from my family,
having to obey my superiors even when I think they are
wrong!" Arthur sets himself apart for God by refusing to
join his peers in the Army's swearing and drinking culture.

8. Fear of the Lord (A bonus point)

I have added this as a bonus for your armour. Living in the Fear
of the Lord means worshiping Him as you step out and know
that He has your situation covered. He has your back. Evoke
this healthy fear as a protective garment of praise that you can
wear.

▲ ▲ ▲

Giles said, "I fear the Lord in my everyday living. I try
to serve Him and worship Him with my heart, mind
and soul, in fact my whole being. This way I know
He has my back and will always protect me. I do not
live a 'charmed life' but a normal God given one".

God is not expecting you to have a degree in theology, to know the Bible
backwards, or to be able to recite every verse in the Bible. He asks you to

have a simple belief in Him, to come to Him, have conversations, dialogue and walk in His warming light.

Open the Door

1. **Visualise** what protection means to you. What is your picture? How do you see God as part of this?
2. **Pour blessings** into your situation where it appears to you that God's protection is absent. Expand this to where you live and nationally.
3. **Choose a Prayer** of protection. Make one your favourite prayer, such as *The Lord's Prayer* or even one verse from this prayer. Say these when asking God for His help.
4. **Write** down times when God has protected you. Has this covered your sins? Is this part of your testimony? Have you shared this with anyone lately?
5. **Imagine** what life would be like for a person from whom God has withdrawn His protection. What do you think their life looks like?
6. **Be familiar** with the armour; commit the protective articles (plus bonus) to memory. How do they relate to your current situation?
7. **Promise** yourself that you will put the armour of God on figuratively, when you leave the safety of your home.
8. **Dress properly** to protect yourself? What is your belt of truth, what does it look like and how do you use it?
9. **Step out in Peace:** What colour are your shoes? Do you step out in peace or do you need to ask God for His grace in calming your interactions?
10. **Lift up** your Shield. What do you have inscribed on it? Can you put your Shield of Faith to use in dispelling disillusionment?
11. **Put on** the Helmet of Salvation. Praise God for this incredible gift, accept your Salvation through Jesus Christ and tell others about it.
12. **Practice** using your Sword of the Spirit. What words and promises will Holy Spirit give you when you are challenged?

Step into God's Warming Light

Dear Lord,

I pray that I will be able to see Your love and protection in my life. I pray that I may daily wear Your armour. I ask Holy Spirit to come and help me to practice wielding Your sword. I pray that I can move with confidence from the practice swords given to children, to handling the grown up version, which is Your Word 'sharper than a double-edged sword'. Lord, do not let any of the 3Ds get past my defences.

Please Lord protect my blind side and that I will keep my faith, continuing to bless people and circumstances even in times when I cannot see Your protection Lord. May my cries of Your blessings rain down upon my enemies. I pray that I can be certain that my place in heaven has been reserved and protected by You. Let me acknowledge Your presence at my side, protecting me in my endeavours.

Amen.

3rd DIMENSION
DISTILLING DISCOURAGEMENT

3rd Dimension

Your Enemy? Fear is not Your Enemy

YOUR ENEMY? FEAR IS NOT YOUR ENEMY

Fear locks God in a Box
REV JARROD COOPER

Fear–Your Friend or Foe?

Is fear your enemy or your friend? If it comes out upon occasion saving your life then it is your friend if it is part of your daily life then it is a foe. Fear is a reaction, the psychological and physical wiring for your protection—your essential vigilant survival instinct. Does your instinct kick in the moment you feel threatened or in danger? This is good as a fear response raises awareness of danger enabling you to take the right action. It acts like an alarm. Your primal response—feeling scared—is a warning to escape harm, attack, or intimidation against you or your family.

It is known as the 'Fight-or-Flight' response. This also includes the 'Freeze' response. As seen in the animal world, survival can be assured by fighting predators, fleeing from them or staying still and quiet, playing dead until the danger has passed. The first person to describe this was Walter Bradford Cannon in 1915. His theory showed how the body releases a mass of hormones to enable you to fight or to flee, a life-saving reaction. The hormones include norepinephrine, stimulating alertness and epinephrine affecting the central nervous system. The adrenal glands, sitting on top of the kidneys secrete chemicals and the neurotransmitters in the brain are activated. When you are frightened, a rush of adrenaline raises your alertness and arousal. Its role is to promote a fight or flight reaction to your given circumstance.

The night is dark and there are unfamiliar shapes coming towards you, do you:

1. Stand your ground confident in your ability to fight if attacked?
2. Run as fast as possible in the opposite direction? Or do you,
3. Stay still convinced that the shapes will pass, unaware of your presence?

You make an instant judgment, your body's rapid response to protecting itself; simultaneously your body is hijacked with hormones heading into overdrive—your body tenses and is primed—waiting for your decision as to what to do next.

The choices are life saving when applied to the right situation. When a car races around the corner towards you and your family, flight is the instantaneous choice—to run out of the car's path is the best option. You cannot fight a 4,000 lb (1,800 kg) speeding metal machine and to freeze will involve harm. You are accustomed to crossing roads without harm; you know this is a one-off experience and therefore it does not affect your regular strategies of crossing a road without undue fear. Thankfully, an out of control car scenario is rare.

More common are the daily challenges in your workplace by competing colleagues, encountering a bully or interaction with an argumentative next-door neighbour—all stimulating your fear response. Even foreboding begins the release of your hormones. Your body reacts with the same power of urgency to smaller incidents as it does if you thought a bomb was about to explode. Your healthy and friendly fear can keep you from danger, make you aware, tell you to proceed cautiously, and stay within support networks as a sensible protection for your safety. It is when fear prevents you from progressing and turns into a freezing scenario you need to question its friendship.

Playing with Fear

Fear is used as a plaything, a toy for entertainment heightening your senses, stimulating the hormonal rush whilst knowing you are safe, for instance, enjoying horror films or reading suspense thrillers. Fear sells. Products glorifying killing, horror or fear are commonplace—it is easy to forget that they are playing with your emotions. Or it can be considered that you are practising for the real eventuality, rather like young animals when they play-fight.

Have you ever ridden a roller coaster? You either love or hate them as they trigger your fear. I have observed the differing reactions to the experience as people step off at the end of the ride. They have experienced the same sensation yet there is a continuum of responses. Their feelings have changed over the duration of two and a half minutes. All are in a hyper state: excited, buzzed, revved and salivating for a repeat, or feeling sick, terrorised, shaky and resolved never to ride on it again.

They are calmed by a release of oxytocin, the hormone which counteracts adrenaline. When this is released into the bloodstream, it compensates the body for submitting to fear. The play between an adrenaline rush and oxytocin overflow can in itself be addictive! The enthusiasts or fairground junkies want more. The roller coaster industry builds higher and faster models each year, catering to the insatiable adrenaline-rush fear addicts.

There is an attraction to fear, or stimulated fear in the consumption of news and information on social media. You are attracted to headlines such as 'Top 10 wildlife creatures that will give you nightmares'. A mouse click on the Internet and, within seconds, fear is placed in your mind just by reading the list!

Manipulated by Fear

Manipulating your fear response is used by the corporate, political, education, medical and media worlds. A subtle power is at work to discourage the freedom of your independent thoughts and choices. This can be under the guise of providing information and protection.

The headline of a recent email caught my eye, 'If you are over the age of 30 and aren't terrified of having a STROKE, you should be'. Maybe you have seen a similar email with Alzheimer disease or cancer? These fear-inspiring headlines may bring helpful information to your attention, with the article proceeding to give positive advice and actions from a medical expert, or it might be to acting as a fund-raiser. Regardless of the intent, it generates a fear response. If I had not been worrying about having a stroke before this unsolicited email arrived in my inbox, then I do now!

▲   ▲   ▲

> My friend *Lynn* was worried; "I saw warnings on Facebook about holiday destinations being possible targets for the next terrorist attack. It was where I had booked a holiday, but I was not going to take the risk with so many militant groups about, so I had to cancelled my holiday plans".

What was the latest 'fear mongering' message you remember? It may have been based in fact but was it intended to discourage and change your mindset?

There are many examples of the discouraging fear messages you probably received each day. They may come from well-meaning friends who caution: "Don't overdo it", or "Be careful about …" Each interaction discourages your own wise sense of being and competence to tackle whatever your day may bring. A caution embroidered on your heart could read, 'Warning: living can damage your health!'

Those Lazy, Hazy, Crazy Days of Fearlessness

Do you remember a time when you were without fear? When the world was your oyster and anything and everything was possible. Perhaps you played as a superhero with yourself in the central role, and you could cut any horror down to size? It was a time when nothing was insurmountable and challenges were there to overcome. You jumped out of bed, ready and happy to face the day, no turning over with a moan for you. The day meant excitement and not quite knowing what was planned. When did this stop? Is it only as a child that this is possible? Were you told, "It is time to grow up" and in a flash 'realism' was born? Is it time to try and recapture those imaginative times? After all, you can fan your courage into flames, rekindling your fearlessness, 'for God has not given you the spirit of fear, but of power, and of love, and of a sound mind' (2 Timothy 1:7 NKJV).

Discouragement Leading to Fear

At the core of all discouragement sits fear—it is a lying 'stopping' agent. The good usage of fear with its short burst of survival instincts has been anaesthetised, and replaced by the accepted norms of a fear-filled 21st Century life. The pulse of daily life is littered with accepted long-term stress and pressure. It is all around you, belittling your resilience and natural survival responses.

Discouragement is the third of the Dimensions—the 3Ds—joining Disappointment and Disillusionment in a terminal trilogy that causes your heart to become frozen. In Disney's *Frozen*, fear is the emotion driving its main character, Elsa. She is taught to be fearful as a child following an accident when she used her magical powers. To control these powers fear is used, isolating her and she is discouraged in everything she tries to undertake. Fear is named as an enemy. This could be your damaging lifestyle if you live with fear sitting on your shoulder. Is fear reigning in your life, preventing you or stopping you from a life experience?

⋏   ⋏   ⋏

Alex had an aptitude for working with people always giving her best. Her boss asked her to present her ideas at a meeting. Alex stayed up all night working on the presentation; she was excited at the prospect of sharing with her peers. She was unprepared for the arrows of criticism from her colleagues the next day. This discouraging experience triggered a fear response to speaking in-group settings— to volunteering her opinion—before long Alex could not enter a meeting without anxiety, worry and panic attacks.

▲   ▲   ▲

Sally's stomach turned, it would not stop growling although she was not hungry. Her head felt light and she was unable to focus on what she really wanted to say. Naturally a confident person able to control nerves easily, today she was worried that her body would let her down and she would begin to shake. It was silly, she told herself, she was the boss and had responsibility for many staff, yet it was as though she was the enemy.

Sally admired *Felicity*; she had chosen her to be part of the senior leadership team because she respected her opinions. Why was it that this professional approach was not returned? Instead, Felicity appears to enjoy instigating dissent amongst the others. The previous meeting had been a disaster and Sally had felt as though she was walking through treacle at the resistance against new policy and procedures. Once a lover of communicating management and leadership techniques, Sally would now like to be somewhere else. Sometimes just looking at Felicity brings out these fearful feelings, compromising her leadership decisions.

Perhaps you have been in a similar situation to Alex and Sally or know someone going through this kind of stress? Fear can be used to control us, consciously or unconsciously as other people promote their own agendas. We believe that our fight is against other people but actually it is not. It could be that they are 'under the influence' of an attacking spiritual force. Fear is the Enemy's weapon of choice.

With this realisation, it is possible to put on the armour of God and protect yourself in fearful situations. The Apostle Paul explained it like this, 'For our struggle is not against flesh and blood, but against the rulers, against the authorities, against the powers of this dark world and against the spiritual forces of evil in the heavenly realms' (Ephesians 6:12). This means Alex and Sally can pray against spiritual forces and not against their individual colleagues and use the healing balm of blessings.

Fear Companions

Fear has two cousins whose names are 'doubt' and 'worry'. They are fear's warm up act; once fear arrives, they are nearby. In the absence of fear, they will act as fear's ambassadors. The acronym F.E.A.R. stands for 'False Evidence Appearing Real'. The 'lies' are buried within a false truth making it a hard to ignore its potency. Gary Busey calls this 'the darkroom where Satan develops his negatives'.

It is the job of doubt and worry to lie to you. Discouragement 'lies' tell you falsehoods such as, if you do an activity you will suffer and be hurt. It tells you how much can and will go wrong. It does not need proof but suggests that it is better for you to feel awful now than suffer terrors later. Discouragement screeches, "Stop!" spreading uncertainly and preventing you from moving into your wonderful plans. When your fear erupts, you become frozen. "I can't", becomes your byword. You freeze; trying new experiences, meeting new people, believing in your ideas or yourself, are relegated to the past. You no longer recognise yourself—you freeze out the encouragers in your life and over time, they give up trying to support you. The extreme version of this frozen reaction is a phobia changing your behaviour to focus with absolute attention on the fear.

▲   ▲   ▲

Seb had a past: he was in a damaging and abusive situation, living with his girlfriend. He suffered: unwarranted criticism, silent treatments, put-downs and isolation, while his girlfriend went off with groups of friends refusing his company. When he tried to leave, she would turn on the charm and persuade him that she would be different, meanwhile carrying on affairs with other men behind Seb's back. His belief in commitment and his own high code of conduct kept him in the relationship for years.

Finally, he broke free and began a relationship with a beautiful girl with a heart of compassion and love. But fear kept rising up within him sabotaging the new relationship. He could not trust himself to believe that he deserved the feeling of happiness. His heart was discouraged—the fear of future disillusionment dominated. Rather than try again, reinvesting with hope and healing, he had anxiety attacks and passed on his fear to his new girlfriend in cyclical patterns. He pushed this relationship to breaking point, escalating his doubts in a warped, self-fulfilling prophesy.

⋀　⋀　⋀

Pippa is known as a worrier. She left the house only to turn the car back after a few miles. Her fears become unbearable. She was tormented by, "I must check …" thoughts, doubting her own abilities. "Have I closed the windows? Did I lock the door? Is the stove ring still on?" When out with friends she would check their status and at the end of the outing telephoned them to check, "Have you got home safely?" Each scenario she double or triple-checks turned out fine with nothing to be fearful about. Pippa's anxious state prevented her from believing in her own competences and she passed this state of nervousness onto others.

A Basketful of Fear
It is surprising how quickly fear can take hold. This is what happened as I researched this book

⋀　⋀　⋀

It started with a moment of doubt, a minute musing needing to be thrown away instead it took hold with the tenacity of a weed. I became concerned about how certain references may be perceived and, if taken the wrong way might mean a court case. Immediately, my imagination catapulted the scene forward; I was appointing solicitors and appearing in the dock!

This is how quickly the thought patterns and mind stories can hop from a minor detail to an irrational major crisis. Psychologists call it 'Catastrophic Thinking'. My thoughts had made the cogitative jump to an irrational worst-case scenario.

▲   ▲   ▲

I reached out to a few friends and was slightly comforted. Then my thoughts rested on my daughter, who had recently received some horrid comments on social media, and my thoughts jumped even higher, beating Javier Sotomayor's record. In the next moment, I had a scenario of her being stalked!

Dr Martin Seligman who established the Master Resiliency Training Programme for the US Army, refers to fear-generated emotional reactions, relating to old beliefs and core values, as 'icebergs'. We are back to a frozen landscape. Icebergs have 90% of their mass hidden under the icy waters, creating hidden dangers—as the *RMS Titanic* discovered.

▲   ▲   ▲

My thoughts carried me, like a passenger on that beleaguered ship, sucking me down to its depth. Fear gripped my heart catapulting me towards a frozen state. I had to take a deep breath and take my own advice. These thoughts were not my reality so I changed and recaptured my thoughts. I replaced the self-talk with positive scenarios, prayed, "God take all my worries from me" (1 Peter 5:7), and injected some humour into my reality. A wry grin appeared—I was writing on 'Fear is not the enemy', meanwhile disillusionment's 'lies' circled around me and caught me unawares, spoiling my evening with a basketful of fear!

Fear Wants Company

Fear is as contagious as a virus. It seeks others to contaminate in its efforts to 'help'. Your fear sends signals transmitting its powerful energy to others whose sensitive antennae receive it. Their response might be to:

1. Commune with it.
2. Conjoining your fear with their own doubt and worry, or
3. Pull on their own reserve, discount and ignore it.

The people who respond as in Number three are encouragers who can choose to seek to reassure those who respond to fear with numbers one and two.

Tina and Gina are sisters and nervous travellers. They take a
flight in an aeroplane to a holiday destination when a flight
attendant suffers a fit of terror. The sisters and the other
passengers become fellow sufferers as a 15-minute tirade
about crashing and terrorist attacks is broadcast. Tina, afraid
of heights with concerns about flying caught the transmitting
fear which rippling like radio waves through the cabin. Tina
insisted on getting off as she was unable to carry on the journey
and now refuses to fly—even to her dream destinations. Gina
refused to believe the outpourings. Her attempts to settle,
reassure and convince her sister failed. She continued the
journey and met her future husband on the aeroplane!

One person's fear may seem trivial to another person but the suffering is the same regardless of which fear manifests itself. Somehow, space has been given for it to enter your life. The damage of discouragement is inflicted. Fear does not care about the subject and attaches itself to anything that comes to hand.

> *Joan* is fearful of poppies. She cannot bear to be near them
> or drive by a hedgerow full of them. During the summer,
> she becomes housebound rather than risk seeing one.
> Remembrance Day is a nightmare for her. She remembers
> being told that they are used for cocaine and are poisonous.

I have heard of people whose natural fears have developed into phobias with other plants such as foxgloves, delphiniums and laburnum.

> It took a long while for *Andy* to become aware of his fear of
> success. He could not understand why his projects would
> get so far and then go no further. He became discouraged
> and fearful of the final outcome. He insisted, "They are not
> good enough" and would re-double his efforts to perfect each
> stage. As this thought dominated his mind, he sabotaged
> his efforts until the project was halted. He realised that once
> finished he would need to move into a new experience and
> have to deal with new people. The prospect of a successful
> completion filled him with fear—a fear of success.

Being Fear Bound

Have you ever tried to help a person who is fear-bound? It is as difficult as trying to make friends with a dog waiting outside a store for its owner! The task involves imparting confidence and assurance when their senses are locked down in an overriding state of fear.

♠   ♠   ♠

My husband, daughters and I had the chance to snorkel across a beautiful safe aquarium at a water park. We took the opportunity; all was fine until a panic attack hit me as the sound of my own breathing flashed up a memory of 'going under' anaesthetic as a child. This introduced uncertainty in my ability and fear joined the swim, preventing enjoyment for us all. I am a strong swimmer but the 250 yards felt like 250 miles. It was only the encouragement from my family that got me across the stretch of water.

♠   ♠   ♠

Tess was paralysed on high ropes on a family holiday. She shared her view on the experience, "It seemed like a good idea at the time but my fear of heights took over. I stopped feeling any pleasure, fun or sense of achievement". Tess had been certain that she would enjoy this sport but had forgotten that having her feet off the ground worry her. Tess said, "It was not until I had traversed half way through the course that the fear of heights hit me and I froze". The instructor and her husband spent over an hour talking her down to ground level—each step to safety was emotionally painful and slow.

Tess and I conquered these discouraging fears. They were faced and lessons learnt. The repeated activities produced different outcomes and more positive experiences.

Have you had to ask for support to overcome a fear? It has to be a concentrated effort bringing in help from those without fear to enable you to combat your fear. Help and support comes from great encouragers who have a different viewpoint towards the activity, they are unafraid and excited by the action. They help you to transfer your unbelief of your own ability into certainty. Certainty once established moves to gaining the confidence that you too can do the activity.

Have you ever observed sportsmen and women? It is with certainty that they approach a race, or they could not enter! They believe they can win. The excitement at the start of a race is palpable: the anticipation mounts in the seconds just before the starter pistol is shot. There is no room for fear or doubt in these moments. Perhaps you have watched a sport with matches, which take longer? In these scenarios, the certainty of the sportsperson has to be sustained over a longer period of time. Consider the tennis match, the opponents have to maintain their certainty but it is possible to see doubt and uncertainty creep in and then that person consistently loses whereas previously they had won the points.

In the same way, watching a football team when the opposition begin to score goals and they do not, the players become wracked with uncertainty and it can be painful to watch. It might be why it is so devastating, for the team, individual, fan, and spectator when they finally lose. The psychology of sport is fascinating but the lessons are the same in life. The psychology of sport is fascinating but the lessons are the same in life. The Apostle Paul talks about this in his metaphors in running a race, 'I therefore so run, not as uncertainly... (1 Corinthians 9:26 NKJV). If worry and fear are allowed space then your certainty is eroded regardless of the subject or activity.

Dr Joanna Martin is a great encourager especially in the field of public speaking. The fear of public speaking tops death and spiders as the number one phobia! Joanna says, "The antidote to fear is certainty as they cannot co-exist".

Can you identify your encouragers? Or, have you been able to encourage someone else to overcome his or her uncertainty and fear?

Misplaced Fear is Entrapment

Fears are a cold comfort, yet how many times do you find yourself controlled by your fear?

Fear displayed in behaviour and lifestyles can be called many other names: anxiety, panic, depression and stress. The feelings are accompanied by a physical change in the body—a hormonal reaction—making the experience intense and harder to control.

Studies into stress from fear by *Professor Amit Sood*, from the Mayo Clinic College of Medicine, Minnesota, have identified changes in brain and organ function with the release of hormones. Levels of oestrogen and testosterone—the primary sex hormones in women and men—change, affecting the way you react to stress. Dopamine is released sending signals to the nerve cells. Serotonin changes your regulation of mood, sleep and appetite. Does any of this sound familiar? Insomnia for instance is only one condition associated with stress, discouragement and fear.

The best description I have read about being entrapped by fear comes from Katharine Welby-Roberts who writes a wonderful blog with the amazing title, *A conglomerate of yodeling hippopotami!*

⋏　　⋏　　⋏

Katharine talks about her fear as a "crushing weight currently dominating the skyline of my future". She speaks openly about her depression and living in fear, describing it as "paralysing, gluing me to the spot". She calls it "my daily battle; fighting off incapacity and pain, the forays are occasionally won, more often lost".

At times Katharine asks, "Where is God?" She knows that He is fighting the battle alongside her saying, "Jesus 'gets' how I feel". She concludes one of her posts with, "Where is God? He is here with me. Enjoying my moments of hope and holding me in the moments of brokenness. He is the promise of a future, He is light in the dark, and He is everything".

I think Katharine and others like her are incredibly brave. I pray that this flagellating fear will be overcome, replaced with the fear of God.

Fear is misplaced when it is impossible for you to forget the circumstance, triggering the fear response: fight, flight or freeze. The memory is held in the body, mind, and muscles beyond its helpful time period. An overactive memory holds onto the past experience refusing to let it go. Animals do not have this problem. A zebra does not relive the experience of being chased by a lioness certain in its ability to flee again when necessary. The animal returns to normal behaviour as soon as the life-threatening situation has passed by.

It could be that you are frozen in a fear situation, each time it is relived, making your past become your ever-present existence with continual release of hormones. Perhaps you are in the safety of your own home where there are no life-threatening scenarios but responding as though they are still happening. This can be identified as Post Traumatic Stress Disorder. It has been described as simultaneously having your foot on both the accelerator and brake pedal! It is a confused state of living, undermining your ability and confidence to live well.

Overcoming Fear in Your Life

It is important to acknowledge your fear and to find its root. What triggered the fear? How can you reverse the discouragement and begin a healing process. Each fear can be overcome. It is an individual process—your individual journey to take. What do you need to come into balance? What step-by-step encouragement do you need? Who or where do you need this help from to overcome your 'stoppage'? It can be a huge commitment to make a decision to take action. You need to reach a stage where fear of not taking action for recovery is worse (because life is so unbearable) than the fear of taking action to break through your fear (experience its full force). Here are a few suggestions:

i. *A cause larger than your fear:* The stories of Oskar Schindler or Sir Nicholas Winton (Britain's 'Schindler'), both involved in saving the lives of Jewish people and children, can inspire you. Many times when they were fearful for their own lives, it was the righteousness of the situation which enabled them to continue. They forced themselves to override their fear. Is there a cause in your life, a motivator of concern for other people which is bigger than your fear? One which could force you to endure your fear and carry on anyway?

ii. *Whistling or singing:* Did you know that whistling a happy tune scares away fears? It is a surprising fact, you cannot feel sad and whistle! Probably because whistling is a physical act changing your hormone levels along with your body language. Next time you feel fear—knowing it is unwarranted—have a whistle! If, like me, you cannot whistle, try singing instead, although my singing will chase away anything and everyone! This change in physiology replaces your fear by self-encouragement.

iii. *Embrace Joy and Hope:* Find situations which produce feelings of joy and hope. Engender these emotions to reduce the release of 'fear' hormones.

iv. *Act 'As if':* Move through your fear by acting as if you do not have this nervousness or anxiety. What are the differences in your attitude and physical stance?

v. *Be around natural encouragers*: Notice how they act and emulate them. Become your own encourager. Ask Holy Spirit to come alongside you and claim your certainty. By claiming your certainty, you can do anything you set your mind to do.

vi. *Choose* to replace a discouraging word with an encouraging one. Beware the 'don't' word. Detect discouragement in conversations and deflect its negative potency. Family members might be rampant in discouragement: reminding you of times when you tried and failed, when a mistake happened, or they want to stop you in case you are hurt. They may only tell their stories of the past within a negative framework injecting, "I tried that", or "A friend of mine tried that, and had a horrid time". They are your dream stealers introducing uncertainty, worry and doubt.

vii. Have conversations with your friends about what phrases are most helpful for you, to encourage you. Encouragers do not use the word 'don't' or phrase sentences in the negative. You may have to rephrase your own words! I had to rephrase my conversation. For instance, instead of saying, "Don't forget your keys" I would say, "Remember to take your keys". It might seem a small change but it made an enormous difference in my thinking. Encourage your friends to become your natural supporters and become their supporters too.

How Much Fear Can a Person Endure?

I enjoyed a TV programme called *Fear Factor*. In this competitive set up, a person was taken to their fear limit. It tested people to see how far they would go before their psychological or physical instincts, or delicate senses, discouraged them enough to stop. The winner was the fastest person to accomplished tasks involving their ability to master their fears. The programme sets challenges or stunts involved having to: touch live or dead insects and creatures, eat raw foods in awful conditions (cow tongues in lard and fish oil—yuk!), conquer the elements: heights, water, speed, temperatures and darkness.

It raised the question as to how much fear a body and mind could endure? The answer depended on a person's will power, hope and beliefs as much as physical endurance. There was real danger of physical injury and mental scarring. My favourite episode involved couples having to work together as a team. It evoked the protective instinct to rescue the person they loved overriding their fear. Interestingly, the episode without a winner was one where the participants were friends; perhaps this took off the competitive edge!

What situations or circumstances incite you enough to override your fear? You may have heard fantastic stories of heroes or heroines who overcome horrendous conditions to rescue others. Many of society's professions; fire, police and military to name a few, face their fears as part of their jobs. A fireman or woman has to overcome a natural fear of fire to enter a building of toxic fumes and overwhelming heat to check for unknown people. Through regular practice they build up confidence in the certainty of their own abilities, the skills of their team members and resources they use and know the probability of success.

Fear as a Tonic

An alternative viewpoint to fear is to embrace it and push through the emotion, knowing that the following emotions will be worthwhile. This seems to be the attitude of many adventurers. I guess that if this was not so, they would not be able to go out and conquer the elements, opening doors for others to have an easier journey when they follow in their footsteps. In this way, the Wild West, Arctic Circles and Space have been explored.

The Irish aviator *Lady Mary Heath,* viewed fear in a different way; 'Fear is a tonic and danger, an ecstasy'. Lady Mary had to face the fear of her own immortality, flying small open cockpit aircrafts in the 1920s. She was the first woman to parachute from an aeroplane. She chose to take a radical viewpoint on fear overcoming it to establish new records in races and long-distance flights.

I will return to a fellow believer who I admire, *Bear Grylls.* Bear is not a stranger to fear but his faith and certainty in his own skills enable him to conquer the fear. He acknowledges fear as part of the human condition, using it to sharpen his reactions—the original survival mechanism. His confidence is enough for others to 'buy into' and use to overcome their own fears and they manage to have adventures they never thought were possible. In turn, Bear has a person in whom he has confidence—Jesus. Jesus is a role model for Bear, as expressed by his quote, 'and Jesus, the heart of the Christian faith, is the wildest, most radical guy you'd ever come across'.

Surprise yourself and identify and acknowledge your fear. What is it for you? It could be the embarrassment of speaking out loud. Therefore you do not saying anything for fear of offending and being disliked, or not giving your own opinion but always keeping a status quo—or another deep-seated fear. Ask Holy Spirit to be with you so that you are not alone. Face the fear by taking direct action and putting yourself in the situation. Reverse your reaction with courageous stepping out instead of allowing your past to keep you back in a state of fearful withdrawal.

Do not allow discouragement to provide fear which acts as a lock. This lock is inside your mind, closing your door on life. It is a door without a handle and many internal bolts. Do you want to remain trapped in a room secured in this way?

Throughout the Bible you will find constant messages warning against fear. "Do not fear", and "Do not be afraid" ricochet in persistent patterns reminding you, and I, of God's love and protection. "Do not fear" is one of the first phrases an Angel will say when you meet one! Purists may argue about the number of times 'fear' is mentioned in the Bible but I love the fact that there are enough encouragements against being afraid, anxious, worried, doubtful or upset to cover every day of the year.

The Fear of the Lord
Fear associated with God can be characterised by respect, reverence, awe, worship and wonder. These fear responses are not out-dated or abstract. They are real emotions aroused by the 'fear of the Lord'. This meaning is being lost from today's vocabulary. A 'lie' of discouragement is behind this disuse, leaving an exclusive understanding within the fight, flight or freeze survival responses. Yet, your survival depends on fearing God.

It is easy to mistake 'fear of the Lord' for other fear responses but they could not be more opposite. Daniel, best remembered for his time, 30 days, in the Lion's Den (Daniel 6:1-28), was a man given visions of God. In these visions, he describes how he felt before and after he experienced fear of the Lord. Daniel said he was without strength, looked deathly pale, fell to the floor and felt helpless. After he had received a vision, he was restored and strengthened.

Daniel had confidence and certainty in the Lord, knowing his 'fear of the Lord' would be a good experience and that he would not be hurt but would gain by seeing a vision. Contrast this with the response of Daniel's companions when God wanted to speak to them. Their fear default was flight, 'I, Daniel, was the only one who saw the vision; those who were with me did not see it, but such terror overwhelmed them that they fled and hid themselves' (Daniel 10:8).

Fear of the Lord may come with accompanying trembling and being struck dumb, but it is not to be confused with the undermining of your confidence and self-esteem, depicted in fight, flight or freeze scenarios. The 'fear of the Lord' is different as it involves communicating with God. You know this because, when God appears, or when you appear before God—at the final reckoning— His presence is unmistakable and tangible.

Fear of the Lord works on the oxytocin rather than adrenaline approach. Your fear encounter is now one of reverence, calm and peace. Defences are lowered as God comes in to commune with you. This fear encourages trust and curiosity, giving you freedom to enjoy being with Him.

The Freeing Fear of the Lord

It is time to add an additional F to the flight, fight and freeze responses. It is F for FREE. God sets us free. He is freeing—delivering you away from life's discouragements. You now have another choice when fear comes upon you—a freeing response. His freeing action towards fear provokes His favour. The next time you feel fearful, can you capture the fear, replacing it with the certainty of God's loving response, incorporating your understanding of 'free', rather than hitting the primitive 'terrorising fear' button?

The Lord our God is One Lord, Love him with all your heart, all your soul, all your mind and all your strength.

Love your Neighbour as Yourself.

The Fear of the Lord

The fear of the Lord is one where God turns fear on its head. Fear is the prelude to loving and longing for God and receiving His favour. You have to follow your passion for our mysterious God to receive your freedom. Did you know it is one of the few 'asks' that God has of you? A commandment for you and me to fear Him, 'what does the Lord your God ask of you but to fear the Lord your God, to walk in all His ways, to love him, to serve the Lord your God will your heart and with all your soul' (Deuteronomy 10:12).

Moses follows this up, saying it is good to talk and share the goodness of God with an emphasis to learn about the need to fear Him. Moses wanted this to be passed down through the generations, he instructs the elders to gather men, women, children and foreigners at the Feast of Tabernacles, 'so they can listen and learn to fear the LORD your God' (Deuteronomy 31:12-13).

The beauty of fearing Him stems from the first commandment, 'that you should have no other gods before Me' (Exodus 20:3). In His teaching, Jesus answered the question, "What is the greatest commandment?" In response, Jesus gave two commandments for you and I to keep, "Love the Lord your God with all your heart and with all your soul and with all your mind..." and "Love your neighbour as yourself".

Fear in the context of 'Fear of the Lord' is about love, loving Him.

By this fear, you will have certainty and confidence in God. It is the responsibility of a believer to hold this fear close and keep His commandments (Ecclesiastes 12:13). The commandments are given for your protection and safety, and to bring joy to your heart (Psalm 19:8). In all His directives, God does not incite fear or discouragement. Moses knew there was no need for this type of fear, 'the Lord himself goes before you and will be with you; he will never leave you nor forsake you' (Deuteronomy 31:8). It is the same today nothing has changed. God is here for you and wants to set you free from the 3Ds.

Showing Fear of the Lord

How do you exhibit the 'fear of the Lord' as worship and honour to Him? The obvious ways are by praying and singing, reverently and quietly or with exuberance, but might it be that you are limiting your communication? The less obvious way is when Holy Spirit evokes the power in you. Have you noticed when Holy Spirit comes 'upon' you, or 'rises up within you', your behaviour alters? You may appear 'out of control'; you cry, shout, fall down, speak in a foreign tongue, laugh uncontrollably, shake and exhibit other reactions. It is the Holy Spirit working and communicating with you, involving Himself in your life, and it could be viewed as manifestations of the 'Fear of the Lord' (just like Daniel!).

▲   ▲   ▲

My friend **Penel**, describes her fear of the Lord as being, "overawed by His majesty". She realised the magnitude of His love for her. Penel said, "I believe His love for all is a mystery, especially as we get so much wrong. His timely direction to keep me and others on the right path, and His forgiveness when we choose an alternative is unlike any relationship with anyone else".

I agree with Penel, His magnitude is so great that I can only glimpse a fraction of it. It is like seeing a star with the unaided eye. I am only seeing it at a sixth of its magnitude. In astronomy, this is termed 'visual magnitude'. This is a measure of brightness. In this way, a 1st magnitude star is 100 times brighter than a 6th magnitude star. We see stars in the night sky and the difference in brightness between the dimmest and the brightest is over one hundred times. The sun is 25,148,408,816 times brighter than the brightest star. Can you imagine how brightly the glory of God will shine? My fear of the Lord is realising His magnitude, it feels me with awe and wonder. In return, He gives you and me significance, whilst He is the one who is omnipotent. Perhaps the fear of the Lord is like having stars in our eyes!

In His Fan Club

It is easy to witness the behaviour of people who are supporters and fans of a person, a club or a place. Perhaps you have a particular interest in a famous person, a sportsperson or pop/film star, or live for the holidays when you can travel to your favourite place? Perhaps you take a particular interest in a member of the Royal Family, or hero worship a particular person? You want to know more about your favourite, to have inside knowledge, and to be an expert on them. You may join a fan club, subscribe to their website, follow social media for instant news, read their books, look at their picture in a magazine, buy their recordings, see their films. You cannot get enough of them; you adore them and become one of their followers. Do you follow God, craving His presence with the same devoted fervour?

What happens when your dreams come true and you meet your hero? Perhaps the expectation is too much; they are different to how you imagined or you become awestruck. You freeze, stop, and focus only on your hero, drinking in the moment; they have your full attention. Nothing else matters and time stands still.

It is a one-sided relationship spending your 'worshipping fear' in this way. Can they give you an individual response, protect you, help you, or love you back? They have thousands of fans and entering into a personal relationship with each one is not their way. Many celebrities refuse to give autographs, or conduct meaningful conversation with their fans, despite the supporters trying to emulate them, look, dress, and talk like them. There is a conditional transaction going on, and at some point, they will disappoint you. They cannot continue at the level you placed them—on the pedestal. They will grow older, underperform, and their esteemed qualities will diminish. They show their human side, feet made of clay and, in the transient nature of fans, they are superseded; the pattern is then repeated with a new hero.

God is unchanging and, as a fan of God I know, a better or newer model cannot replace Him. He 'gives back' responding to my and your worship making the interaction a two-sided relationship. His warming light puts you in the spotlight. He gives you far more than any idol possible could, 'every good and perfect gift is from above, coming down from the Father of the heavenly lights, who does not change like shifting shadows' (James 1:17). He even adopts you into His family (Ephesians 1:5).

In God's fan club, you receive God's promises and there are many! The young King Uzziah asked Zechariah for instruction to fear the Lord and was known as a successful King, 'as long as he (Uzziah) sought the Lord, God gave him success' (2 Chronicles 26:5).

Fearfulness in God

Miracles are close by when you fear the Lord. God wants not only to show you His amazing power but also make it available to you. He ends wars and heals the broken-hearted. Here are the top ten responses from God's to your fear in the Lord.

1. Commandment: (Deuteronomy 10:12).
2. Learning: (2 Chronicles 26:5).
3. Blessing (1 Samuel 23:5, Psalms 128:1).
4. Serving (Joshua 24:15).
5. Remembrance (1 Samuel 12:24, Joshua 4:24).
6. Leadership (2 Samuel 23:3).
7. Responsibility (2 Chronicles 19:7).
8. Life giving (Proverbs 10:27, 14:27).
9. Prosperity and Success (2 Samuel 23:5, Psalms 34:9).
10. Wisdom (Job 28:28, Proverbs 1:7, 9:10).

They can be considered as evidence for choosing fear of the Lord and as part of your salvation and deliverance.

God's Hierarchy of Need

If you were to put a Hierarchy of Need together from a perspective of a relationship with God, I wonder what it would look like? I have put it together in this way, with Fear of the Lord as the foundation base, as without this fear you cannot get off the starting blocks! At the top is the hardest commandment of them all, 'love your neighbour as yourself' (Mark 12:31) which would be comparable with Maslow's self-actualisation. To achieve it, you need to work through the other tiers. By the way, baptism would mean baptism in the Holy Spirit.

Forgiveness
Blessings
Joy, Self-control
Love & Peace
Love thy Neighbour

Wisdom, Understanding,
Counsel, Knowledge
Gifts & Fruits

Baptism, Fasting,
Meditation, Devotion, Favour
Passion for the Bible

Discussion, Communication, Prayer, Hope, Deliverance,
Identity, Purpose and Meaning
Relationship with God

Awe, Reverance, Worship, Praise, Salvation, Faith
Fear of the Lord

God's Hierarchy of Need

Fear of the Lord Favours You

The Bible has been described as the 'Book of the Law and Instruction'. It is a source for learning about God, His character, promises and love. It is a starting point for your relationship with Him. The Holy Spirit teaches us, using the Bible as a tool in His rapport with you. When the disciples were building the Church throughout Judea, Galilee and Samaria they were encouraged by Holy Spirit, 'living in the fear of the Lord and encouraged by Holy Spirit, it (the Church) increased in numbers' (Acts 9:31).

The fear of the Lord comes with enormous favour, standing alongside prayer and blessings. It forms a trilogy of offerings to God. When God gives his favour it can come in like a flood, bringing a torrent of good things for your benefit. Jesus taught on the bountiful generosity of God as your Father, "How much more will your Father in heaven give the Holy Spirit to those who ask Him?" (Matthew 7:11, Luke 11:13). You only need to ask.

This fear is one to be practiced and developed as an informed, enthusiastic and passionate choice. It brings you closer to God. The Psalmist says, 'The Lord confides in those who fear Him; He makes His covenant known to them' (Psalms 25:14). Are you in His confidence? Would you like to be? Like a muscle, it is a case of 'use it or lose it'. This fear needs to be used—it is NOT your enemy. Draw on your ability to discuss private matters, secrets and problems with God. Check that you are not in danger of losing your 'fear of the Lord'.

King David on his deathbed, in his beautiful poetic way, spoke about the connection between the fear of the Lord and receiving His favour. David's last words of wisdom are like a baton being passed for those in leadership. As a leader, the majority of his life had been spent commanding others; ruling over people with fairness, goodness and justice. David acknowledged God in everything he had accomplished.

> *"The one who rules in the fear of God is like*
> *the light of morning at sunrise,*
> *like a morning without clouds,*
> *like the gleaming of the sun on new grass after rain"*
>
> (2 Samuel 23:2-4).

Current law systems were set up under the principles of the fear of the Lord. King Jehoshaphat when appointing judges, wanted them to operate in the fear (honour) of the Lord, with these three standards in mind: impartiality, justice and to withstand bribery (2 Chronicles 19:7). The standards have never been replaced since circa. 914 BC!

Searching for knowledge and gaining information is high on most people's agenda and is why the Internet and search engines are so popular and well used. The fear of the Lord is about understanding the difference between right and wrong and celebrating the contrast, 'the fear of the Lord, that is wisdom, and to shun evil is understanding' (Job 28:28).

God's favour is received in different ways. Your portion will be different to mine. As Isaiah explained, 'the Lord teaches you what is good for you' (48:17). Would you like to learn from the master? All four gospels recount a similar story, a woman anointing Jesus' feet with oil (Matthew 26:7, Mark 14:3, Luke 7:37 and John 12:3). This woman, or women if it happened more than once, was given a blessing from Jesus that she would be remembered. Jesus acknowledged her, "Truly I say to you, wherever this gospel is preached in the whole world, what this woman has done will also be spoken of in memory of her". The gospel writers have fulfilled this promise. But what happened to prompt this promise? She acted in the fear of the Lord. To express her love for Jesus, she worshipped him and gave a most precious present, anointing his feet with expensive perfume. She overcame her fear of criticism and possible rejection (even the disciples were affronted by her actions) replacing it with her fear of the Lord, appreciation and devotion for Jesus. She was a great example to the disciples and part of their learning.

Jesus' blessing of her continues today as we read her story. There is an incredible website called the *Alabaster Jar* (www.alabasterjar.org. uk). It remembers and celebrates women who have done something beautiful for Jesus. It acknowledges the contributions of women who have preached to, and led, the church.

Time to be Frightened of God

The only time you need to cower in front of the Lord in a fearful state of shame and terror is if you incur His wrath. God's anger is different to the anger exhibited by people. It is a righteous anger against evil and those who persist in it. You are wise to be afraid of God's anger. One image from Isaiah describes it: 'His anger burns, comes in dense clouds of smoke, a resentful indignity on His lips, looking for vengeance and punishment and His tongue a consuming fire' (Isaiah 30:27). The prophet Nahum spoke about the God who is, 'slow to anger but great in power, so will not leave the guilty unpunished', but who 'avenges His foes and stands up against His enemies, fierce and raging. But God doesn't lose His temper. He's powerful, but it is a patient power' (Nahum 1:2-3 The Message).

Would you expect anything else if you break his commandments (Deuteronomy 5:6-21)? What happens if you choose to commit murder, or adultery, to envy or steal, to blaspheme or practice idolatry, to lie about people or hold poor priorities in your life? What if you dishonour your parents, give insufficient time to God, or reject Jesus' commandment to love one another as He has loved you (John 13:34)? If there is any breakdown to the commandments, and you are truly sorry, then you may receive the grace of God who forgives you. I believe His full anger is for those who are unprepared to be disciplined or corrected by Him. People who show no remorse for their behaviour or actions and do not seek to make amends. They are recognised as being proud and arrogant, choosing to be used for evil purposes—hurting others.

Fear Choices

If you are overtaken with fears that are stopping you, change the fear pattern and replace it with the fear of the Lord.

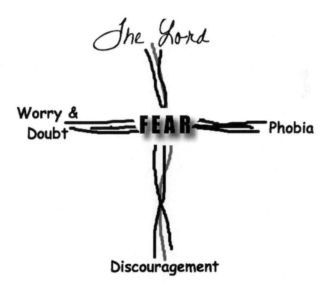

It is like standing at a crossroads. Your fear reaction is your choice but you need to take control of your thoughts. There is no need to be a victim and become discouraged. It is time to become a victor, bringing your fear points to God; asking Him to change it into fear of Him. Your encouragers are Jesus and Holy Spirit.

Jesus is the best encourager you can have. He has the solution to any fear that upsets you. The Apostle John reminds us of this fact, 'Perfect love drives out (all) fear' (1 John 4:18). Jesus is Perfect Love and He says:

1. "Yes you can, just ask me" (John 14:13-14).
2. "Be like me" (John 14:12).
3. "Heal like me" (Matthew 10:1).
4. "Believe in me and have an untroubled heart" (John 14:1).
5. "Love the Father as I do" (Matthew 6:14, Luke 11:2-4).
6. "Love the Holy Spirit whom I will send" (John 14:27, 20:22).
7. "I give you Life" (John 3:16, 14:6).
8. "Fear only God" (Matthew 10:28).
9. "Love one another" (John 13:35, 15:12).
10. "Know there is a better life waiting for you" (John 18:36).

This is your challenge to shine the light of your encouragers (Jesus, Holy Spirit, friends and family) into your fears while being persistent in your fear of the Lord. God is the only person who can bring you out of darkness and into light. It is His light, revealing your heart. He wants to unburden you, ensuring that you are not a slave to anything, including the 3Ds and fear. A final word comes from the Apostle Paul, 'It is for freedom that Christ has set us free' (Galatians 5:1).

Open the Door

1. **Recognise** the warning signs of fear. Which part of worry and doubt can you recognise as arriving before an onset of fear?
2. **Identify** your flight/fight/frozen responses? When has fear paralysed you and what did you do to move forward again?
3. **Remember** the days when you were fearless? How can you recapture them?

4. **Resist** feeding your fear? Do you allow worry and doubt to have centre stage in your life? Which strategies are you going to use to reverse this choice?

5. **Check out** your basketful of fears. For each fear place a stone in a basket, feel how heavy it is. Replace the stones with pieces of paper with encouraging words on them.

6. **Choose** freedom from your fear. Be prepared to change your response and look for deliverance from God.

7. **Memorise** a Bible verse beginning with, "Do not to be afraid". Speak this out loud when doubt, worry or fear creeps up on you. Remember there are enough verses to cover each day of the year! Therefore, there must be enough to cover all your fears.

8. **Choose** your dream team of encouragers. Make a list of these people. Ask them to help and support you through the processes of overcoming your fear. Are any of these people your role models?

9. **Aspire** to fearlessness as your new state of mind, body and soul. Be free and recognise this new way of being. How can fear of the Lord play a part in your life?

10. **Celebrate** with others who fear the Lord and demonstrate using the fear of the Lord in your daily life.

11. **Review** the Ten Commandments (Deuteronomy 5:6-21). How much bearing do they have on your life?

12. **Confide** a secret with God today and show God that you are His No 1 Fan.

Step into God's Warming Light

Dear Lord,

May the fear of God come upon me, flooding me with a fear stemming from His favour, imparting love and strength to me. I pray that my fear, worship and reverence for You will grow so that Your blessings are reflected in my life. May my need to use the fear responses, fight, flight or freeze be ever more rare and the freeing response used in abundance ripping away all discouragement.

I pray that I may be delivered from fear's unhelpful manifestations and that I will know God's freeing power. May I be reminded of Your great promises, God. May I learn more each day about the fear of the Lord, where I can be lost in wonder, awe and respect. Thank you Holy Spirit for your gifts, for teaching me how to use and share them with others.

Amen.

YOUR LOVE WILL FIND A WAY

To love another person is to see the face of God.
VICTOR HUGO

Where Will Love Take You?

There is a saying, 'A little love goes a very long way', and it goes further than hate. It opens doors. When you have love inside you it finds a way out: it is like a beacon attracting others to you—calling—for it overflows, contagious in its need to be shared. Is it an emotion or a state of being? It is a permanent light with self-chargeable batteries and it cannot run out. Love exchanged is palatable; it is the language of the heart.

You and I speak about the heart in many ways, feeling happiest when doing an activity that keeps our heart content or feeling at our worst when heart-broken. Your heart began to beat four weeks after you were conceived and will not stop until your final day. As a foetus it beat twice as fast than as an adult, beginning at 150 beats per minute to, once grown, dropping to around 70-75 beats when relaxed or resting. The symbol of the heart decorates many cards, not just on Valentine's Day and the heart is used to adorn necklaces and lockets. The © shape is universally recognised as the symbol for love.

'In a heart beat' is a phrase used when you do something that you do not need any thinking time to respond with a 'yes' as it is, as coined in another phrase, a 'no-brainer'. Your heart is the most energetic organ in your body, physically, psychologically, emotionally and spiritually. It creates energy pumping into your 'will' and 'free will', convincing you to get up in the mornings! Did you know that your heart creates enough energy to drive a lorry (truck) 20 miles every day? So where is your heart of love driving you today?

मधुर

रति

प्रिय

love

कामिता

Your Love Will Find a Way

Yes, love can be complicated but it is the necessary healing component to overcoming most problems stemming from the 3Ds, in particular, unnecessary fear. Without fear, you can do so much more and you will be amazed at how far love will take you—across many miles and in many directions. Have you noticed? Love shines its light in the darkness and, smilingly, takes no prisoners!

The Existence of Love

In the 1950s, Dr Harry Harlow conducted controversial experiments on young Rhesus monkeys that involved removing them from their mothers. In some cases, the young monkeys were isolated from all contact with their species and this continued for a minimum of 24 months to the whole of the animal's life. The experiments in themselves were as disturbing as their results. The learning from them has shown how isolation and separation from loving care, especially a mother's love and care, produces fear, leaving severely disturbed creatures.

Harlow reported his results in a paper entitled *The Nature of Love*. The experiments were cited as progressive in their time, albeit cruel. They have informed the world about attachment theories and human need for love. It subsequently supported professionals in helping children to develop well. It is strange to me that, to prove the need for love, Harlow and his team had to first remove love! On one of the monkeys' autopsy report, the cause of death was cited as 'emotional anorexia'. A fortunate consequence of these experiments was the rise in the animal liberation movement.

The experimenters themselves had to be without love, certainly of the monkeys—it would have been impossible to conduct the experiments otherwise. In a radio interview (Pittsburgh Press-Roto, 1974) Harlow said, "The only thing I care about is whether a monkey will turn out a property I can publish. I don't have any love for them. Never have. I don't really like animals. I despise cats. I hate dogs. How could I like monkeys?"

Depersonalisation and dehumanisation is how cruelty for animals, people and the environment occurs. It is the separation or alienation of yourself from another person. It is possible to legitimately discount that others have feelings when you come from a place of pride and superiority, convinced that your view is the only one that matters. It is even worse when pleasure is gained from subjecting others to pain, fear or destruction. It is an open door for hate, fear and discouragement and the antithesis of the love of God.

Eyes of Love

Survival is possible without love but it is, at best, a very basic endurance—joy and pleasure are missing. To aspire to love is the ultimate and highest goal you can place before yourself. To be a healthy holistic person, love calls to be satisfied within your mind, body and soul. Love is about being and behaving beyond yourself, as it is about reaching out to others and thinking about more than just you. In Greek mythology, Narcissus only loved himself, rejecting love and disdaining those who tried to show him love. He drowned because he was unable to leave his own beautiful reflection. So, love has to involve genuine two-way relationships.

By showing love, you can achieve great things for it is the secret ingredient in all accomplishments. This is can be from micro one-to-one relationships of marriage and friendships, to mammoth achievements attained throughout history. This has been shown in the fields of literature, sport, music, architecture, humanity, and so much more.

The only way to understand another person and their actions is to love them. Through the eyes of love, you can see the essential potential in someone else. You can recognise that they can gain the confidence needed to make their possibilities come true. Love promotes positive action—it is an overcomer— shining a light through desolation and darkness, and hence overcoming death, fear and any of the 3Ds.

There is a great debate on the nature of love, ranging from love expressed as contentment or lust, and from gratitude to the fear of God! People who study linguistics have a field day in their debates! The number of words used in different languages to describe love have been counted resulting in 96 love words in Sanskrit, 80 love words in Persian, 30 love words from Ancient Greek and one love word—love—in English.

As a 'Brit', I think the word love is also contained in tone of voice and body expression, so when I talk about my love for books or favourite foods it has a different connotation than telling my husband that I love him. How I express my deepest love for Denis also differs according to our mood and activity. In this way there is more than one word being expressed!

Standard practice has reduced the love words from the Greek into seven categories:

1. Agape—self-giving love for others.
2. Eros— erotic and passionate love.
3. Ludus—feelings of fun and affection.
4. Philautia—self-respect.
5. Philia—shared experiences.
6. Pragma—enduring pragmatic love.
7. Storge—family committed love.

Whichever way it is explained or categorised, the emotions of love are essential for a meaningful life. Love is the antidote to discouragement, being as strong as death, burning like a blazing fire with a mighty flame (Song of Solomon 8:6). With this kind of power, it is impossible to be discouraged when you love what it is you are doing, or to discourage another person if you love them. Love can override the 'dream-stealers' and the naysayers in our lives. They cannot understand your passion and, until they show their love ungoverned by fear, they never will. Therefore, it is by choosing who you listen to that will determine how much discouragement you will accept.

Tough Love

Do you love someone enough to demonstrate tough love? This is love which will stand back when your loved one is doing something wrong so they can learn from it themselves. It involves waiting rather than providing an immediate answer or doing something for them when they can achieve it themselves. At the start of your life, you are dependent on others and in the circle of life; others will become dependent on you. For instance, you are there to support a child when he is learning to walk, but you had to let him fall in the first place so he could learn about picking himself up and trying again. You have to stand aside when a child becomes frustrated while learning new skills, such as: reading, writing, maths, or riding a bike. You step in with timely encouragement and a piece of advice but it is only by experiencing the frustration, seemingly failure, that the skill will be discovered and developed. If you did everything for a child, they would never learn.

Standing back, but still supporting is harder when a child is grown, making adult decisions and being hurt by other people. Try to let go of your parental instincts to protect and take care of them and, instead hold onto your belief that God is for them and with them. After all, He is their Father too. Like you did, they will grow through the experience despite the hurt.

▲　▲　▲

Marie is angry with her parents as she says they do not love her. She is in debt and knows her parents could easily afford to pay them off for her; they have done so in the past. This time they deny her with a firm "No". They are offering support in other ways, providing meals and accommodation but want Marie to budget and give up her luxuries until she has paid off her credit cards. It is time for Marie to learn the hard way. Her parents are exhibiting tough love but it is a painful and upsetting time for them all.

▲　▲　▲

Jeremy's face is screwed up in concentration. He wants to join the conversation. He gestures and shouts in his excitement to contribute. He has learning disabilities but his views are important. His mother knows exactly what he wants to say and could easily interpret for him to their friends. Instead, she gently encourages, "Use your words Jeremy". He tries again; his words come out haltingly, in staccato bursts, enhancing the conversation. The courage it takes for Jeremy to force his brain to work harder and to achieve what everyone else takes for granted, is amazing. The courage of the mother to step back and show appropriate tough love is touching, and, unseen God smiles down on them.

God showed his tough love for me by allowing me to experience life's trauma rather than stopping them. Instead, he loved and protected me through the situations. He was using the experiences to refine my faith and character, deepening my relationship and reliance on Him. His encouragement was ever present despite the gloom of other people's discouragement. I had to choose to open the door to His warming light.

Fairy Tale Love

A true love's kiss is the central theme of many fairy tales spinning their romance. Disney is the undisputed animation expert in retelling fables and stories with romance in mind. These have included Cinderella, Sleeping Beauty, and Rapunzel, to name just a few—but one of the first to have a twist that was not defined by Eros love or dependent on a romantic 'living happily-ever-after' was Disney's *Frozen*. The romance was a side theme but it was the love between two sisters that was the central theme. As part of the research, *Frozen's* Creative Team called a 'Sister Summit' (Solomon: *The Art of Frozen*). The team spoke with sisters about their relationships, from trivial matters like squabbling over clothes, to deeper issues of supporting one another through life threatening illness. This information was then used to enhance the depth of characterisation between Elsa and Anna.

Many marriages have suffered from unrealistic expectations formed by ingesting stories of fairy tale love where neither person has any faults. These contrasts with real, sustaining love, which overcomes faults and is wonderful to behold. I recently attended a wedding where hope of love abounded. The central focal point was the couple. This is perhaps an obvious statement, but I watched with interest as the guests were fascinated and mesmerised by seeing them together. The focus was sustained for hours, with countless photographs being taken to capture each and every moment. It was as though the guests wanted the public display of love, transmitting from the couple, to touch their lives too. This was alongside their genuine hope that this love would fulfil their vows to one another and continue to be life affirming and last a lifetime. This is what God's love for you is like. He is there for you throughout your life.

God *is* Love

Where you and I see love as an emotion and a feeling which we can choose to bestow or not, this is not the case with God—'He IS love' (1 John 4:16). It is a simple statement of truth and informs you and I about God's nature and character. This quality of love cannot change and it makes a big difference to the way love is viewed. It is an absolute and it is why I have chosen to serve Him—the God of love.

The Apostle John also speaks about how knowing God is manifested by the ability to love. It is easy to love those who love you, and God first loved you (1 John 4:19), so it is a case of 'Right back atcha God'! Love becomes more complicated when I want to be selective in whom I love and how much I choose to love them, based on merit. In John Gill's exposition, he calls God's love, 'free, sovereign, distinguishing and unmerited', enabling you and I to be able to return it so easily.

It is not as easy to return love to your fellow man or woman. It is effortless to love those who you have kinship with or who are your friends, but what about those people who seem unlovable? I was challenged in this direction when I read the verse, 'if I do not love others then it is not possible for God to live in me' (1 John 4:20).

▲   ▲   ▲

Clive was hard to love; he was obese and suffered from depression. Living on his own since his wife's death he became housebound rarely moving from his broken chair. He had a dog and a cat living in his small home, defecating wherever they wished. Clive's bedding had not been changed for months. The grass in his garden was chest high and his kitchen sink was piled high with dirty dishes, empty cans and half eaten ready-meal packets. His clothes were ill fitting and marked with dripped food. He chain-smoked and drank heavily. Added to his suffering were health problems: diabetes, emphysema and a heart condition.

My family and I were repulsed by his living conditions and there was very little to recommend him to us. However, God challenged us to love him and show him God's love. I asked my mentor, Frances Marchant, about the situation and she wisely asked me, "What do you think Jesus would do in this situation?" With the help of Holy Spirit we slowly built a relationship with Clive. We discovered a joint interest in playing cards, and in this way enjoyed his company. We took him out in the car, looked after the dog when he was in hospital, and did a house 'make-over' for him. Clive slowly began to take an interest in himself again and we found a website which had 4X sizes enabling him to have new clothes.

For a short time he attended our church for special occasions. We had to say goodbye to our interaction with him when we moved to another county. We prayed that the improvements in his life have continued and he remembers our kindness as God's love for him.

It was not until we took the effort to try to love that we discovered Clive's personality and the fact we could find him lovable. God knew this—he already loved Clive.

Jesus is Perfect Love

Cheryl Ford, in her commentary in *Pilgrim Progress Devotional,* asks her readers to imagine Jesus' decision to come to Earth to become our example of perfect love:

"Let's ponder a moment ... High aloft in his celestial kingdom, all is eternally resplendent majesty, purity, truth, righteousness, joy and love. However, Jesus Christ, King of the universe, royal Prince of this celestial kingdom was not content. He looked through Heaven's window down to the Earth where he saw human beings, made in his image, languishing and dying in the poisonous garbage dumps of wilful sin. Amazingly, (because) he loved them (He) decided to do something bold, something extraordinary. Pure love is like that".

Jesus commanded us, 'to love one another as HE loved us' (John 15:12). He loves you and I enough to exemplify this love throughout his life and finally, in love, to sacrifice his life for our deliverance. Jesus said, "Greater love has no one than this to lay down one's life for one's friends" (John 15:13). As God, Jesus is the 'Perfect Love'. You and I are imperfect but we are not without knowledge of this love. The least we can do is to try to expand how we give our love to others. This can be from the simplest way of controlling our own emotions, by loving strangers who behave disrespectfully, to holding a love for another nation. Love in action can be shown by your graciousness towards people, your generosity—both financially and spiritually—and sharing the love of God with them.

Decisions Taken Without Love

Saul, before Love named him Paul, was a man without love. He was a persecutor filled with a righteous malice. He travelled throughout Israel, Cyprus and Antioch persecuting Christians. Imagine being an early believer! Come with me and let us go back to a moment in time and learn about a fictitious character I have named *Pedroc*.

▲   ▲   ▲

Pedroc was a man who loved God and served his fellow Jews in the synagogue, praying regularly and seeking more knowledge of God. Pedroc was enjoying a beautiful peaceful morning of prayer, when a friend approached him. His friend, *Shemlock*, was bouncing with excitement about to explode with some gossip or the latest titbits of news and his outlet was Pedroc. Pedroc sighed, knowing his peace was about to be shattered as his friend spotted him, and changed direction towards him.

Shemlock confirmed the rumour which was circling in the temple, about a forthcoming visit by Saul. Due to Saul's passion in eradicating blasphemers he had been nicknamed *Shechita*, meaning the 'Sanctifying Slaughterer. "Did you know Shechita, is honouring our synagogue with a visit?" Shemlock delighted in whispering as though they were conspiring together. Without waiting for a reply he continued with his news, "He is dropping in on the way to Damascus. But the best bit is that the Disciple Philip and others are nearby preaching". Shemlock's face turned red as he related this, and he gave a dramatic pause. He is too impatient to wait, "Can't you see?" he bursts, "We can witness a cleansing first hand. The Priests are at this very moment making a list and writing letters".

Pedroc had a feeling of foreboding but did not have to respond, as Shemlock was off to tell others his 'good news'. Pedroc was not one to make a decision based on other people's opinions. He decided to take the opportunity and resolved to go and meet with the disciples himself. His friends warned him to wait especially in light of Saul's imminent arrival. Everyone knew about Saul. He was without mercy, killing many people who believed in Jesus. It meant that the men and women who followed Jesus had been scattered. It was said that Saul was on a mission for the heads of all the disciples and how proud he was of the coats laid at his feet when he had approved Stephen's death by stoning. This made Pedroc more determined to meet Philip and the other disciples. Despite his friends' fears, he found the details and travelled to the place.

He was surprised at the number of people surrounding Philip, and the joy and passion of the disciples' speech. He saw miracles, heard about the teaching of Jesus, and believed. The disciples could not stay long because they also knew Saul was on his way. Pedroc did not expect his world to be turned upside down. But, on hearing the remarkable stories of what Jesus did for people, he committed his life and joined the queue (line) of those waiting to be baptised by Philip. His love for God was now three-fold.

Pedroc knew the day Saul arrived in the city. He came with a fanfare of soldiers, a colourful troop of men, rich in confidence, authority and arrogance as a righteous race. The High Priests fêted them, celebrating the numbers of people whom Saul had cleansed from their synagogues. The High Priests had given Saul letters of authority. They knew he would find people either in the synagogue or at their homes; he was authorised to supervise the soldiers as they pulled men and women out onto the street. Saul was renowned for being zealous in violence and showing no mercy. These believers in Christ would be beaten, scourged and tortured to confess. They might talk about their love for Christ but, according to Saul and the Priests, this was blasphemy.

Pedroc was terrified that this would happen to him. Pedroc's position in the synagogue meant he had an invitation to dine with the others to celebrate Saul's arrival in the city. It was an invitation he could not refuse. Pedroc did not even have time to take his place on the cushion. It was as if Saul had inbuilt radar for believers. Saul took one look at Pedroc and knew. Petroc's love for Jesus radiated from him. His speech was humble and he was, is and would ever be for Christ. Saul was on the hunt and Pedroc was his quarry.

Pedroc stood before Saul with the Psalmist's words on his lips, 'Even though I walk through the valley of the shadow of death, I will fear no evil' (Psalm 23:4). In that moment, Pedroc knew he would never see his family again and prayed to God for their protection. That night Saul locked him in prison, and with the authority from the Chief Priests, cast his vote against Pedroc, sentencing him to death with a thumb down. After the visit Saul travelled onto Damascus.

Saul's actions are documented in his testimony to King Agrippa (Acts 26: 11-12). Jesus loved Pedroc and all the other saints who were (and still are) tortured and sacrifice their lives in his name.

Love, Light, Action!

There comes a point when God has to intervene in the horrors and atrocities which man commits against one another. These acts may be performed through ignorance and unbelief, or deliberately in the grip of evil. In the point in history that God intervened in Saul's life, changing the man everyone knew as a murderer and hater of all Christians. He put in place another plan. Jesus had a word in Saul's ear causing a dramatic conversion; Saul had been blind to the damage of his actions and the misuse of his authority.

Jesus met Saul. He came to him in light. The light from heaven flashed and shone all around. Saul and his men fell to the ground in fear. It would appear that Saul was the only one to hear the actual words which were spoken. Jesus revealed himself to Saul making His identity crystal clear. He asked Saul, "Why? Why are you persecuting me?" I think this was a rhetorical question! Jesus then tells Saul to wait for instructions, when Saul shakily rises to his feet he realises he cannot see and is blind (Acts 9:4-8).

What is it like to be blind? Close your eyes for a moment and feel the darkness. What can you not do now that you could a moment ago? You cannot read this page. In fact, in many ways you are now helpless. Saul was humbled physically and mentally. Physically he had to be led and rely on other people to help him. Saul had to wait a further next three days to be told what to do, in this time Saul did not eat or drink anything (Acts 9:9).

For a highly intelligent man how did Saul spend this time? It had to be pondering on the experience, rewinding it in his mind and asking himself questions. Jesus had brought him face to face with his actions and asked, "Why?" What was his answer? The blood of innocent people was on his hands. Jesus promised, "You will be told what to do". Saul was no doubt waiting for a punishment. He knew he had offended his God. He understood God's wrath and believed it was coming his way. It was Saul's three days of radical reflection.

⋏　⋏　⋏

A disciple named Ananias was the next person God spoke with (Acts 9:10-19) through a vision. Ananias was told to go to Saul and heal his sight by laying on hands. Ananias was unaware that Jesus had spoken to Saul. He had to overcome his fear of Saul's persecution power, enter the house of an enemy and heal him. His fear of the Lord was an act of obedient love.

Through Ananias, Saul regained his sight, saw Jesus as a God of Love, was baptised changing his character from a persecutor to a persecutee! He may have been forgiven but he would have to make amends, as God had reassured Ananias, "I will show him how much he must suffer for my name" (Acts 9:16). God did not humiliate Saul He humbled him.

Saul has another family name—Paul (Acts 13:9). It makes sense that he would want to disassociate himself from the intimidating name, inspiring fear in people, in order to be able to inspire God's love in them. Quite a reversal in message! Perhaps his change in name was motivated when he encountered another Paul, Sergius Paulus, a Proconsul, or Governor of a Roman province. This story (Acts 13:6-12) also involved blindness and the evidence of the work of Holy Spirit also changed Sergius Paulus into a believer.

Saul is now known as the Apostle Paul. He has written much to the world about the meaning of Love. His treatises on love contain the most famous words about love (1 Corinthians 13:1-8). Apostle Paul knew what it was like to be without love, acknowledging that actions and words without love are worthless. He proclaims, 'If I have a faith that can move mountains, but do not have love, I am nothing'. His most known and repeated sayings are used in wedding ceremonies across the world. You may remember them, they begin, 'Love is patient, love is kind...'.

God will respond in the same way to the persecution and heinous crimes in our current history. God's love for you, others and me is too great for wicked crimes to be allowed to continue forever. It was why He sent Jesus and why He will return.

Showing Sincere Love

God wants you to be authentic and sincere in showing your love. The Apostle Peter wrote, '... obeying the truth, so that you have sincere love for each other, love one another deeply, from the heart'. What would your world look like if everyone did this? What would your world look like if you took this advice?

'A friend loves at all times' (Proverb 17:17) is one of many verses you can draw on from the Bible on how to behave in a loving way. The Apostle Peter counsels you and I to, 'love each other deeply because love covers a multitude of sins' (1 Peter 4:8). This is because you are not to judge others or keep score of their mistakes. This is hard to do, I know, but the danger is if you withdraw your love, it is as though you have given a punishment. If someone feels that they have been disciplined without permission it prevents change and damages the relationship. A more loving way is to overlook personal slights, offences or affronts instead bearing them and forgiving the person.

These values may need to be woven into your personality as you grow in your walk with Christ, 'be ready to do whatever is good, to slander no one, to be peaceful and considerate always ready to be gentle towards everyone' (Titus 3:1-2). It might not happen overnight and you may need to fight your Goliaths for the transformation to take place.

Have you noticed that when you have difficulty with someone it is hard to show that person love? You cannot forget their offence, and they appear everywhere and the situation becomes as large as *Goliath*.

▲   ▲   ▲

The man she thought she loved had made *Crystal's* life a misery. He controlled her with fear and his hands. She was able to leave him after a couple of years. However, as she repeats the stories and his treatment of her, he never really leaves. He became a Goliath in her heart but she refused to believe that forgiveness would help her.

Fear and discouragement can be the resistance you face when trying to show love in adversity. But, you will emerge stronger as you choose to make changes in your personality and in your life. It is rather like a caterpillar transforming into a butterfly of love.

Open the Door

1. **Notice** when you felt most discouragement and ask if love could transform this.
2. **Consider** how you can demonstrate your love for other people, creatures and the environment?
3. **Name** the different words and feelings you have to describe love. Discover some descriptions of love from other languages.
4. **Describe** what tough love means to you. Have you experienced this or have you ever had to use it? Has God ever demonstrated His love for you through tough love?
5. **Look up** love verses in the Bible and spend a day following them. Can you increase the number of days using them as you go about your business?
6. **Strategise** how you can chase away fear and discouragement with His love in your life?
7. **Ask** Holy Spirit to show you how to give love to a stranger?
8. **Think** about the times you have shown love to someone. On a scale of 1-10 (with 10 being the highest) how close to God do you feel when you are acting in a loving manner?
9. **Write** notes in a diary for a week of how many times you are gentle, considerate and loving towards people and note their reactions. Notice whether you found it hard or easy to behave in this way.
10. **Give up** criticism of others and find ways to give encouragement instead. Operate radar for criticism even in the smallest of behaviours.
11. **Describe** the difference it has made to you to belong to, and serve, a loving God.
12. **Be sincere** in how you show your love. Do you have any Goliaths who need to be felled? Pray about this today and notice the difference.

Step into God's Warming Light

Dear Lord,

I pray that I can know Your love for me. I accept that You first loved me before time itself and You continue to do so today. Please may I be drawn towards You accepting this love and reflecting it back to You. I accept that You loved me so much that You sent Your only Son, Jesus Christ, to die for me.

May His love be shown in my face when I speak of Him to others. May my family also recognise the Trinity knowing Their love for themselves. I ask that I can feel the strength of Your love helping me to overcome any and all obstacles in my life. May Your love change my mind-set, remembering that 'love will find a way', in order that I can achieve my heart's desire, especially in seemingly impossible circumstances!

Amen.

YOUR SACRIFICE

In some ways suffering ceases to be suffering at the moment it finds a meaning, such as the meaning of a sacrifice.
VIKTOR E FRANKL

Your Sacrifices

Your life is full of sacrifices—these may be small—seen in the moments you genuinely put someone else's needs before your own. Discouragement cannot feature in sacrifice, making it possible to push discouragement away when you choose to sacrifice your own feelings and desires as a conscious courageous decision. In adverse conditions, it can be considered as 'being the bigger person'. In baseball, a person will sacrifice their individual moment of glory for the good of the team. It is called a 'sacrifice bunt' or 'hit' and is a game changer.

As I watched Disney's *Frozen*, I was touched at Queen Elsa's surprise and amazement when Anna, her sister, had died to save her, and because of her deep love she was returned to life. It showed love in a new light or did it? In my mind, I transferred this entertainment into reality. My immediate thought was, "I know a person who willingly died for me and was raised to life three days later". It was the ultimate sacrifice of love, 'this is how we know what love is: Jesus Christ laid down his life for us. And we ought to lay down our lives for our brothers and sisters' (1 John 3:16).

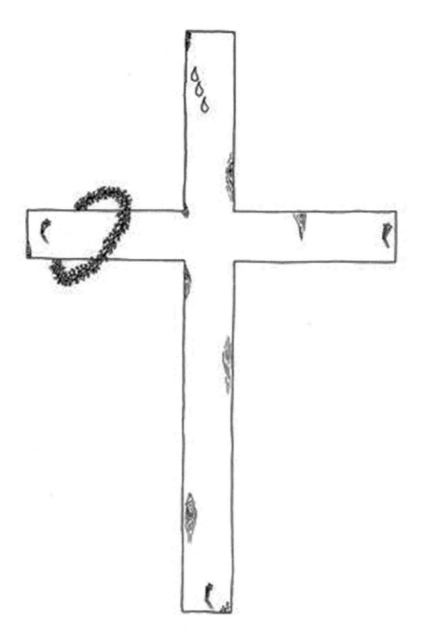

Your Sacrifice

To sacrifice your life is the ultimate gift anyone can give for a friend, relative or indeed a stranger. We have many examples of this from stories of military life when a soldier puts himself in the firing line and saves his comrades to circumstances where ordinary people will give their lives in exceptional moments. It can be a mother giving her baby life knowing her own life will be forfeited by this choice; a hostage giving their life to save others and, as I write this chapter, the tragedy of a cinema trip in Lafayette, Louisiana unfolds. In the face of senseless drama, two teachers took risks. They were willing to sacrifice their lives to raise the alarm and save others who had chosen to watch a film that fateful night. As the gunman chose to go on the rampage, their choice was to help each other. One also shielded the other and her actions prevented her friend from taking a bullet in the head, they both sustained non-fatal gun shot injuries.

Reasoned Sacrifice

There is a difference between sacrifice offered as an instant response in abnormal situations and sacrifice offered as a reasoned decision to honour God. Offering a sacrifice to God is demonstrated throughout the Old Testament. These could be burnt or peace offerings and were used as communal sacrificial meals. It was a way to atone for sins—a means to say sorry for wrongdoing. It was done in the third person, a priest atoning for the people. It was part of worship, drawing people closer to God. In Western cultures, this kind of custom seems alien to our understanding. It was a choice to give the first and the best to God, and for it to be distributed for the benefit of others. You can consider harvest festivals and tithing in this same way.

Such sacrifice is a reasoned choice not spontaneous. God made the decision to send His son Jesus to be humankind's sacrifice. This was not coincidental. It was a planned action to show the world His love. It was a way for all our sins to be taken away once and for all. It replaced sacrificial ceremonies with the Communion or Eucharist. Jesus' sacrifice was an action which changed EVERYTHING. If this was not so, why have people been arguing and debating this event ever since? It was a demonstration of ultimate love, bringing people closer to God with such finality and ending the need for blood sacrifices forever. This is still for your, mine and humankind's benefit, 'this is love: not that we loved God, but that he loved us and sent his Son as an atoning sacrifice for our sins' (1 John 2:2, 4:10).

Taking in the enormity of this sacrifice sends me to my knees as I am in awe and in fear of the Lord at His generosity to me. He has given His life so I can have a full relationship with God in mine. This melts my heart. I know the 3Ds no longer have a place in my life. I discover, to my joy, that I can bring Him a praise offering as part of thanksgiving. What feelings do you have when you reflect on His sacrifice?

Sacrifice of Forgiveness

Forgiveness is a hard discipline but essential for your well being and necessary in order to rebuild and restore your life. There are numerous stories of people who have had to come to terms with forgiveness as the only tool to free them from past experiences. Whether these are huge accomplishments from wartime or smaller ones of everyday relationships, to forgive takes a person from ordinary to extraordinary.

Some extraordinary people who survived and had to deal with extreme experiences are those who were tortured and imprisoned as a consequence of war. In recent history, we commemorated the ending of World War I and II and each year more stories are revealed. Each and everyone is a hero, although they do not see themselves in this light. We celebrate anniversaries of Victory over Japan Day, Victory in Europe Day, Battle of Britain Day and Armistice Day; the emerging stories are inspiring telling the individuals' recovery journeys. Some people return to the camps where they had been imprisoned, meet their former guards, persecutors, and some have forgiven them, even becoming friends. A possibility that was impossible at the time of the experience.

Corrie ten Boom lived in Amsterdam and when the Nazis occupied the Netherlands, she and her family saved and protected Jews and members of the resistance movement. Her family were Christians and were later betrayed to the Nazis and sent to the Ravensbrück Concentration Camp.

Corrie herself was released from the camp due to a clerical error; it was one week before the remaining prisoners were annihilated. Corrie went on to establish a rehabilitation centre in the Netherlands, and become a worldwide speaker and author. She talked about her ordeal during the Holocaust and on the concepts of forgiveness and God's love.

At one event, she was faced with not just talking about forgiveness but having to put it into action. In 1947, she was speaking in Germany; unknown to her, in the audience was a former Ravensbrück concentration camp guard who had been one of the cruellest guards. He approached Corrie at the end of her talk. She realised how reluctant she was to forgive him and prayed to God to help her. She later wrote, 'for a long moment we grasped each other's hands, the former guard and the former prisoner. I had never known God's love so intensely as I did then'.

▲　▲　▲

Eric Lomax tells his story in the book and film called *The Railway Man*.

Eric was captured and brutally tortured by the Japanese in the Second World War. He was forced to be one of the labourers used to build the Thai-Burma Railway. Years later, he decided to track down one of his torturers, Takashi Nagase, who had chosen to live and work at the site of the railway camp. The two men met and over a period of time, there was forgiveness and the two men eventually became friends. God uses everything for His good and it is an incredibly moving true-life story.

▲   ▲   ▲

This story features my personal friends. My friends travelled to the service at St Martins-in-the-Field to mark Victory over Japan Day (70th year), also attend by the Queen and Prince Philip.

Many years earlier, *Dee* had suffered as a baby and little girl, imprisoned with her family during the Japanese occupation of Hong Kong during the Second World War. She was a believer and later married a man who became a Minister. As part of life as a Minister's wife, it was with shock and horror that she had to accept Kikusaburo (Kiku) Horinouchi and his Japanese family when they joined the church she and her husband pastored.

This caused a lot of buried pain and feelings to surface. Dee felt a great deal of anger and bitterness towards the Japanese people because of her past.

One evening there was a service to commemorate Victory over Japan day (50th year). Kiku said, "I was moved by God to stand in front of the church to confess and repent what the Japanese had done against British POWs during WW2. After I apologised, Dee came up to the front, accepted my apology, and hugged me".

Her husband *Geoff* says, "I'll never forget the evening service when she and *Kiku* stood together at the front of the church and embraced each other".

The forgiveness process has been a journey for Dee supported by God and Geoff. It has involved visits to Japan, ongoing support for Pilgrimages of Reconciliation for FEPOWS and their families.

Once more God has used negative experiences for good. Dee and Geoff became great friends with Kiku and his family and they now live less than a mile away from each other.

I am sure God was at the centre of this sacrifice of forgiveness and enjoyed the reunion of friendship between His children.

Sometimes, it is the everyday forgiveness sacrifices that need to be undertaken. For the individual they are as meaningful as forgiving atrocities and must not be undervalued.

▲   ▲   ▲

Violet, told me about her issue with another member of the worship group. "I had been upset by some criticism that I had received which I felt was unwarranted. It took me months to come to terms with it. The person who ripped into me had no idea how much I suffered or how long it took me to get over it! I avoided speaking to this person and each time we were in the same room, my mind would go over their words, poisoning my heart with each meeting. It was as if I could only focus on this person and how much I disliked them and could see no-one else."

One Sunday morning, Violet watched as the worship group prepared to serve the church. All she could see was this person, the dislike in her heart grew ever large and she could not see anyone else in the group. Her total focus zoned in on to the singer, emitting animosity and feeling victimised.

"I realised that I had taken the situation out of proportion—to Goliath proportions. I might have an issue with this person but God did not and God loved us both."

"A song was sung and my irritator took the solo part, I was deaf to the beauty in her voice could only look at her with dislike, unseeing and unhearing of the rest of the band. I prayed, "Please God help me to forgive". In front of my eyes, the person's position and the issue diminished, shrinking down to the right proportions. I forgave, stopped repeating the argument and I was able to move on with my life." Violet realised that in forgiveness she could feel the energy of God's love rest on her and knew that she had received as much forgiveness for her frozen attitude as her friend.

Does this resonate with you? How easily do you give your freedom away by focusing on one issue and not letting it go in the practice of freeing forgiveness? Sacrifice means giving up the hurt feelings and it takes practice and training.

Get into Sacrificial Training

When was the last time you did some serious training? Was it learning a new sport, or trying a new skill? Can you remember how you struggled at the beginning?

▲   ▲   ▲

Robert gasps for breath. His breath is forced and laboured. He sounds asthmatic, struggling to get air into his lungs. His throat hurts and he can taste blood in his mouth. It did not look like this when he watched the guys in the yellow shirts on TV—why is this happening to him? He thought he was in good shape but his legs are communicating with his brain telling him otherwise. They are shaking, his muscles hurt, conveying urgent complaints as they painfully burn lactic acid.

The message is clear, they are unused to this level of work and their ability to cope is being stretched. Robert takes one more gulp of air to bring in more oxygen to his protesting body, wondering if another swig of water would also be prudent. He does not want to whine but is coming very close to it. His partner cycling by his side, grins reassuringly, "It'll get better with practice".

Robert perseveres with the cycling, he conditions his body to accept a new regime, strengthening, developing and improving his abilities. He eventually enjoys the discipline of his chosen sport.

It is the same with sacrifices to God; it takes discipline which is as welcome as a visit to the dentist! To do this it is helpful to remember the initial inspiration to start, keep in mind the 'why' and your 'desired end result'. It motivates you to carry on, overcoming physical hurdles and any mind games—including 'lies' from the 3Ds—that mock you saying, "You cannot do this, let alone master it".

Sacrifice involves the discipline of surrender—you are giving up something. To make this choice, you move from your current behaviour to a new demeanour. You plan to become different for Him. Any discipline is tough. Whenever you attempt a new challenge, it requires you to step away outside your 'comfort zone'.

To learn well you need to accept that, at first, you may fail and you need to be 'corrected'. This type of discipline—another hard challenge—is for some adults a gargantuan leap! It is why the Apostle Paul pointed out, '...we take captive every thought to make it obedient to Christ' (2 Corinthians 10:5). This is never more apparent as when you are learning to walk through God's open doors; there will be many arguments to persuade you otherwise.

Your negative thoughts are what keep you from completing your sacrifice. They are as persistent and domineering as chocolate looking most tempting when you are on a diet, or the fear of looking foolish when you speak a foreign language for the first time. Remember it is only you who controls your thoughts and your own mind.

Sacrifice as Self-Improvement

Sacrifice is a natural part of self-improvement and any progress you make may meet discouragement and resistance to your success along the way. Steven Pressfield points out, 'The more important a call to action is to our soul's evolution, the more Resistance we will feel about answering it. But to yield to Resistance deforms our spirit. It stunts us and makes us less than we are and were born to be'. Does this sound familiar?

You can monitor how near you are to reaching your goal by how much resistance comes your way! Gaining and congratulating yourself at each stage, without expecting too much of yourself, will meet the 3Ds head on and not allow them to get the upper hand.

Often, the temptation is to want to miss a stage, to go from beginner to expert overnight, or to crave expert results from your novice attempts and without doing 'the work'. In a culture of instant results, in which you can have a meal cooked within three minutes, whereas expertise requires patience. Keeping 'in the present' will help you here, rather than hurrying into the future as soon as the first activity or milestone has been completed. I have heard it referred to as, 'enjoying the journey rather than the destination'. God blesses your efforts and they are never wasted, 'so, my dear brothers and sisters, be strong and immovable. Always work enthusiastically for the Lord, for you know that nothing you do for the Lord is ever useless' (1 Corinthians 15:58).

▲   ▲   ▲

Zoe was worried; she wanted to know what was happening in the life of a couple in the church. She does not know them very well but she concluded that as they attended the same church this must make her a sister in Christ! She had heard that they were experiencing difficulties within their marriage. Perhaps she could help. After all, marriage was sacred wasn't it? She tried to make up her mind, should she talk to them or shun them? Does she need to take a side? Who could she ask and how could she phrase her questions without being seen as gossiping? The dilemma mounted in Zoe's mind as she pondered the situation.

The challenge Zoe faces is about making a choice? She needs to examine why she wants to know about other people's lives. It might not be a healthy interest. God will honour her if she can sacrifice her 'need to know' and leave it to Him. If her friendship is wanted or needed then a door will be opened without her interference.

▲　▲　▲

The pub was full; drinks orders were being yelled at the harassed barman, elbows were poked in *Justin's* side as he jostled for position. He caught the barman's eye and within minutes was carrying his tray of drinks high above his head through the throng who had spilt out onto the pavement. His mates had secured a table, their laughter and near-to-the-knuckle ribbing carried across the room. Swearing was just part of their conversation peppering the other words as if to enhance them. If Justin asked his buddies how many times they used a swear word they would look at him in amazement, unable to comprehend the question. They even write swear words on social media and when texting one another. Swearing is as much a part of them as their eyelashes, and they would demand, "So, what is the problem?"

Justin decided that his sacrifice to God was to give up swearing. He might not be able to influence his mates but he can start with himself. Occasionally he slips back into bad habits, in the same way as a person's accent and colloquialism naturally changes when visiting another region. It is part of the subconscious to mimic local language to bond and fit in with others. He wondered how long it would take his friends to notice that he no longer swears?

Giving up a specific behaviour is a sacrifice. It shows your way to honour God. It might need to be done in small stages. Start with replacing old behaviours with better ones. What would happen if instead of saying the F*** word it was changed to Fiddle-de-dee? Ok, perhaps not that word you do not want to be laughed at, but you could change it to another daft one! Perhaps you would not want to say the new word in public, but there are times when you are alone that you may swear; as an irate reaction to a driver who queue (line) jumps, or when you hit your finger with a hammer or drop a plate. Would humour change your annoyances into realising these small things are not worth swearing about?

This is what makes it a sacrifice; you have surrendered something of value to others in exchange for a value to delight God, 'offer your bodies as a living sacrifice, holy and pleasing to God—this is your true and proper worship. Do not conform to the pattern of this world, but be transformed by the renewing of your mind' (Romans 12:1-2).

Other Ways to Sacrifice

As a sacrifice of praise or praise offering there are other ways of surrendering earthly values and replacing these with godly ones. You can replace the time that an activity would take and give it to God in the form of prayer and praise instead. These can be times when:

- Normally you would put your own interests and hobbies first.
- Eating a meal, replaced with fasting.
- Doing something for someone else when you would rather be doing or had planned to do something else.

Try to give your sacrifice cheerfully, without fanfare or martyrdom!

Cost of Sacrifice

When you practice sacrificing a behaviour, you might find other attitudes are challenged!

After my husband and I were baptised and as 'new' Christians, we decided we would not laugh at others' misfortunes or poke fun at them behind their backs. In our circle of friends and family, it had become general practice. It was a sudden change

and when we no longer joined in or laughed, it shocked them.
They thought we had been brainwashed by our new belief.

Sacrifice might be unpopular to those who are around you, as you challenge their social 'norms' by refusing to conform to unwritten rules within a family tradition, peer group or work culture. Resistance may come as part of a backlash response.

Finally, sacrifice is a process involving discipline and it has a cost. This was shown by the parents of thousands of children who were evacuated during wartime. Parents sacrificed being with their children in order that they would find places of safety in the countryside away from enemy bombers.

▲　　▲　　▲

Marleen and Phillip sacrificed everything to support their
son in his quest for the Olympics. They re-mortgaged their
home, took on second jobs, and forgoed holidays to pay for
training and coaching. Their time was spent travelled around
the country taking him to competitions and events. They
wanted to give him possibilities and experiences which were
not available to them when they were younger, Phillip said,
"He is worth the sacrifice and we love him—what else could
we do when we realised his talent?" It did not matter to them
if he succeeded or not, but they wanted to ensure they did
everything, regardless of the cost, to give him the opportunities
he needed to use his skill, fulfil his potential and attain his dream.

What cost are you prepared to pay? How do you feel about those who have made a sacrifice for you and how do you receive their offerings? If it does not appear to you that your prayer, sacrifice, blessings or love is making any difference and that God is silent to your petitions then increase the dosage. There is no plan B in God's Kingdom. After all, He made the ultimate sacrifice, so keep going, you are doing great.

Open the Door

1. **Notice** your language; how do you speak and what words do you use? If you are tempted to swear, for instance, do you need to make any changes?
2. **Listen** to your own conversation and how you talk about other people. Do you pass on other people's news or keep it confidential? Make sure that you compliment them when you speak about them in a sincere edifying manner.
3. **Consider** how you will lovingly react when someone speaks openly about Jesus in a derogatory manner.
4. **Ask** Holy Spirit to reveal areas you need to sacrifice for God in your behaviours and actions.
5. **Start** sacrificial training today. Change one thing at a time so building your esteem and setting yourself apart for God.
6. **Read** 1 Corinthians 13:5-6 and, in your own words make a list of wrongdoings or sins. Can you change your habits? Is it possible to make them into a praise offering?
7. **Describe** the meaning of Jesus' sacrifice to you?
8. **Remember** a person in your life who has made a sacrifice for you. What was it? Send them a note of thanks for this as a sign that you are honouring the memory of their actions.
9. **Record** the times when you have received a 'backlash' to your sacrifices to God from other people. From your heart send them prayers of forgiveness and bless them.
10. **Contemplate** where you think discouragement stands in the light of Jesus' sacrifice?
11. **List six** habits you can give to God as a sacrifice of praise.
12. **Choose** sacrifice as your expression of the 'Fear of the Lord'.

Step into God's Warming Light

Dear Lord,

Thank you for giving me Jesus who sacrificed His life so that no sin barrier can come between me and You. I pray for my heart to melt as I prepare to be a sacrifice for my fellow man should I be asked to do so. I pray that I will be content to let 'God's will be done' in my life. I pray I can be challenged in practising sacrifice in my life, giving up 'worldly ways', so that I can be edified and built up, showing my sacrifices as honouring You God.

Amen.

4th DIMENSION
DAZZLING DELIVERANCE

4th Dimension

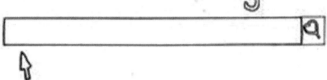

Your Searching Heart

YOUR SEARCHING HEART

*Your real, new self won't come as long as you are looking
for it. It will come when you are looking for Him.*
C S LEWIS

Desperate Searching

Searching involves emotion as you are looking for someone or something precious. Deep down you know your life feels lessened by its loss or the frustration of not finding it. These are some life stories from my memory bank.

▲   ▲   ▲

Dusk crept upon him, the light dimmed, threatening to disappear as night stalked it. A feeling of desperation settled upon him. Soon it would be time to give up for the second day in a row, the time already spent searching felt worthless. "It cannot be far: only a moment ago it was here", he murmured.

The coolness of a Scottish autumnal afternoon breezed in, unsympathetic in its approach. The smell of autumn filled the air and laughed at the dismissed summer. He looked at the all too familiar light brown earth and exploded, "How far can a ring go?" He had been helping in the garden. As he threw a tuft of turf over into the field, his wedding ring had gone flying through the air with it. The regrets and 'if only' began, "If only I had taken it off before I started the clearing", he criticised himself, as he raked through the sods, and continued to search.

He was upset but keeps a stiff upper lip, determined that if he looked long enough it would appear. The memories came flooding back. Was it really only four years ago when he married the girl of his dreams? So much had happened in that time. He looked across as his wife walked towards him; she was expecting their second child. He could hardly meet her eyes, feeling ashamed that his carelessness had lost the symbol of their love. He remembered the day when they bought the ring; they had fallen out and argued all the way home. He wanted to laugh now at the memory. It had been a stressful event, not least because they had been financially strapped and the cost of the ring had pushed their budget to breaking point.

He looked for the condemnation in her eyes at his failure but he saw only love as she joined in and searched alongside him. Perhaps if he borrowed a metal detector from a friend he might have more success?

Fruitless hours were spent looking. They never did find the ring. It remained buried in a field in Morayshire. Perhaps someday, someone will find it and benefit. Yet, a symbol of love was replaceable and a new ring was bought without angst. His and my love was blessed with its fullness carrying beyond 35 years.

▲   ▲   ▲

"Where was he?" He promised he would be here, agreed the time and this particular spot but I began to fret, "I cannot see him". Thoughts tumbled through my mind as I desperately searched for him. My eyes hunted through the crowd, unfamiliar faces discounted as I sought the one familiar one I wanted to see. There were so many people in the stadium it seemed impossible to find him.

"What was he wearing?" I questioned but I could not remember. Tears of self-pity pricked my eyes. "Oh yes, wait, a green shirt". I looked once more into the crowd, I segregated the green shirts, but when did so many guys (and gals) start wearing green? There were so many and there was the possibility that he had changed into the newly bought T-shirt, emblazoned with the event's logo.

I knew that he had been sitting across the stadium whilst I was on duty at the other side. I also knew that at the end of the day we would find one another as we boarded the church minibus but for now, in this moment, I wanted to see his face. I was desperate to share the moment with him and enjoy the music of celebrating Jesus at the one-off event, *Champion of the World.*

My fear of not finding him turned to frustrated anger, silly disconnected thoughts entered, "He has let me down because he is not here", and "If he loved me he would be here". I was miserable in a throng of happy worshippers. I craned my neck in an effort to grow taller to see above the sea of people in search of the one frame that I was seeking. I made out a familiar shape in green my heart beat faster. My eyes brightened for a second, only to dip down in disappointment when I realised that the man was too tall and not as handsome as the one I was looking for.

I checked my watch. It would not be long before I would have to turn back and go on duty again. Doubt set in. I began to get despondent and asked myself, "Would we meet up or miss the opportunity?" It was a time before mobile phones and other electronic devices become commonplace, so we were dependent on our senses. I send up a prayer to God begging Him to help us. I heard a voice calling my name and turned around, there was my husband, Denis, grinning at me.

▲   ▲   ▲

"She was only three years old; where could she be?" I
was not paying attention and in seconds, my world
changed into a mother's worst nightmare. My child had
disappeared. If only I had not been engrossed in reading
my book. She had been nearby, playing shops, and I
thought she was safe in the house. The back gate swung
on its hinges as it squeaked a chastisement to me; the
last time I had looked, it had been shut and locked!

The clue is there, she must have gone out. I looked down the
street, frantically calling her name but there was no reply. I asked
passers-by, "Have you seen a little girl wearing a blue dress with
a cat on it?" They replied, "No" and carried on walking, their
world still intact. I ran across to my neighbours' house where
my best friend lived. Mo answered the door, her smile froze as
she took in my distraught features, "She's gone", I cried "and
I cannot find her". Tears began to stream down my face.

My friend dropped everything, joining me in the search. She
asked the necessary questions: "How long had Candice been
missing? Had I checked all the rooms in the house? What was
she doing when I last saw her?" To the last question I replied,

"She was playing shops" and, then the penny dropped.

"Shops, Mummy, let's go", her little voice had said.

"Yes, yes in a minute", impatiently I had replied. She
must have gone to the shops. I started to run in the
direction of the corner shop, my mind now imagining other
dangers. Has she managed to cross the road safely? My
friend stopped me saying, "You stay here in case she
comes back, and I will go and look for her at the shops."

My forehead was creased how would I make this painful
decision to stay and wait or to go out and search?

The next moment a child's wail filled the air. It was the sweetest sound I have ever heard in my life. My daughter tottered down the path, crying loudly because the shop had been closed. I gathered her up in my arms, our tears mingled. I kissed her better. I promised that we would go together when the shops opened. Her tears comforted my soul.

Have you had an experience of a search bordering on desperation? The relief when it is all over, regardless of the outcome, is immense. There is a searching, which permeates throughout your life. It might rear its head occasionally or be a constant companion. It can be recognised as a questioning of your life's purpose or even the meaning of life.

Life's Search

What exactly is the purpose of your, or my, life? The search for identity, meaning and purpose is a universal hunger. It is far more than the number 42 given by *Douglas Adams*! Today, young people's meaning seems to be restricted to the number of friends on Facebook, the number of hearts in Periscope, the number of followers on Twitter, or anything that ranks one person above another. Statistics have taken over. So, what *is* the meaning of your life? *Donald Miller*, put it this way, 'every human being is searching for a deep sense of meaning, and yet we're all chasing success. We've confused one for the other'.

Could this be the essence of the problem and a 'lie' of discouragement? Lies are often coated with a semblance of truth. Society considers it 'admirable' to look for success but making it your life's focus is dangerous, opening the door to discouragement. Rather like a hamster in a wheel, success always seems the next rung away. As your expectations, rise success becomes just out of reach and more becomes an overriding need—tagging it as 'Insatiable Success'. I wonder which is worse, this or travelling through life, searching and not knowing what exactly you are looking for?

The Fourth Dimension

Up until now, the 3Ds described have negative connotations in your life. Now it is time to reveal the Dimension that brings with it the positive transformation of His warming light. A light to brighten, warm and transform your life—it is called Deliverance.

Try saying the word Deliverance out loud. Possibly it is a word you have not said for a long time, if ever. Can you hear it in today's context even though it is an old fashioned word, hardly ever used in today's conversations, and rarely from the pulpit or church lectern? A word as old as Middle England and yet, not so long ago, it would have peppered sermons and Christian conversations alongside words like: sin, repentance, salvation, redemption, atonement, reconciliation, purification, righteousness, end-times, sacrament and fear of the Lord.

So why should deliverance still be important to you? Do you think you need deliverance? If your answer is, "No, I am doing OK, thank you" then perhaps it is time for you to think again, and then think some more. If your deliverance means you can overcome the 3Ds by stepping into His warming light and enjoying communion with God on a one-to-one basis, would you reconsider?

▲　　▲　　▲

"There's got to be more to life than this…, oh no, what is wrong with me?" *Louise* looked around and checked that she had not said the words aloud. Her husband was stretched out on the sofa, the guy whose lovemaking she had enjoyed earlier this morning. He smiled widely at her and returned to watching the sports programme while she lived up to the title 'domestic goddess', ironing away. Louise enjoyed housework and felt it therapeutic and not the chore she knew others viewed it. Her thoughts drifted on, "Is this what a mid-life crisis feels like—a life without struggles, mortgage payments covered, but an unspoken feeling of being dissatisfied with life?"

Her musing was interrupted by the yells which filtered down from upstairs; her three children were in the middle of a sibling spat. It was a normal life. She enjoyed her job, friends, and family and yet something was missing, it was as though she was searching for something but could not put her finger on what it was. Out loud, she said, "Why don't we go to church?"

▲   ▲   ▲

Lewis would like to break out, away from the boredom, the tedium of his life; made up of a dead-end job, friends with whom he constantly quarrelled, and a wife who looked at him in puzzlement as if trying to recall why they hooked up in the first place? He wondered if a drink would help, or drugs, but actually this depressive state was preferable to the bother of reaching out in that destructive direction. He thought, "I want to experience freedom, freedom to be the person I wants to be, to like himself again, and do the things I want to do. How do I find it? He felt puzzled, "When did I become so lost?" he wonders. He welcomed a reprieve from his thoughts as his wife appeared with a cup of tea and a leaflet. She made a suggestion, "Why don't we try this church thing?"

Are you searching for God? He can be found in many ways, as your heart knows. It is your heart that understands that searching for God and His search for us is ongoing. It is your heart, with its more holistic view of nature, that recognises Him in creation and in life. This can be seen by the wonder of nature, seeing the life of animals, plants, insects and fish: from artistic creation and expression, or from manufacturing, engineering and medical breakthroughs. Saint Augustine of Hippo (living in modern day Algeria) recorded his search for God in his writings *Confessions*. Born in 354-430 AD, it took Augustine until the age of 31 to complete his searching. Augustine discovered deliverance and then began a new journey. God took him from skeptic to Christian sage.

A search begins with a single step and the prompt from a still small voice. It can be stimulated by:

- A conversation with a friend about life.
- A neighbour inviting you to come to Church, or start an Alpha or similar course.
- A reminder about a time when you attended church and then stopped.

Each prompt suggests it is time to get to know God better. You never know when these seeds will drop, quietly germinating and growing until the time is right. It was the death of my dear friend, Bob Young which prompted my searching for what comes after life. It took my search for God to another level, and there was no way I was going to leave my husband behind!

Do you remember when you just knew your need to search? It comes from the depth of your stomach, the centre of your being. Believers recognise this as the still small voice of Holy Spirit within us all.

My Dad, when he really wanted me to hear him spoke quietly. In this way he would get my attention far more effectively than if he had shouted! Elijah saw spectacular expressions of God's power and heard His voice but it was when God spoke in a gentle whisper, in a still small voice, that He gained Elijah's direct attention (1 Kings 19:12 NKJV). Have you noticed, heard or responded to the still small voice inside you?

Meaning of Deliverance

Deliverance means to be liberated and to be saved. Imagine being saved by an awesome loving God who has promised never to leave your side. A God who sent Holy Spirit to guide and teach you, and the God who sacrificed His only Son to give you eternal life.

If you are still unconvinced—have another think—you have time. Hold a debate with God. He loves it when you question Him directly. Take all your arguments to Him and see what kind of reply you get! Make a note of the 'serendipitous' follow up events and let me know. In the meantime, consider deliverance as the Fourth Dimension—the winning dimension.

This dimension is chosen not to overwhelm you but to change the way you view your disappointments, disillusionment and discouragements, the recognised negative 3Ds. This fourth dimension takes you to a whole new level (if you will pardon the pun). It is about stepping through the Open Door and feeling the warmth of His Light.

HE Finds You

God loves you so much that, if you are lost, He will find you. Being lost can be when you are suffering and feel isolated or without hope, making decisions that you know are not wise. It might explain the Apostle John's claim, 'He first loved us' (1 John 4:19). He knows you, and therefore His search is not a frantic one because He knows where you are. This has been the same from Bible days to present day.

King David puts it best in this Psalm:

Where could I go from your Spirit?
Where could I run and hide from your face?
If I go up to heaven, you are there
If I go down to the realm of the dead, you are there too!
If I fly into the radiant sunset, you are there waiting.
Wherever I go your hand will guide me;
Your strength will empower me.
It is impossible to disappear from you,
Or ask the darkness to hide me,
For your presence is everywhere
Bringing light into my night!
(Psalm 139:7-12, The Passion Translation)

God knew where Adam and Eve hid themselves from Him; He found David in the caves and spoke to him. Elijah was one of God's greatest champions and prophets. Even when Elijah went into hiding, going as far as pulling his cloak over his face, rather like a child whimpering, "if I cannot see you, you cannot see me!" God spoke to him and said, "What are you doing here, Elijah?" (1 Kings 19:13).

God promises to search and seek for His people, "I, myself will search for My Sheep and seek them out" (Ezekiel 34:11,). Later, God talks about 'delivering them from everywhere they have been scattered'—this also applies today—for you and me.

Jesus talks in his Parables about how intensely the Father will look for you. You can find this in the stories of the Lost Sheep, the Lost Coin and the Prodigal Son (Luke 15:4-31). Each parable contains this promise by God, He will look out for you and when you call out to Him—He is there.

I believe that relationship and partnership are the distinguishing features that God looks for in the seeker. He gave you and me free will. He's longing and desire is that we will choose to meet with Him. It is not a game of hide-and-seek but a true regard God holds for you. He will reveal Himself to you when your search is motivated by your free will—a genuine interest in finding Him. God promises His love, 'I love those who love me, and those who seek me find me' (Proverb 8:17). Martin Sheen, the actor, revealed, 'I have long since returned to my church. I have never forgotten that, even though I turned my back on God, in my time of greatest need, he came to find me'.

Your Search for God
Finding God may be as simple as saying the 'Sinners Prayer'— an unsexy title—makes you want to rush to read it doesn't it? It is also known as the 'Salvation Prayer' and I have included it in Your Bonuses.

The preacher was droning on. "When did sermons get so boring?" **Marty** thought, "It is the same each week". He recognised the feelings of dissatisfaction and disillusionment that bubbled up inside him. Marty glanced around, he felt alone in the crowd, and he knew that before long the songs would begin and hands would be in the air. He wonders, "Should I put my hands up, to be the same as everyone else?"

He does not want to. "Where is God, He is supposed to be here isn't he?" Marty longed for this 'relationship thing' he has heard others talk about.

"If Christians *have* got it all together, why do so many of them look so miserable?" he wondered, "Oh Crumbs", the preacher was talking about the speck of dust in my brother's eye compared with the plank in my own. "How did he know my thoughts?" Marty glanced around, "Don't be daft", he comforted himself, "it is just a coincidence".

"I want to know more about you God", he mumbled to himself, "perhaps I can then be free of these feelings of obligation and frustration!"

Marty is in the right place as he has set aside time for God by attending the service. He is not going anywhere else. And, yes, Christians can get stuck and lose the first love they experienced when they first met God. Has this happened to you? If so, you need to have faith to begin your search for God.

Everyone who searches for God needs some faith that they will find Him and their questions will be answered. Your faith does not have to be very large to begin with, less than a mustard seed in fact, as Jesus told His disciples when they had failed at a task. Nonetheless, 'without faith it is impossible to please God, because anyone who comes to Him must believe that He exists and that He rewards those who earnestly seek him' (Hebrews 11:6). God reaches out to everyone at their individual level. He is in the business of waiting. When a person reaches out in faith—'ask and you will receive'—He will hear and respond to your every prayer.

God is an Open Door

What if the finding of the meaning of life was much simpler than you have ever considered? If it is found in a two-way interaction because God is simultaneously wanting to find you! He only wants good things for you and, if you make Him your treasure, you will find satisfaction and wholeness in your life, 'For everyone who asks receives; the one who seeks finds; and to the one who knocks, the door will be opened' (Matthew 7:8).

I love the painting by the Pre-Raphaelite artist, William Holman Hunt, entitled *The Light of the World*. It was inspired by words from the Apostle John's final book, 'Here I am! I stand at the door and knock. If anyone hears my voice and opens the door, I will come in and eat with that person, and they with me' (Revelations 3:20 NLT).

There are three versions of Hunt's pictures; one, completed in 1853, is held at Keble College, Oxford; the second completed in 1854-5, is displayed at Manchester Art Gallery, Manchester; and a latter one, painted 50 years after the first was presented in 1908 to St Paul's Cathedral, London. Like all great paintings, it is the viewer who interprets the painting and allows the painter's original purpose to speak. In the picture, the door has no handle, and once more God—Jesus—is quietly waiting. He is waiting for you.

What or Who is Your Treasure?

The search for deliverance is a re-valuation of what is important to you. You have the ability to choose, for God has given you free will. If your whole life is taken up with working, or with an "It is OK as long as I'm not hurting anyone" attitude, it might be worth considering the Apostle Paul's words. '… you might have the right to do anything but not everything is beneficial' (1 Corinthians 6:12).

Choosing a selfish life where you can eat as much as you want, look, say or buy anything without any boundary is a life where God is not your priority. If these are your first thoughts, and your passions and interests are to gain riches, possessions and wealth then you may be replacing and devaluing God, 'for what profit is it to a man if he gains the whole world and loses his own soul?' (Matthew 16:26 NKJV).

Are you searching for a better life? To gain this you may buy a lottery ticket—as it is buying into a dream of changing your current life-style with money. It might be that you say, "Yes, but if I won I would share the prize, giving money to my family, to charity and even to the church". This may be so, but the search for your dream of another life-style is incongruent with trusting God with your life and finding Him as your prize and treasure.

In Anderson's *The Snow Queen*, Gerda's treasure is her friend Kai. She is pushed to search for Kai to the ends of the earth in her efforts to return him back to his true self. Along the way, she has resistance and distractions to overcome. She meets and makes new friends and is given a reindeer as a gift for her perseverance to help her continue in her search.

What is your treasure? Is it God? Can He be part of your treasure? If you draw near to God, He will come near to you (James 4:8 NLT). How many distractions or mis-directions have you had in your heart's search for God? Do other things come in the way, taking your attention somewhere else, persuading you that He is unimportant in your life? Can you recognise this type of 'lie', taking you away from His dazzling, healing and delivering light?

Recognising God

God can be persistent, blunt and very direct in getting your attention. It is like the pistol going off at the starting line, or the mother eagle giving her eaglet an extra shove out of the nest, as He reminds you and me to seek Him. He can use any situation, illness, failure and impossibility to show you His face.

"I was driven into church, pulled by invisible threads to the church, any church", says *Pamela*. The day was 13 March 1996, Pamela was away from home on a training course and had just heard the news bulletin on the radio. There had been a massacre; a gunman had gone on the rampage, shooting sixteen children and one teacher in a Primary School in Dunblane, Scotland. She was beyond understanding the motive for the waste of so many young lives and had many questions for God. She found herself in a pew of the Lady Chapel of an unknown church crying out in her heart for these unknown families.

When you are at your most desperate, this is where God is illuminated and His light is at its most visible.

By contrast, the times you are in good health, basking in success and good fortune, it is easy to miss Him. I think this is the meaning behind Jesus cryptic comment, "It is easier for a camel to go through the eye of a needle, than for someone who is rich to enter into the kingdom of God" (Matthew 19:24, Mark 10:25 and Luke 18:25).

Just like knowing God's plans for you, how do you know when He has spoken to you?

It may be different for each person but for me I know when I have heard His voice when I feel at peace regarding a decision or action. But I have to beware of false 'voices' and attributing them to God, aware of imitation and distractions, as these are not signs of God's presence. Where love is—there is God. He may be found even amongst destruction and devastation. He was there for the families who suffered the Dunblane shooting.

Recognising God can come by asking the question, "Is this you Jesus?" If the answer is yes, then you have confirmation (1 John 4:2). God is excited to hear your voice, are you excited to hear His? It is your choice to turn towards Him and have adventures in deliverance, or to turn away from Him and continue in the self-condemnation of your own ways.

Where is God?

If you are have difficulty sensing the touch of God's presence, consider it to be like seeing His fingerprints—and they are everywhere. HE is there in the small details of your life and in your environment. What delights your eyes?

- a wildflower,
- the beauty of a baby,
- an exchanged smile with a stranger in the supermarket,
- an unexpected compliment,
- an animal playing in the park,
- a friend with cancer making a joke,
- your children saying thank you? Or,
- something else?

He comes down to earth all the time to be with you but the 3Ds' 'lies' include distraction and uncertainty, so He is not seen. I love the writing of Micah which has a great image of how God comes to earth, 'Look! The Lord is coming from his dwelling place; he comes down and treads the high places of the earth. The mountains melt beneath him and the valleys split apart' (Micah 1:3-4). If mountains can melt why can't your heart?

Do you need help to see God's presence and His fingerprints, like the police using Carbon Black and other powders to show up human prints? In the UK and internationally there is a great programme called *Alpha*, written by Holy Trinity Church, Brompton in London. It is delivered through thousands of churches across the globe. The interactive sessions give space to ask any question about God, Jesus and Holy Spirit, and to discover your own answers. This is the Christian version of forensic dust powder!

This poem encapsulates your and my searching:

The Spirit was
there before us
and then God
created us to share, and
we fly and
rise with Him.
And sometimes
we need to rest
on Him and
other times we
need to dive
into His arms
to be transformed.
© Donna Drouin (April 2012)

Warnings

Any journey of searching takes you along different paths where you uncover new experiences. The New Testament is the good news of God's love, grace and mercy, offering you the free gift of deliverance. This will be for your freedom, though there are a few warnings to look out for:

1. Getting nearer to God may incite distractions and diversions from the spiritual Enemy who tries to block the (door) way to Him and puts uncertainty in your heart. This is a sure sign that you are close. Remember, it is resistance.

2. Once you start searching, you cannot fail to see Him and then you will say, "How did I not see Him before?" It is a bit like when you buy a new car, all of a sudden the same model is everywhere!

3. When you have found Him, you may become fervent in wanting to know more, to seek His face, His name, His character, His will and to become more like Him.

Finally, I conclude with the blessing the Apostle Paul gave when writing to people who had just heard the good news of Jesus. Paul wanted them to know the strength and power when filled with the fullness of God: '... that Christ will live in you as you open the door and invite Him in' (Ephesians 3:17 The Message).

Open the Door

1. **Remember** your feelings when you search for something or someone you thought you had lost. How did you feel?
2. **Describe** what deliverance means to you and how Holy Spirit has moved you in this area.
3. **Categorise yourself** are you lost or found? Do you like to go your own way? How often do you find that you have become a lost sheep and have to return to God?
4. **Scrutinise** your beliefs on free will. What does it mean to you and how important is your free will?
5. **Ask** Holy Spirit how you can seek God's face, find out about His character and get to know Him more deeply.
6. **List** five ways you can seek and search for more of God. What doors has God opened for you in your searching journey?
7. **Notice** any patterns in your life for searching out God? What advice would you give to another seeker?
8. **Help someone else** who is searching. How would you recognise this state and what could you do to help them and open doors for them?
9. **Examine** where you find your treasure. What does your heart love? Where is God in this mix?
10. **Listen** and get to know your 'still small voice'. How do you recognise His voice and how do you respond?
11. **Consider** how God searches for, or speaks, to you? Is it through the Bible—His word, or creation, or 'quiet time', or worship or another personalised way?
12. **Invite** God's searching gaze into your heart today. You may find Psalm 139 helpful, especially the last two verses.

Step into God's Warming Light

Dear Lord,

I thank you, Jesus, for my salvation and deliverance. May I know the full meaning of my life and walk in this fourth dimension—deliverance. May I search and find You as my treasure Lord. Please let the unbearable seeking be over and my natural search for knowledge to know You more be increased.

I want to know, to the deepest depth of my soul how much You—God—love me and how You search my heart to find my treasure which is You at my centre. May I continue to find myself, using my free will. May my balance and my spirit align with Yours as I step into Your dazzling and warming light.

Amen.

YOUR HEART, HIS CREATION

I would rather be what God chose to make me than the most glorious creature that I could think of; for to have been thought about, born in God's thought, and then made by God, is the dearest, grandest and most precious thing in all thinking.
GEORGE MACDONALD

Dust

What is dust? Have you looked at it lately? Is it merely something you chase off with a duster or sweep away with a broom?

▲   ▲   ▲

"What *is* this white stuff everywhere?" my friend *Pauline* exclaimed. We looked around in disbelief; the cupboard where we stored the mosaic supplies was covered with a light, white powder. It had got everywhere. In the kiln a porcelain piece had exploded and although the door was still firmly shut, the dust had leaked, discharging itself to cover all that it touched, giving it a new veneer.

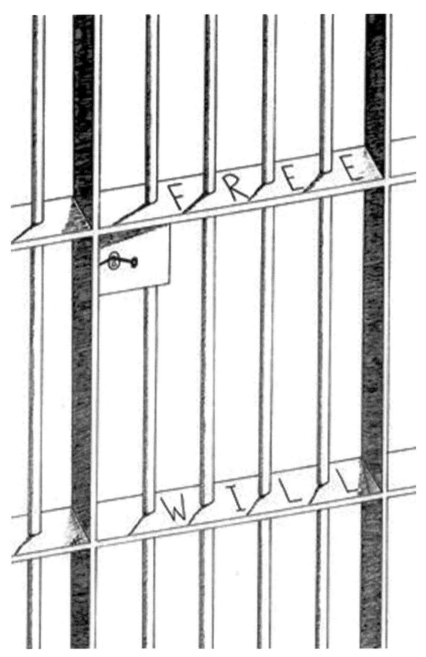

Your Heart, His Creation

▲   ▲   ▲

Barbara lived for a while in the desert as part of her husband's tour of duty. She recalled her fight against dust, "When the sand storms arrived it became a battle against the elements. No matter how tightly I closed the doors and windows, the dust would get in, penetrating through the tiniest of cracks, and the next days were spent trying to clear up. It seemed that we no sooner cleaned it up when we were attacked again".

I remember the pictures of people covered in smoke and dust from crumbling buildings, in the aftermath of 9/11. Dust was the suffocating substance that stuck in the throat. As pictures were televised across the globe, clouds of dust enveloped New York. It made the buildings and people invisible or appear as ghostly shapes. The dust was as much a killer as the fire and the toxic dust legacy has plagued thousands of people. It has been impossible to get this dust out of the body and it has had devastating effects. The initial symptoms have become known as 'World Trade Centre Cough', first coined by Dr David Prezant.

Have you tried to weigh dust? A particle of dust feels weightless. Try holding a single particle in your hand; it is almost impossible to see. It consists of a small, fine piece of dryness, yet get a speck of dust in your eye, and it feels enormous and the stinging reaction is immediate. Dust is a disintegrated or decayed substance without life although, when it contains organic matter, especially flakes of human skin, it quickly becomes heavily colonised by dust mites that can cause eczema or bring on asthma attacks. Dust on the top of soil is a covering which the wind can move from one place to another place, and it only becomes part of the soil when 'dampened down'. As a substance it is formless and empty. Yet, it was the earth's original surface, which God used as the base for creating our ancestor Adam.

Creation's Song

I get goosebumps when I hear the words, "In the beginning …" I know the following words will construct a story, a poem, or a song and retell the origins of something magnificent. Our world, God's creation—His gift to us— is awe inspiring. Each time I read Genesis 1 and 2, I remember His creativity and whenever I look around me, I see the evidence and beauty of His creation.

'The earth was formless and empty, darkness was over the surface of the deep' (Genesis 1:2) making it a watery sphere, a shapeless mass, shrouded in darkness. God's presence, word and breath took this unproductive, inanimate, deprived waste and gave it form and life. The Holy Spirit hovered over the deep darkness, and God's first recorded words (noted by Moses) were spoken, "Let there be light!" (Genesis 1:3). Light, His Light, gives life. Can you imagine this as a place to long to be—in His warming light, to feel His beginnings for you, which takes you back to your origins? Here is the account of the creation of your origins (Genesis 1:1-2:4):

Day 1: God speaks and Light enters the void, making a distinction between light and dark, day and night.

Day 2: God separates the water, to give a sky and a horizon.

Day 3: God calls for dry land and waters to be distinct. Land and Sea appear. God breathes life and orders vegetation, seed-bearing plants, flora and trees.

Day 4: God makes the moon, stars and the sun, setting their trajectory, their courses and purposes to put the seasons in place and the plant life self-sufficient.

Day 5: God creates all living creatures of the sea and air. He fills the sea with fish and mammals, the air with bountiful bird life.

Day 6: God breathes life into wild animals and livestock. He creates man and woman in His own image. You and I were made in the image of God the Father, Jesus and Holy Spirit—the Trinity. This image tells us that we were made

for relationship—with God and with one another. He created man and woman to be in harmonious relationship together and so to rule over all the creatures and plant life.
Day 7: God rests.

Once you have searched for God, found him and sought to know Him more, then it is fully reasonable to believe that He could and did speak this universe into being. It is the Truth and makes more sense than any other theories.

The difference between man and woman is in their creation story. Adam (man) was created from dust whereas Eve (woman) was created through man, from his rib. Perhaps this is why ladies often give their fellows a dig in the ribs to remind them of a different view! We can see from this verse, 'So God created mankind in his own image, in the image of God he created them; male and female he created them' (Genesis 1:27). This shows that woman was not an afterthought but part of His original plan.

One of the amazing differences about women is—
we were not made from dust!

Whereas, God took dust of the ground, breathed into his nostrils the breath of life to make Adam a living being (Genesis 2:7). But for his wife, 'The LORD God made a woman from the rib he had taken out of the man, and he brought her to the man' (Genesis 2: 22). This, to my mind, explains the bonding between men and women and is the foundation of the Christian view of the nature and purpose of marriage (Genesis 2:24). This harmonious togetherness is God's wisdom and intent.

Your Free Will
How important is your freedom? People will run and risk their lives to have a freedom to live their life as they choose. Just consider a refugee or asylum seeker who is no longer prepared to stay in an oppressive, persecuted, conflict zone or poverty-stricken country. They are seeking a

better life for themselves and their families. The risks they are prepared to take include forfeiting their lives, as, for them, no life is preferable to staying where they were.

When I was growing up, the news was filled with escapee stories from the Berlin Wall; today it is via a port called Calais. How desperate do you think a person is who chooses to attach himself or herself to the bottom of a coach or hide themselves in the wheel arch of a vehicle? One of numerous people trying this was *Ahmed Osman* who risked and lost his life at 17 years old.

Free will is highly prized and God gifted it to you and me. In the beginning it was given by God when He gave responsibility to men and women for everything else He had just created. What an amazing gift, to look after the land, all its fauna and flora—to be a partner with God over His creation. But with responsibility come choice, the choice of decision-making and the freedom to choose.

God loves and values you; He also values your free will. He can guide you in the choices you make and it delights Him when you freely give your will back to Him. Leviticus is full of details, given to the nation of Israel, about sacrifice and giving to the Lord freely. These are termed 'free will offerings' and especially when given enthusiastically, 'God loves a cheerful giver' (2 Corinthians 9:7).

What do you think it would be like if you did not have free will? Imagine sacrificing, fearing and serving the Lord as an automated action. It would not include a conscience or love. You would not have the ability to think for yourself, only behaving and reacting as programmed. The fact that you have free will proves that God is not a dictator and looks for relationship with His people. He knows the Truth, so can help us to deal with all the different counter productive arguments surrounding Him as we each try to figure it all out!

Free will is a higher level of intellect as freedom means making choices—between right and wrong. Animals do not have this ability and cannot show remorse for their actions. They do what they do because that is their make-up and how God created them to be. When you consider the mess that Man makes of our world with good and bad choices, it would be a nightmare to throw in the mix other beings doing the same! God knew this and gave the responsibility to us. Even with all the risks, He would rather have a world of free people than a robotic automated world. Where would the pleasure in the latter be? Where would love be?

The problem with free will is that it is easy to become proud. Consider the proverb, 'Pride comes before a fall' (Proverb 16:18). Do you think it is true? I have witnessed pride puffing me up, and I think I can do anything in my own strength and without the help of anyone. When I have been in this position, I have had to repent of this fault. God is gracious and merciful when you and I say sorry, and a better outcome occurs when I align my free will with His will. I know God will not force me to do anything; it is against His collaborative nature. In the First Century, Saint Augustine remarked on God's intent on free will boundaries, 'He who created us without our help will not save us without our consent'.

God Values Your Freedom

God understands how easy it is to lose your freedom, usually by another person choosing to take over in power, wanting all other lives to bow to his or her decisions. It is a scramble for power which is not godly power. The paradox is that God gives His power freely, so it is already available, but selfish people want their own version of power so they can enjoy depravity and cruelty. He values your freedom so much that, throughout history, He has intervened whenever oppression becomes too much for people to bear. Liberating His people was first seen when He used His power through Moses, 'so God looked on the Israelites and was concerned about them' (Exodus 2:25). The fight for freedom was demonstrated via plagues and miracles like the parting of the Red Sea.

God intervenes in our history, providing freedom for people at every turn, rescuing us from others' bad free will choices. It seems that humanity's free will has a propensity towards sin leading to slavery, seduced into the condition, preferring sinful pastimes and turning away from God. The sending of Jesus was also a rescue mission. One in which God revealed himself, inline with the prophecies (Isaiah 53). God's timing for this rescue mission was perfect, 'but when the fullness of the time was come, God sent forth his Son, made of a woman, made under the law' (Galatians 4:4).

I am intrigued as to what featured in the timing of this piece of history making? Why this particular time as the essential moment for Jesus to come, changing history's calibrated calendar from BC to AD forever. Looking at it more closely the following circumstances were in place:

1. The first taxation system was put in place by Caesar Augustus and operated through a census. This counting of people ensured that Jesus' birth was recorded (Luke 2:1-7). No one has been able to dispute that Jesus existed.

2. The Jewish people, having returned from captivity in Babylon and Persia, were hungry for the fulfillment of the scriptures that foretold the arrival of the Messiah.

3. It was a fulfillment of prophecy that Jesus was pierced (by nails) while innocent (Isaiah 53 and Zechariah 12:10). Roman crucifixion did this, whereas Jewish law would have killed him by stoning or strangulation. Although innocent Jesus was tried under both Jewish and Roman Law, and a death statistic recorded and documented by Roman, Jewish and Greek historians.

4. Rome, through military action, had conquered much of the world and unified it. This allowed freedom of travel for trade and artisans, providing a vehicle for news and the message of the Gospel to travel. The Gospel would travel with believers in the Roman army, which is how it first arrived on Britain's shores.

5. The Greeks had conquered the world from a philosophical, linguistic and scientific point of view. They brought a culture with a commonality in language, enabling written communications and artistic works to be maximised.

6. Non-Jewish people (Gentiles) had begun to realise that pagan religions were inadequate and did not satisfy people spiritually.

Their meaning of life was being disintegrated with a world awash with despair and confusion.

God does not make any mistakes especially regarding His timing. Over 2000 years ago was a time of slavery and huge differences in class structures. Jesus still is the key to setting free anyone in bondage. This is what His death on the Cross, the Crucifixion, was all about—your deliverance. Times have changed and further freedoms have been bought at great cost via wars and battles. Today's danger could be that we do not recognise that we are still slaves, albeit a slavery hidden within new technology.

Today's Loss of Freedom

The bondage to slavery continues today, you may recognise it in the elementary things in life; the inability to get along with one another, immigration fears, the rich-poor divide, work pressures, incessant immediacy of social media, hypocrisy of politics, hijacking of health information, powerlessness or apathy, and the worldliness of wealth.

⚓ ⚓ ⚓

Roderick looked around him. He was one of the fortunate ones. He had everything he wanted albeit most of it owned by others. The mortgage belonged to the bank for another 15 years, which forced him to work in a job managed, in his opinion, by inept bosses. Despite the hours he worked, his weekends were his own where, he tried to make up to his wife and kids for time snatched away by other pressures.

He had just bought his kids new personalised computers so they could be entertained watching their favourite movies, listening to their music—which he no longer understood— and playing games. He knew his wife would appreciate some time to herself. He was not worried that his credit cards were hitting their maximum. He was about to book the annual holidays abroad as it was important to the family and they all deserved a break. It was part of their pattern for a good life. With his wife's earnings they always managed the minimum payback amount to satisfy their creditors.

He looked around, his life was good, he was successful and the envy of his friends, wider family and neighbours. He wondered what they would have for dinner tonight—it was take-out night. The choices were wide open, Italian, Indian, Chinese, Thai or Fish and Chips. Sometimes the kids would fight over the choice as if they were overwhelmed by the variety. He hoped they would make up their minds tonight without squabbling. It was different to his childhood when Pizza was only available if you travelled to Italy and no one on his estate could have afforded that. "His kids did not know how lucky they were" he exclaimed.

The news was on the radio; it is a local station with an international flavour. He shook his head as news blares out about immigrants being arrested in his country. "How did they get through the check points?" he wonders. There is a sound bite about the High Street being full of beggars, which he discounts as "people wanting to scrounge off decent people like him". Another clip talks about guns and gang warfare. It was happening in the next county but he was sure that it was not as bad as they were making out. They would be talking about drugs, prostitution and child slavery next. He shook his head again; they talked as though it was just down the street from him but he knew that it was not part of his life so he did not have to worry about it. He shrugged his shoulders; there was nothing he could do anyway. Best to leave it to the 'do-gooders' and the 'God-botherers'!

He took a drag on his cigarette and felt satisfied with his life. He considered the cross trainer he had set up in the corner of the sitting room, but dismissed it with the promise that he would go to the gym tomorrow. He made a cup of tea, imported from India, picked a thread off his shirt, imported from China, and relaxed uncaring about how the products got to him. "Everyone would be OK if they had jobs", he thought, "and got off benefits".

He did not consider that he was a slave of modern trappings and worldly thinking. Roderick had bought into the 'lie'. His favourite song came on the radio, sung by a winner of a TV programme. He remembered he had voted for the singer's place in the final.

The telephone rang, Roderick responded quicker than a Pavlov dog. His friend chattered at the other end, and invited him to go 'off-roading' in his 4x4 Land rover. "Yes", Roderick punched the air with his fist, "Life was good". He knew that he and his family were privileged.

There are elements of Roderick in me; putting myself before others with an interest in luxurious life-styles and instant gratification. What about you?

Slave to Culture

It is impossible to live in this world without some part of your riches coming from the slavery of unknown people in other countries. We are all part of this circular problem. The 'lie' says, "today's abundant living is proof of our freedom"—you have liberty. It takes you off course, away from God's deliverance. If anything, Roderick, like many, is an unwitting slave to worldly goods, oblivious to their trappings and has forgotten God. This is really dangerous as forgetting God, following other gods, worshipping money or our own pleasures will result in our destruction (Deuteronomy 8:19).

Another danger is coined in an English proverb, 'familiarity breeds contempt'. In this loss of freedom, the Bible, and anything religious, is discounted, as it is too familiar, rather like a favourite record which has been played too many times, losing the pleasure of originality. The memory of life with a believer's heart is forgotten. One of the 3Ds' 'lies' is that original need is forgotten and reasoning can be disrespected, rather like the time when whooping cough was deadly and streets were full of drawn curtains symbolizing the death of a child in that house; with modern vaccinations this is no more. Consequently, generations later, whooping cough has almost been wiped out, parents contempt of vaccinations creep in and the need to have them is lost, until this dreadful contagious bacterial infection returns. I am reminded of God speaking to Hosea, the minor prophet, known as the prophet with the broken heart. In 790 BC God said, "When I fed them, they were satisfied; when they were satisfied, they became proud; then they forgot me" (Hosea 13:6).

It could be considered that spiritual blindness, lack of awareness or contempt for ourselves fall into this bracket. In the first century Saint Augustine wrote, 'People travel to marvel at the mountains, seas, rivers and stars; and they pass right by themselves without astonishment'. It is the same today. You are a marvel to God as His creation and yet this is the hardest truth for you to take on board and believe. Consequently, your search continues without seeing Him right in front of you.

⚓   ⚓   ⚓

My friend received this message from Holy Spirit to our church:

'Our church is full of sinners. Why wouldn't it be? We are all human, BUT we are God-filled. We know right from wrong. We know we should lead righteous lives—and that includes not bowing down to idols. Idols of social media: bowing our heads to check our phones and tablets for text and emails. Bowing down our heads to the weighing scales in the morning. Bowing our heads to take money from our wallets and purses to buy stuff we don't need, bowing our heads over food that our bodies don't need as we have already eaten sufficient. The list goes on and on'.

'We need to repent and ask God's forgiveness, to ask Him for strength to turn aside from the idols we worship; to ask Him for strength to lead a righteous life'.

I think we have received an important message; it could apply to your church too. I would add that He wants us to live a righteous and creative life in Him. Is it time to humbly say, "Lord, help us, we need rescuing again?"

The Second Coming

Jesus told us that He would be back, "And if I go and prepare a place for you, I will come back and take you to be with me that you also may be where I am" (John 14:3). We do not know when He will return as Jesus would not say. The Apostle Mark reports on Jesus' words, "But about that day or hour no one knows, not even the angels in heaven, nor the Son, but only the Father. Be on guard! Be alert! You do not know when that time will come" (Mark 13:32-33).

His return is called *'The Second Coming'* and is describe in amazing detail in the book of Revelation. However, as God created the universe in the first place, He can create a new one. The new one holds many more promises, a new life and a new body for you. A world so unlike this one where there is no more death, mourning, crying or pain. Heaven will be a utopia. Just for you and me, still retaining your free will but with so much understanding that worshipping God will be a 'no brainer'. Meanwhile, we may live in today's broken world but we can be creative in our worship to Him.

Creative Beings

God is a creative being, creative beyond your imagination—just watch the colours of a sky at sunset for the proof. He also created you and therefore knows everything there is about you. You cannot surprise

Him but you can delight Him, just like children delight their Father by being themselves. I like to be reminded of His loving knowledge of me through David's Psalm:

'Lord, you know everything there is to know about me.
You have examined my innermost being with your loving gaze.
You perceive every movement of my heart and soul and
understand my every thought before it enters my mind.
You are so intimately aware of me Lord, you read my
heart like an open book.
And you know all the words I am about to speak before I
even start a sentence.
You know every step I will take before my journey begins!
You have gone into my future to prepare the way,
And in kindness, you follow behind me, to spare me
from the harm of my past.
With your hand of love upon me, You impart a
Father's blessing to me.
This is just so wonderful, deep and incomprehensible'.
(Psalm 139:1-5 The Passion Translation)

As a human, you cannot help but be creative and this may mean more than the arts. Creativity can be seen in every sphere of life as progress beyond an original is developed. As a believer, it is wonderful to harness your gifts with His will, which inevitably involves other people. Can you see how bringing together like-minded people who want to express their creativity in a specific way, learning from each other and offering their skills as an outpouring of worship to Him, is an example of this?

I have seen this in organisations such as Christians Artists Together, Worship Academy and Transform Work UK. Professionals open up the door for believers in the various disciplines, such as the Lawyers' Christian Fellowship, the Armed Forces Christian Union and the Christian Dental

Fellowship. You name it; there will be a group of believers practising their creativity and common love of God together.

Your Creativity

He created you to be creative. It is recognised that Walt Disney was one of the most creative people to be born. Walt did not keep this creativity to himself, it was by sharing and bringing together of other creative people that enabled Disney's dreams to come true and a business empire to be born. One of Disney's ancestors, Robert d'Isigny, was a Frenchman and travelled with William the Conqueror in 1066 to England. The name was eventually Anglicising to Disney. I do not know how many great greats this makes, but I live 15 miles away from a village named after one 'great' grandfather—Norton Disney in Lincolnshire. Walt Disney visited on July 30th 1949. In light of the inspiration for this book, I think this is a great piece of creative serendipity.

In Disney's *Frozen,* creativity is shown when Princess Elsa makes a snowman as part of her creative play with her sister. In this memory-building activity of love between two sisters in the creation of a snowman, provides a connective moment. It also introduces one of the central characters, Olaf, who will appear later in the film.

Creativity shared encourages bonding. When you share in creativity, how does this bond friendship or communing with others? Did you find you were more creative as a child than as an adult? If so, is this something to address?

Your inner creative spirit wants to be expressed and can be revealed in any craftwork, scientific, technological or building endeavour. It is a return to the 'you' that God intended you to be, revealing a holistic wholeness, the 'you' full of personality and character. You can use your experience allowing your creativity to come out in a better version of yourself. Add this to your and His plans. Now, let your creative plans begin!

Have you ever heard the phrase, 'God threw away the mould when he made you?' He does not want a template to repeat your personality—how would that exemplify freedom? I can only copy to produce art, whereas He is the originator of all art—including you. You are awesome. Believe it.

Open the Door

1. **Be clear** on your beliefs about the source of Creation and ask God to reveal to you His truth.
2. **Examine** dust, try weighing it, looking at its substance and consider how you could make something from it?
3. **Calculate** how important your freedom is to you. What would you be prepared to give up for it?
4. **Describe** your free will offerings to God.
5. **Be alert** to living your life so that you can be ready for the Second Coming. How will you wait?
6. **Consider** whether you are a slave to modern trappings. How would you describe this bondage?
7. **List** six things which might control you, check out how this entrapment is happening and consider how you can change it.
8. **Imagine** being on God's lap, sitting on your Father's knee and telling Him of your dreams or your problems. Feel His delight and know, beyond a shadow of a doubt, that He will do anything to protect you in His love for you.
9. **Think back** to how creative you were as a child. What were your passions as a younger person? Have these developed as you have grown? How is your creative spirit shown today? Ask your family and friends and you may be surprised at how much creativity they see in you.
10. **Consider** whether your creativity can be shared. How could this positively affect other people?
11. **Research** a group or organisation of believers meeting together around a creative subject or profession. Consider joining them.
12. **Believe** in yourself as a unique person created without a copy by God.

Step into God's Warming Light

Dear Lord,

Thank you for creating me, breathing Your Spirit into my life and making me part of Your wonderful creation. Allow me dear God to return Your love and praise You for my life. May I never forget You, as the One who made me, knows me and celebrates my uniqueness.

I want to worship You deeply, show my own creativity, and feel my heart melt in the warmth of You. Help me to see creation from Your eyes and in all Your glory.

Amen.

Your Heart's Reunion

Your Heart's Reunion

He has created us for Himself and our heart will not be at
peace until it rests in Him.
SAINT AUGUSTINE OF HIPPO (345-530 AD)

Your Room

"No room, no room" may be words remembered by *Mary*, Mother of Jesus from her past. At the beginning of her labour, this was the message from the Innkeepers but "No room" has nil currency in God's Kingdom. You are welcome—always. However, there is "No Room" for life's 3Ds: disappointment, disillusionment or discouragement. There is only room for deliverance.

Remember, Jesus has prepared a room for you in His Father's house; did He not say so? "I am going there to prepare a place for you" (John 14:2-3). God's Kingdom is one of celebration because there are daily, if not moment-by-moment, reunions. The arrival of believers is greeted with trumpets and great rejoicing as they meet Him face-to-face. Imagine your feelings when your heart is reunited with Him?

Reunion Scenes

Reunions conjure up images of great homecomings. The best part of any story is the scene, usually at the ending, when there is a reunion. The boy gets the girl; the family is reunited at the airport; the animals are reunited with the family as in Shelia Burnford's *The Incredible Journey;* the son and father, daughter and mother, or siblings are reunited at the deathbed. In book and film, it is the tearjerker ending. Romcoms have scenes where one lover is rushing to the airport to prevent the other's departure! Watching or reading, your heart swells with well being, you feel safe because it has all worked out well in the end. Life has been made better, lessons learnt and the characters' love for each other expressed and shared in their moment of reunion. It gives hope for the times in real life when reunions seem far away.

It warms the heart, even those cheesy TV programmes when long-lost relatives are reunited. The directors have to schedule this moment for the end of the programme, with a dramatic build up because reunions are awash with emotion and tears rendering further conversation impossible.

My favourite real reunion scene was the newsreel of servicemen returning to UK from the Falklands War. Let me take you there.

▲   ▲   ▲

It was a remarkable victorious reunion, returning home triumphant, docking at Southampton on July 11th 1982. The **SS Canberra** sailed into view, she travelled among a flotilla of tugs, steamers, and speedboats. Homemade banners were slung across the side of the ship, matching the family creations that lined the Port walls. The soldiers from the Parachute Regiment and the Royal Marines sang out of tune which strangely created a harmony of happy voices. The military band entertained the crowds, adding to their excited anticipation of the safe return of their men and womenfolk after a three-month South Atlantic separation. Thoughts of reunion radiated, their jubilation was tangible. Officials released balloons of the national colours, red, white and blue, which filled the sky in passionate exuberance. The SS Canberra announced her arrival; the ship's whistle sounded a deep hello responding to the cheers and exuberant cries of the awaiting friends and families.

The soldiers filed out, conditioned to disembark in a
disciplined orderly fashion, making their way homeward. *HRH
Prince Charles* was present and walked with his security posse
towards the returning heroes. Suddenly, a woman broke free
from the crowd; her focus was to reach only one person. She
dashed past the Prince and into the arms of her beloved. The
Prince smiled and continued with his duties. It must be one of
the few occasions when royalty was ignored and discounted!

Visit any airport, go to the Arrivals Gate and watch the various reunions
taking place. The human drama is evident; television producers have
even made programmes recording real life's dramas. Here is a reunion
from my family history.

▲　▲　▲

She cannot wait to leave the last holding bay. She looked
out for the piece of ribbon which distinguished her case
from a cascade of cases descending onto the conveyor belt
before they begun their loop around the carousel. The
aeroplane has shunted its cargo of people to a room where
they gathered at the edges of the carousel, like stock traders
awaiting results. They were on the last stage of their journey,
collecting their earthly possessions within a cardboard and
plastic container before being dispersed to different parts
of the country. It is a lottery as to whose case would come
out first, yet the margin of the belt thickened with bodies as
if crowding would make their suitcase magically appear.
　　"Excuse me", she says, as she stretched towards her
rucksack with the ribbon flapping, looking bright and out of
place, defiant on its journey to be reunited with its owner.

Across the hall, beyond corridors and behind security barriers, less than 100 yards away, her family awaits. The plane had arrived an hour ago; the Arrivals Gate streamed with people like the rush of a 'salmon run', but did not include the face they sought. Whoops of joy, dispersed the boredom, as others were reunited, interspersed with bored, fatigued looks from businessmen, as they found their names marked up on pieces of cardboard held by equally bored looking taxi drivers.

It had been two years since they had seen her, letting her go to live her life and have the adventures she needed. Skype, letters and phone calls had filled in the blanks but it was nothing like holding their girl in their arms once more.

"I must not cry", he told himself, but his baby, albeit now in her 30s, would be back from Australia at last. For a millisecond, internally he panicked in case she had changed so much he would not recognise her, or perhaps she had already passed him and he had missed her. "Don't be silly", he scolded himself; he was as impatient as only a father could be. The years without her had been long ones and he had missed his first-born terribly.

She spotted them first. Her sister waved the joke name card above her head. She dropped her rucksack and ran, they screamed and embraced her. *Abbirose*, their beautiful daughter, was back in the bosom of her family, and her father cried.

I am sure you have reunion memories. These can be personal or observed, from family or work occasions, perhaps at a wedding or family occasion where long lost relatives are reunited, or perhaps by attending a school reunion after years of little or no contact. Through such an event, you are brought back in touch and able to rekindle long-forgotten relationships and friendships.

Homecomings

Homecomings for military families are regular occurrences as there are continual leavings. *The Lovely Leave,* a play by *Dorothy Parker* sums up the joy and pain of short reunions. Set during World War II, this dramatic story communicates the timeworn emotions of reunion infected by separation's pain. It shows how experiences gained individually while apart affects the reunion. Even today, the joy of reunions can be tempered by the readjustment of reuniting—who has authority over the remote control!

For a reunion to occur there has to be a passage of separation— it is part of the deal. Love finds being apart difficult. There is an element of disengagement. Some people detach themselves from their loved ones emotionally, as well as physically, as part of their coping mechanism. This puts a strain on the relationship, especially in light of an individual's love language. *Gary Chapman* has identified love languages in his sterling research. If your love language is touch or time, then the apartness can feel like disconnection and you can feel a sense of abandonment during the separation. Does this make the reunion sweeter?

Reunions can have a surprise element, like work or social reunions. Reunions are joyful when the separation has been combined with communications and contacts in the time interval. Reunions where the leaving process has been fractious or interspersed with difficulty can feel bittersweet. Each reunion is different and a reflection of the complexity of the relationship.

Scenes of Reunited Love

In Disney's *Frozen,* the reunion scene is a tearjerker—the two sisters acknowledging the love flowing between them. Their adventure has deepened the bond between them and they vow never to be separated from one another again. Fear has lost its power to divide them and trust is given an open door for love to blossom and the deep freeze to melt.

I do not have a sister but I am thankful for the unconditional love I witness between my daughters.

▲   ▲   ▲

As Abbirose and Candice have grown older their sisterly bond has strengthened. They are both creative in their own ways and have different experiences and outlooks on life. Life choices separate them by geography and busyness so they do not see each other as often as they would like. Yet, when they are together the separation disappears, the bond has the elasticity to stretch without breaking and bounces back on reconnection. God has blessed both them and me.

Perhaps you have friendships like this? You and your friend have not seen one another for ages—years—but when you finally meet, it is as though the years never existed. The time drops away like the original water clock and you pick up conversations where you had left off—as if you had spoken only yesterday.

In the Waiting

Have you waited for someone to arrive? It is a frustrating time, as nothing can be done to quicken their arrival. Prayers of patience are needed. Perhaps this is why God is known as a God of Patience—He awaits for your realisation that He is part of you, so important in your life, which is meaningless without Him. As a giver of free will, He will not force you to return and reunite with Him. He is there in the waiting.

In his book *The Pilgrim's Regress*, C S Lewis said, 'One road leads home and a thousand roads leads into the wilderness'. I wonder how many times I get misdirected and veer off track. The other multitude of tempting roads invariably leads me to a lost place and I have to wait for Him to find me like the Good Shepherd that He is.

Alternatively it takes me a while to realise I have gone off track and I need to find the path back to Him. Has this happened to you? For those who like maps and can ask for directions the route back onto His path can be retrieved. It must be much harder for those who find it near impossible to ask for help.

Two half-brothers who in Bible history have created the largest divide between believers had to reunite. Isaac and Ishmael, reuniting to bury their father Abraham (Genesis 25:9). In this moment of joint grief at their father's death, they came together. The brothers took seriously different paths. God's promise to Abraham was that *all* his descendants would inherit the earth. These included *all* the offspring from Abraham's two wives, Sarah and Keturah, the servant girl, Hagar and his concubines. It must break the Trinity's heart to see his descendants in such disarray and at war with one another!

Separated from God

I wonder if somehow in the growing up process you and I became separated from the Father and now need to find a way to recognise Him? He looks and feels nothing like your earthly father. Amazingly, there are numerous stories told by parents about their under-fives who are worried and ask questions about God. There appears an anxiety about the separation from Him. Some of these children are not brought up in a Christian household but they still ask about God. It proved impossible to find the originator of the following story but I love it anyway and believe it is more than an urban myth. It is my turn to retell it.

⅄   ⅄   ⅄

The homecoming of Mum and baby was particularly gratifying after the months of waiting. Proud Mum and even prouder Dad could not wait to introduce the new arrival to their two-year-old son. Their son asked to hold the child. This was dutifully done, with Mum nearby. When the baby was put into the infant's arms, he surprised his parents and said he wanted to be alone with his new brother. Understandably, the parents were perturbed by the request and promised, "Maybe later".

After a few months, their eldest son, now turned three, was still insistent that he wanted to be alone with the baby. In fact, his demands grew evermore persistent. Finally, they agreed and left the two young children alone together for a few minutes. They stood just outside the room listening intently for anything out of the ordinary. This was what they heard:

The young boy asked the baby, "Tell me what God is like, cos I'm starting to forget".

Is it as simple as this? As God put you in your mother's womb—knew you from the beginning then you and I have always been on loan to this world! The plan is you will return to Him. Is it possible that apart from an innate instinct, you and I forget Him as earthly life takes over? It is necessary to re-learn, become re-connected and feel the touch of God's light upon you once more.

The Reunion of His Warming Light

Reunion with your Creator pulls together all the loose ends, discards your painful past, defeats disappointment, dispels disillusionment and distils discouragement to 'champion' your life into balance once more. The reunion of man, woman and child to God, in this world or in the next—is to be celebrated.

You can wait till the end, your death, for your meeting with God and the final encounter will be one of dazzling triumph but terrifying judgement. So why would you put it off? In His kindness and by His Grace, He gives opportunities for you to reunite with Him while living here on earth. These could be termed mini-reunions. His presence can be part of your life. This is an invitation to step into God's warming light. Are you interested?

There are numerous points of union and reunion with God. This is why collective worship is so popular, a dedicated time to immerse yourself in the presence of God and connect into relationship with Him.

There is continuum along which you travel in your union with Him. You can mark your times of union or reunion with Him on the line below. The end marked 0 represents those self-declared atheists and agnostics who have spent their life rejecting God's offer (and encouraging others to do the same) whereas 100, the other end are those who have accepted Him wholly (and encouraged others to do the same). Like me, you may be somewhere along the line, bobbing up and down. But as you move towards Him—stepping fully into His warming light—you understand more and give more of yourself to Him.

0   50   100

Along the way are mini-reunions which help you traverse in your journey towards the 100 mark, the full light of His presence. Reunion with God changes the course of your life. They can occur at any moment—subject to His behest.

Reunion Events

The following are events where interventions and reunions with God may take place. I have listed a few of life's events, although by no means an inexhaustive list as God is a game or plan changer, 'in his heart a man plans his course, but the Lord determines his steps' (Proverb 16:9). If He wants to intervene in your life, He will.

Baptism is an outward ceremony, recognition of salvation. It symbolises death, burial and resurrection. It is about you giving up an old life and choosing to step into a new life with God at the centre. During my baptism I could not stop giggling as the Spirit of God came upon me.

Do you remember what happened at Jesus' baptism? 'As soon as Jesus was baptised, he went up out of the water. At that moment heaven was opened, and he saw the Spirit of God descending like a dove and alighting on him. And a voice from heaven said, "This is my Son, whom I love; with him I am well pleased" (Matthew 3: 16-17). This fulfilled the prophesy, 'out of the stump of David's family will grow a shot, yes, a new Branch bearing fruit from the old root. And the Spirit of the Lord will rest on him…' (Isaiah 11:1-2 NLT).

The following references will guide you if you have any questions regarding baptism (Mark 16:26, John 3:3-5, Acts 2:38 and Romans 6:4).

Christening, Dedication, Confirmation, Bar and Bat Mitzvahs are important steps towards our union with God. Any ceremony involving children and young people brings joy to His heart. Jesus was indignant when his disciples tried to stop the children from coming to Him saying, "Let the little children come to me". As a tactile person, Jesus took the children in His arms (Mark 10:13-16).

On another occasion, Jesus called a child to him as a teaching tool; he demonstrated with the physical presence of the youngster, how we all need to be as trusting as a child if we are to enter into His presence—the Kingdom of God (Matthew 18:2-6 and Mark 9: 36-37).

This also comes with a warning against harming children, and I believe this includes physical as well as spiritual harm. Jesus said, "But if you cause one of these little ones who trusts in me to fall into sin, it would be better for you to have a large millstone tied around your neck and be drowned in the depths of the sea" (Matthew 18:6 NLT). Jesus does not mince His words does He? My daughters are adults but they are still my children. Even as you grow up you will remain a 'child' of God. There are over 70 Bible verses about His acceptance of you as accepted as one of His children.

Communication and Conversation are areas in which God excels. He can cope with arguments—heated anger too. Just bring your thoughts to Him and He will respond. The Apostle James recommends, 'If any of you lacks wisdom, you should ask God, who gives generously to all without finding fault, and it will be given to you' (James 1:5).

Communion is a lovely time of remembering Jesus and the words He spoke while taking the bread and wine at The Last Supper. This enactment, whether you are of the persuasion that communion can only be passed down through priests. Or, if you, like the early believers, directly partake in communion with other believers, 'they devoted themselves to the apostles' teaching and to fellowship, to the breaking of bread and to prayer' (Acts 2:42) God will be there with you.

Conviction or Conversion is when God can turn your life around and towards Him. Regardless of a person's former belief, an awakening of God and His majesty can happen. Consider the changed lives of Saul to Apostle Paul, Augustine of Hippo to Bishop of Milan, or writer Gilbert Keith (GK) Chesterton from dabbling in the occult to Catholic Apologist.

Conversion and new convictions are not done by force but with His Spirit working intensely but kindly within you, 'God can do anything, you know—far more than you could ever imagine or guess or request in your wildest dreams! He does it not be pushing us around but by working within us, his Spirit deeply and gently within us' (Ephesians 3:20 The Message).

The most powerful of testimonies are when God reaches in and transforms a person's life. Jesus uses the Parable of the Lost Sheep to illustrate the reaction in Heaven to a conversion. He said, "Rejoice with me; I have found my lost sheep. I tell you that in the same way there will be more rejoicing in heaven over one sinner who repents than over ninety-nine righteous persons who do not need to repent" (Luke 15:6-7).

Death is part of the final reunion from which you will never be parted from Him again. It is an eventuality that greets you and I, and, for those in union with God, need not be feared. When I lose someone, it is this bereavement that raises the most questions about the way I am living my life, how they lived theirs and how God will receive them and me.
Death has been swallowed up in victory by God (Isaiah 25:8, Hosea 13:14 and 1 Corinthians 15:54); we are reminded of this when singing the words 'Death has lost its sting' in hymns and songs. This line is used in over 120,689 songs according to *Go Song* website!

Dreams and Visions are some of the ways in which God talks to you. Have you had a significant dream that you know was God communicating with you? Joel spoke about this (Joel 2:28) and the Apostle Luke also says, 'in the last days, God says, "I will pour out my Spirit on all people. Your sons and daughters will prophesy, your young men will see visions, your old men will dream dreams" (Acts 2:17). *Fellowship and Church Gatherings* are times to share together a hymn, song, lesson, revelation, tongue or an interpretation. They are meetings to build up and edify everyone's faith, 'we proclaim to you what we have seen and heard, so that you also may have fellowship with us. And our fellowship is with the Father and with his Son, Jesus Christ' (1 John 1:3)

Holy Spirit Encounters are exceptionally special times when you know, without doubt, that He has spoken with you. He communicates in numerous ways; it might be in your quiet time, a message, a prompting, speaking in tongues or a way in which only you recognise. The Apostle Paul wrote, 'Now the Lord is the Spirit, and where the Spirit of the Lord is, there is freedom' (2 Corinthians 3:17).

Judgment. Regardless of your beliefs on earth, you will be asked to give an account of yourself when you die and meet God face-to-face. He is the only person capable of fair judgement and even in this last rendezvous He will listen to your story, 'so then, each of us will give an account of ourselves to God' (Romans 14:12).

Marriage is a physical and spiritual union between a man and a woman. With God at the centre of this relationship, their love will be as strong as a three-stranded cord. It is wonderful to involve God in preparation for marriage and in marriage itself. My husband and I have facilitated *The Marriage Course* on a number of occasions and it really is an MOT or health check for any married couple. We highly recommend it. During the good and not-so-good times of marriage, a personal relationship with God will help to keep you together. King Solomon talks about the mystery of this relationship (Proverbs 30:18-19).

The Apostle Matthew records what Jesus said about this union, recognising that it is God who joins two people together; and this is what is spoken in today's Wedding Ceremonies (Matthew 19:6). The author of Hebrews writes that God expects marriage to be honoured, 'Marriage should be honoured by all, and the marriage bed kept pure, for God will judge the adulterer and all the sexually immoral' (Hebrews 13:4).

Obeying His Commandments is about being in alliance with God. It is your choice and a call for reunion directly from God, '"Ever since the time of your ancestors you have turned away from my decrees and have not kept them. Return to me, and I will return to you", says the LORD Almighty' (Malachi 3:7).

Offerings brought by believers through worship, praise sacrifices and the fear of the Lord. I cannot help but sing (or sign) and praise Him. My record/CD collection contains songs written by many Christian artists. Offerings of praise to God are not only my favourite usage of my life; they uplift me in exceptional ways. My best experiences are when I use British sign language (BSL) to the worship songs. I wave my hands in intrinsic vocabulary, interpreting words and music in this beautiful lexicon.
King David was a master of worship and captures its essence.

'Praise the LORD.
Praise God in his sanctuary;
Praise him in his mighty heavens.
Praise him for his acts of power;
Praise him for his surpassing greatness.
Praise him with the sounding of the trumpet,
Praise him with the harp and lyre,
Praise him with timbrel and dancing,
Praise him with the strings and pipe,
Praise him with the clash of cymbals,
Praise him with resounding cymbals.
Let everything that has breath praise the LORD.
Praise the LORD' .

(Psalm 150:1-6)

Did you get the hint to praise Him?

Poverty, Pain, Grief and Suffering is part of life that you do not like to endure but He will be there with you during these times. In the final reunion he promises, 'He will wipe every tear from their eyes, and there will be no more death or sorrow or crying or pain. All these things are gone forever' (Revelation 21:4). Lean on Him during these times.

Prayer is the time when you can grow close to God. A place for you to give thanks and raise petitions, asking Him for anything for yourself and others. The Bible offers helpful tips on how to pray from Jesus teaching the Lord's Prayer to His example of drawing himself away early in the morning (Mark 1:35). These can be individual prayers alone in your room, as prescribed by the Apostle Matthew (6:6) or they can be prayers with more than one person, 'when two or more gather in my name, there am I with them' (Matthew 18:20).
Never underestimate the power of your prayers, 'therefore confess your sins to each other and pray for each other so that you may be healed. The prayer of a righteous person is powerful and effective' (James 5:16). If you need any encouragement to pray then, listen to the Apostle Timothy, (simply add women in the relevant place!) 'Therefore I want all men everywhere to pray, lifting up holy hands without anger or disputing' (1 Timothy 2:8).

Siblings are significant to God. I do not believe it is by accident that you have the brothers or sisters by blood, or indeed those through God's family. You might not always like them, or they you, but the bond that relates you with them is steadfast. God demands that you show love to one another.

The Apostle John is unequivocal about this, even citing you as a murderer if you hate your brother or neighbour (1 John 3:15). Perhaps this is an example of 'tough love'? He continues, 'whoever claims to love God yet hates a brother or sister, is a liar. For whoever does not love their brother and sister, whom they have seen, cannot love God, whom they have not seen' (1 John 4:20).

Traditions and Customs such as Easter and Christmas are celebrations of your union with God. Where it has not been taken over by commercialisation, it is a beautiful time to worship and bring God into your daily life. My family delights in Christmas, we decorate and pour out our love as a worship declaration to Him. Recognising one another and giving gifts is an old tradition as Queen Esther relates, 'that is why rural Jews—those living in villages—observe the fourteenth of the month of Adar as a day of joy and feasting, a day for giving presents to each other' (Esther 9:19).

It might be an obvious statement but there cannot be a reunion unless there had been a previous union. As your Creator, God has known you from the beginning; hence reunion is uppermost in His mind. God is dependable because He does not change. There is a consistency about Him, recorded throughout the Bible and across other areas of evidence, not least evidenced in the faith of His people. God says, "I am the Alpha and the Omega, the First and the Last, the Beginning and the End" (Revelation 22:13).

His Created Light
Light is important for life and was the first element God created when He commanded, "Let there be light" (Genesis 1:3). Without light, there would be no life, as light is as necessary as water and carbon for your existence. For your well being and welfare, the warmth from light is needed.

▲   ▲   ▲

Kelly knew when depression would hit; she smelt it in the air. The smell of summer, a dryness welcoming sun to skin and tantalizing its promise of relaxation was giving way to the smell of autumn. A fresher wind, "change is in the air" it whispered. The trees began to anticipate winter as their leaves change colour, the light shifts and herein lays the problem.

"When the daylight hours reduce and night-time creeps in earlier and earlier I feel miserable", she says, "I sleep a lot more and wonder whether hibernation would be a good idea for humans?"

Kelly's condition has been diagnosed as S.A.D Seasonal Affective Disorder. Researchers have discovered that this condition is seldom found in countries within 30 degrees of the Equator! Like Kelly darkness, lack of warmth and light affects you and I in different ways.

It can be the darkness of nighttime, when sleep patterns are disturbed, either with insomnia or nightmares. If you suffer from either you will know the relief of morning arriving. Usually because 'normal' activity can resume and the darkness often associated with aloneness will change.

First World countries have light (whether artificial or natural) available for everyone 24/7. This is a huge change in social and cultural development, and a symbol of richness in comparison to other countries that have blocks of the day or night without electricity and so experience times of enforced darkness. Consequently, I would like to share 'did you know' moments on light and heat. This is an abridged version, composed largely with thanks to *Bill William* for his writing, *A History of Light and Lighting*.

▲   ▲   ▲

Did you know?
- Caveman in the Neanderthal period drew light and warmth from the sun, with the first man-made source coming from fire. It is

recorded that fires were kindled in the caves of Peking man as early as 400,000 BC.

- Glass (c2500 BC) was made and used.
- The Sundial (c1500 BC) was invented using light to measure time.
- Pythagoras (c582-c500 BC) proposed the understanding of particles to explain the ability to see objects.
- Archimedes (c200 BC) used mirrors to reflect sunlight to ships, setting up a communication system over distance.
- The Pharos of Alexandria (c290-270 BC) is constructed as the first lighthouse. A 440 ft tall building with a fire burning at the top as a beacon to ships approaching from the Mediterranean. Cited as one of the Seven Wonders of the World.
- Aristotle (384-322 BC), Greek philosopher and scientist, believed that the heart was the body's source of heat whereas the brain merely served to cool the blood.
- The candle (c400 BC) was used as the main source of light until the 14th Century, and you may well use them today for atmospheric light. In 1761 AD, 3000 candles were used at the coronation of King George III.
- Alhazen, Roger Bacon and Giovanni Porta (c1038) refined the Camera. They advanced the camera from a small pinhole for light to pass through onto a screen, to one in which it passed through and onto a mirror—humble beginnings for today's digital camera.
- Sir Isaac Newton (1642-1727) whose birthplace Woolsthorpe in Lincolnshire (14 miles from my home) proposed the theory of light and from the use of a prism, the colours of the spectrum. Does this bring back memories of your science lessons?
- Olaf Romer (1675) calculated the speed of light.
- William Herschel (1800), an astronomer, discovered infrared.
- Johann Wilhelm Ritter (1801), a German physicist discovered ultraviolet light.
- Goldsworthy Gurney (1823) discovered limelight. Taking lime, a material used in building he found it glowed brilliantly when

heated by oxygen and hydrogen flames. He then invented the ox-hydrogen blowpipe.

- Thomas Drummond (1826) devised the Drummond Light, based on Gurney's invention, he invented the spotlight or follow spot. London Theatres used this light regularly up until 1910. It gives the origin of the sayings 'being in the lime light' and 'being in the spotlight'.
- John Walker (1827), a druggist, developed the match; you probably have some in your cupboard. They were originally named friction matches and were nicknamed 'Lucifers'.
- Herman Sprengle (1865), a German chemist, pioneered the light bulb.
- Thomas Edison (1874) successfully marketed the electric filament light bulb.
- Samuel P Langley (1880) invented the Bolometer, an instrument to measure light from stars and heat rays from the sun.
- Heinrich Hertz (1887) discovered the relationship between ultraviolet light and electrodes.
- Albert Einsteen (1905) postulated on the theory of relativity and calculated the speed of light as 186,000 miles per second.

All this, and more, from four simple words—God's words—
"Let there be light"!

Appreciating God and benefitting from the above inventions and many more not mentioned helps me not to be blasé when I open my curtains in the morning or flick the light switch. I am also thankful to God for His light shows the Sun, Moon and Stars. There are cosmic phenomena, lightning, the Aurora Borealis and Aurora Australis (the Northern and Southern Lights). I look forward to seeing them live one day. Other tributes are bioluminescent creatures. They form living lights such as fireflies, glow-worms, lantern fish and Atolla jellyfish. All are awesome!

His Warming Light

The other light that you need for your existence is His warming light. God knows your reliance on light, physically, emotionally and spiritually, and how debilitating it is to be without it. Darkness was the ninth plague that He sent as a means to change Pharaoh's heart and release His people from Egypt (Exodus 7-12). For three days, He took away all light from the Egyptians but the Israelites still had light where they lived (Exodus 10:21-23). It was a darkness that penetrated your soul, a physical feeling— like a fog enclosing you in a chilly cloak of invisibility on a dark winter's night. Would it have made you re-think your approach to God?

Another Bible story tells of a person left in darkness. This was Job. Job describes his time separated from God's protection in this way, "How I long for the months gone by, for the days when God watched over me, when his lamp shone on my head and by his light I walked through darkness!" (Job 29:2).

You do not have to be like Job whose separation from God was due to exceptional circumstances. It is different for you and I because God provides His light to disperse all troubling darkness. He tells you that He is the best hiding place to seek refuge when there are problems (Nahum 1:7-10) and that He does not intend to leave you as an orphan (John 14:18).

One day Jesus was speaking in the Temple Courts and He called out to the crowd, "I am the light of the world. Whoever follows me will never walk in darkness, but will have the light of life" (John 8:12).

God does not want you to be separated from Him therefore He sent the Light (Jesus) to come into your life. The Apostle Paul wrote these words to the church in Turkey in which he acknowledges that the past has gone and that, with Jesus, in your life, you are changed—words which still apply to you and me today: 'For you were once darkness, but now you are light in the Lord. Live as children of light' (Ephesians 5:8).

What does it mean to 'live as children of light'? If God is Light then as His child you can shine your own individual light too. Your centre glows when you live in your authenticity and make purposeful plans. The Apostle

Matthew gave the following advice, 'In the same way, let your light shine before others, that they may see your good deeds and glorify your Father in heaven' (Matthew 5:16).

The light—Jesus—chases away the darkness of unhappiness, depression or evil and His warmth flows through you. It melts anything in your mind, body or soul which has been frozen or hardened. It is why this invitation to you to step into God's warming light is urgent.

Your Reunion

The final proof for you is that He knows your name. Your name is already recorded in Heaven (Luke 10:20). To show you that He has not forgotten you, your name is written on the palm of His hands (Isaiah 49:16). Remind yourself of His goodness by reading the Bible aloud and inserting your name where it says I or me. This example uses Daniel 2:22-23:

> 'He reveals deep and hidden things to (add your
> name); He knows what lies in darkness, and light
> dwells with Him. I (add your name) thank and praise
> you, God of my (add your name) ancestors: You have
> given me (add your name) wisdom and power ...'

If you have had an answer to pray, you can adapt the end of verse 23 by taking out 'the dream of the king' and putting in your request instead:

> '... You have made known to me (add your name) what I
> (add your name) asked of you, you have made known to
> me ...' (add your name and the answer He has give you).

This is not being disrespectful or irrelevant it is taking in His word directly into your heart. The Bible was written for you as surely as Jesus was sent to die for you. There is no offending God in this; 'But now, this is what the LORD says, He who created you, Jacob, He who formed you, Israel: "Do not fear, for I have redeemed you; I have summoned you by name; you are mine"' (Isaiah 43:1).

Your special relationship with God is consummated when He writes your name in His book of Life (John 10:28-30). His people will be given a new name written upon a white Stone (Revelation 2:17).

This is all part and parcel of your Deliverance given with the promises of your dazzling God. It is summed up by King David, a man after God's own heart who wrote, 'The Lord is my light and my salvation ...' (Psalm 27:1).

Is God Reunited with Everyone?

The door for deliverance, salvation and reunion is open to everyone but not everyone is prepared or able to step through the door. This is why it is not carte blanche that everyone will be forgiven, or that entry into heaven is automatic. The Apostle John says, "We know that God does not listen to sinners. He listens to the godly person who does his will" (John 9:31). Jesus speaking with the disciples, commissioning and instructing them in their ministry said, 'But whoever disowns me before others, I will disown before my Father in heaven' (Matthew 10:33).

In the book of Hebrews there are verses about people grieving or upsetting the Holy Spirit. It also speaks about those who turn their back on God after having received gifts from Holy Spirit warning, 'It is impossible for those who have once been enlightened, who have tasted the heavenly gift, who have shared with Holy Spirit, who have tasted the goodness of the word of God and the powers of the coming age and who have fallen away, to be brought back to repentance. To their loss they are crucifying the Son of God all over again and subjecting him to public disgrace' (Hebrews 6:4-6).

The final word (naturally) goes to the Apostle John who gave a revelation of heaven, visions of the 'second coming' and describes our final reunion with God. He writes, 'But the cowardly, the unbelieving, the vile, the murderers, the sexually immoral, those who practice magic arts, the idolaters and all liars—they will be consigned to the fiery lake of burning sulphur. This is the second death' (Revelation 21:8).

He Will Be Back

Placards embossed with the words, *the end is nigh* are no longer commonplace; missions to find the Holy Grail or stories of the Fisher King have been relegated to past times. What cannot be relegated is the promise of Jesus that He will be back. He even put this within a personal context, "for I tell you I will not drink again from the fruit of the vine until the kingdom of God comes" (Matthew 26:29 and Luke 22:18). This is remembered when you say Grace or take Communion it is said with the belief that Jesus will return.

There will be a 'second coming'; this time the ferociousness of the battle will make His recognition unmistakable. Jesus did not know when this would be, so to stop speculation he said, "It is not for you to know the times or dates the Father has set by his own authority" (Matthew 24:36, Mark 13:32 and Acts 1:7,). However, the Bible does give indications of what to expect in the time leading up to His return.

One could be the reunion of East and West to fulfil God's promise given to Abraham back in Genesis, 'I will establish my covenant as an everlasting covenant between me and you and your descendants after you for the generations to come, to be your God and the God of your descendants after you' (Genesis 17:7). This could be an interpretation of the words of Pope John Paul II:

In 1998, The Metropolitan John of Pergamon was in discussion with Pope John Paul II. He referred to earlier words spoken by the Pope, 'As Your Holiness has aptly put it some years ago, East and West are the two lungs by which the Church breathes; their unity is essential to the healthy life of the One, Holy, Catholic and Apostolic Church' (Orthodox Research Institute).

A third person believing in the need of a reunion between East and West is James Goll in his important work *Praying for Israel's Destiny*. This would be a generational reunion.

If, this is impossibility for humankind, then nations will wage war on one another. War disturbs the environment to such an extent that natural disasters occur. Mankind is good at destruction and producing wastelands of dust! It may well be only the final intervention of God that can save everyone—by His return.

Open the Door

1. **Remember** a reunion that you have experienced. How did it feel? What were the highlights of the occasion?
2. **Recognise** moments and times of separation. How do you manage separation times from your loved ones?
3. **Describe** your relationship with God and how you discovered the journey that leads to your union with Him?
4. **Decide** if you would like a reunion encounter with God.
5. **Mark** your place on the reunion continuum (put a x on the line in the book) and check again in a year's time.
6. **Define** your mini reunions and talk with friends about them.
7. **Recall** your favourite reunion moment which involved God or when you knew God's presence with you. How has this supported your ongoing relationship?
8. **Reminisce** on the point of your conversion, where were you before God came into your life? Make this part of your testimony and consider baptism if you have not already been baptised.
9. **Demonstrate** God's light in your life. Think about ways to show your shining light and help others to discover theirs.
10. **Personalise** verses from your Bible as a daily reading. Have fun with this and realise that this book is the Living Word from God.
11. **Read** the Believer's Prayer in the Bonus section once more. Commit or recommit yourself to His Service.
12. **Step** into God's warming light today. Ask Him for more of Him.

Step into God's Warming Light

Dear Lord,

Thank you for the reunions you have shown me in my life, with my family, and friends. Please let me live in harmony and union with others. I pray that I can fully know union and amity with You, dear Father God. Please give me more of these glorious experiences and make periods of separation short.

Please fill me with your Holy Spirit and may I have many adventures with You, feeling Your presence upon my life, my plans, and my actions. I pray for the time when I am finally called home to You; for the reunion to be full of joy and happiness, and that I may hear the words, "Well done, good and faithful servant, come share in My happiness and drink wine and break bread with my Son".

Amen.

Your Full Circle

YOUR FULL CIRCLE

When we are no longer able to change a situation, we
are challenged to change ourselves.
VIKTOR E. FRANKL

Travelling Your Full Circle

Life patterns are cyclical, seasons are cyclical, your emotions and learning are cyclical. According to Shakespeare's *Seven Ages of Man*, your life from birth to old age travels a full circle. Unfrozen takes a circular route as reunion is about reconciliation with your past. As you pass through the doorways of hope, healing, love and creation, each one asks you to consider your 'melting point'.

There is little choice as to your birthplace. You cannot choose whether you were born in a country with a cold or a hot climate. However, the condition and attitude of your heart can be chosen. Are your emotions and psyche running hot or cold? It is your choice, whether to live your life's journey and purpose in a balmy temperate way, embracing life with fluidity, or to live in an arctic, glacial manner, becoming unfeeling in your coldness towards others and yourself. You can choose to have a frozen or an unfrozen heart.

Sink Your Boats or Burn Your Bridges

Be brave! Like explorers and leaders of armies, you are in a battle. The weapons of the enemy are the unhealthy 3Ds, disappointments, disillusionment and discouragements. To arrive at the destination of deliverance you need to let go of your past with all its betrayals and fears.

Take a lesson from Cortez, the Spanish explorer, who sunk his ship thus preventing his men from retreating. They could not go back to safety only forward into the new land. In a similar way, the Roman leaders burnt bridges behind them, cutting off any idea of retreating and going back. Can you be as brave by refusing to return to past hurts, by thought, word or deed?

In the shops there are multitudes of 'Keep Calm' motivational products for sale posters, mugs, bags, books and T-shirts, etc. It is seen on any printed surface or item in unique, personalised designs, customised to suit your hobby or work situation. Here is another to add to the craze, 'Keep Calm and Know God will fight for you' (Exodus 14:14).

Trust in the Lord, knowing He guards your back. He will protect your back, and your front and sides too! Remember to put on the armour of God every day to protect you throughout each day (Ephesians 6:10-18). If you are stuck in a frozen state, your view of daily life is dismal. You are in survival mode rather than shining with His light.

Living in a victim rather than a victor lifestyle and the future is seen from a fatalistic approach—'que sera sera' meaning 'whatever will be will be'. This approach 'gives up' and 'gives in', surrendering your own input or belief in making a difference. Whereas, Unfrozen hearts are about savouring each moment, bringing the sweet taste of success, like rich amber nectar, into your life.

The Lies of Life's 3Ds

Together, we have explored the devastation of Life's 3Ds, uncovering the 'lies' of these states of mind. These lies come from only one person who is the 'Father of all lies'. The Enemy's strategy is all about deception, making lies appear real, and distorting your understanding. God's truth frees you from these 'lies'. Jesus' viewpoint on the devil includes a full description of his deceptive and destructive nature (John 8:44). He truly sees him as the Enemy.

You can choose whose child you want to be. I want to hear from God, grow in my understanding of Jesus' teaching, become engrossed in His plans and fulfill my potential. My prayer is that you will choose this way too. The Apostle Paul, in his role as mentor, wrote this to his dear friend, 'Timothy, guard what has been entrusted to your care. Turn away from godless chatter and the opposing ideas of what is falsely called knowledge' (1 Timothy 6:20).

Lies often mirror truth, rather like a one-sided coin. They are clever in their deception, containing an element of truth twisting it slightly to fool you, and so making the 'lies' more believable.

Disappointment Lies
- I am in the right and I am justified in my resentment against that person.
- I am being told this for my own good.
- I am a disappointment.
- You are no good; it would be best if you were to end your life.
- You have made a mistake and no one will forgive you.
- You are hopeless and cannot get anything right.
- It would be best for everyone if you were to run away and hide.
- Criticism will help another person to grow.
- Making tomorrow your total focus today.
- Constructive criticism never hurt anyone.
- Someone I love has rejected me; therefore, I am unworthy of love.
- I have not been healed, meaning that God does not like me or want me to be well.
- He does not listen to my prayer.

Disillusionment Lies
- They are on your side, even when the evidence is to the contrary.
- I can discredit this person because people need to see their faults.
- There is someone better for the job than me.
- I am doing this because I have a higher purpose.
- It is personal.
- On the receiving end of blatant untruth against you.

- A betrayed trust from a friend.
- You feel confused in a situation where previously you had confidence.
- You feel doubt and an unsettling in your spirit preventing you from going forward in a natural positive way.
- The values you hold dear to your heart are shattered by the opinions of others.
- Other people's opinions discount your worth.
- Darkness is good and cannot harm me.
- A false witness giving testimony against you.
- God is not real, he does not exist.
- God is an unjust God and you can curse Him.
- You can have success and it does not matter what it costs you.
- Work hard and give your life to your work.
- Life is all about having the latest gadget and living in luxury.
- Fame and being rich are goals which must be achieved.
- You have a free life without Christ.

Discouragement Lies
- You must have committed evil for this circumstance to be in your life.
- You are a bad person or this would not be happening.
- It is time you 'got over' your problem.
- White lies are OK and do not grow into bigger ones.
- False evidence appearing real.
- Imagining the worst-case scenario.
- If you take a particular action, you will suffer and have a bad experience.
- You have never been any good at this particular activity so why do it now?
- Any worry or doubt.
- You will be hurt if you do this, as you cannot take care of yourself.
- All fear is your enemy and gives you a spirit of fear.

- You can be proud and superior to others because you are better than them.
- Be like us, you do not need to be your own person.
- As a believer, you do not need to make any changes.
- There is no room in God's kingdom for you.
- You will never be reconciled with this person, reunion is impossible.
- Fear of the Lord is outmoded.
- God can lie.
- Hell is unreal.
- Opposition to the Bible, its origins and source.
- God will forgive anybody, even the vilest person; they do not even have to say sorry.

God never lies or indeed changes His mind (Titus 1:1-2 and 1 Samuel 15:29) and it is this hope which you and I can take as an anchor for our souls. It is a sure and steadfast hope (Hebrews 6:18). This means that all His promises are true. He will fight for you just as he fought for King Hezekiah. King Hezekiah ruled between 715-686 BC and was one of the forefathers of Jesus. When King Hezekiah received a particularly nasty letter from a neighbouring warring King, he brought it before Lord. The Lord then went out and put to death a hundred and eighty-five thousand in the Assyrian camp. (2 Kings 19:14-35)

This remains the law of God, that it is He that takes vengeance for His children. Do you have a nasty letter, email or contract that you would like to lay before the Lord? He is the same yesterday, today and tomorrow.

Deliverance Destroys all Lies

The truth is much simpler than a lie; it does not need to go on ad infinitum. The truth just 'is' or is understood as 'I Am' (Exodus 3:14). Be careful what you choose to believe, check it out, and give it the deliverance 'acid' test. Does it match the Holy Spirit's gifts or fruits? 'Therefore do not let what you know as good be spoken of as evil' (Romans 14:16), while the Apostle Peter gives the following great guidance, 'Therefore, rid yourselves of all malice, all deceit, hypocrisy, envy and slander of every kind' (1 Peter 2:1). There are no lies in deliverance, only the promise of salvation—to save your life.

Feel free to add the following to your armour to counteract the lies, in the same way as Jesus had to counteract the lies, when He was tempted in the wilderness (Matthew 4:1-11). Here are the counteracting statements:

Deliverance Truths

- My survival depends on God.
- I am God's dearly loved child; He wants a relationship with me.
- God loves me and He will never leave or forsake me.
- God created me.
- His warming light is nourishment for my body, mind and soul.
- Jesus is the way, the truth and the life.
- I believe in, God the Father, God the Son and God the Holy Spirit.
- It is true that Jesus Christ came to save me, died by crucifixion on a cross, and was resurrected to life with God in Heaven.

Closing Your Circle of Life

Each step you take towards God moves you into the fourth dimension—deliverance. He is stretching out His arms to welcome you home—a huge hug awaits. Can you find your place in His everlasting arms? Never forget that, 'the eternal God is your refuge, and underneath are the everlasting arms' (Deuteronomy 33:27).

Find your melting point and make Unfrozen your way of life. Contact me via the website as I would love to support you in tackling the 3Ds in your life and praise Him for your wins contact me at Ladeyadey.com. Together, you and I can celebrate a new state of being—a natural, relaxed and life-giving reality—called *UNFROZEN*.

YOUR BUOYANT BONUSES

1. THE SINNER'S PRAYER OR YOUR SALVATION PRAYER

Your Invitation

This is a prayer for you to invite Jesus into your life and begin a personal relationship with Him. It is the START of your commitment to a life with God. Please say the prayer below from your heart.

Lord Jesus Christ,
I am sorry for the things I have done wrong in my life.
I ask your forgiveness.
Thank you for dying on the cross for me
to set me free from my sins.
Please come into my life and
fill me with your Holy Spirit and
be with me forever.
Thank you Lord Jesus. Amen.

Follow up this prayer by joining a church, meeting with believers, finding a Christ family that you are comfortable with and who will support your growth in HIM.

If you are already a believer and supporting someone else, praying these words with them please remember that you are now joined with them and have a 'mentoring' role. Expect lots of questions and be ready to carefully nurture your friend as a 'Newbie' in Christ.

There are numerous 'Sinner's Prayers', the Internet cites 423,000 results! I recommend a simple prayer such as this one from *UCB Word for Today* (reproduced with permission).

Note: Free issues of the daily devotional are available for the UK and Republic of Ireland, UCB Word for Today, United Christian Broadcasters, Operations Centre, Westport Road, Stoke-on-Trent, ST6 4JF or www.ucb.co.uk

YOUR BUOYANT BONUSES

2. THE LORD'S PRAYER

How to Pray

One of the first questions a new believer asks is "How do I pray?" Jesus taught the first 101 'how to' in The Lord's Prayer. Below is a version I learnt as a child. Jesus taught us, "Pray then in this way":

Our Father
Who art in Heaven
Hallowed be Thy Name
Thy Kingdom Come
Thy Will be Done
On Earth as it is in Heaven
Give us this Day our Daily Bread
And forgive us our trespasses
As we forgive those who trespass against us
And lead us not into temptation
But deliver us from evil
For Thine is the Kingdom, the Power and the Glory
Forever and ever, Amen
(Matthew 6:9-18 and Luke 11:2-4)

Feel free to personalise this to: My Father, replacing 'our' to 'my' and 'us' to 'me' or 'I'. Alternatively, you can place your name in to personalise it further. It is your prayer to Him and a private prayer. It is also great to say it together with other believers.

YOUR BUOYANT BONUSES

3. PRAYER OF BLESSING FOR OTHERS

Prayer of Blessing

This Prayer of Blessing is effective for melting your heart towards others. In the blank spaces at the start of the blessing, put the name of the person you are thinking about or replace the word you with the name of the person.

I have found that saying the prayer out loud helps to focus my mind on the person I am thinking about. It can be said without the knowledge of the person, I've used this *Prayer of Blessing* in my life when I needed to forgive someone's actions and keep myself away from vengeful thoughts towards them. Bob Oldershaw is a generous and humble gentleman who I have the privilege to call a friend. He welcomes you to use this prayer in anyway that suits you and gives permission for its use.

_____ I bless your eyes that you might see spiritually the things of God. That you might see the wonderful works that HE has done. That the eyes of your understanding will be enlightened and that you might know what is the hope of HIS calling and what are the glorious riches of HIS inheritance in the saints. I bless your eyes that they will no longer be darkened and blinded

by the god of this world, but that you might
be truly set free to see with spiritual eyes.
_____ I bless your heart, that it will be softened
to be receptive towards the things of
God and not of this world, that your heart
will be melted by the love of Jesus.
_____ I bless your ears that they may truly hear the good
news of Jesus Christ. That your ears will be attuned
to the voice of God. That you will hear the still
small voice of God in the quietness of where you
are, as you sleep and as you wake and, hearing His
voice, you will respond and turn towards HIM.
_____ I bless your mind that it will be creative, that
you will have a sound mind. That creativity will
flow and that you will be totally renewed and
refreshed in body, mind and spirit. I break any
power that the enemy has over your life and
that you will be totally released and set free.
_____ I bless the work of your hands that they
may be diligent and creative.
_____ I bless your feet that you might walk a straight path.
_____ I bless you to be released into all the
fullness of God for your life.
_____ I bless you when you rise and when you sleep.
That God will be in your thoughts while you are
awake and that while you sleep you will have
dreams of Jesus and revelations from HIM.
_____ I bless you that you might be released into all the
plans and purposes that HE has for your life.

©2012 Bob Oldershaw

YOUR BUOYANT BONUSES

4. PRAYER OF SAINT BRENDAN

Saint Brendan's Prayer

As I completed the first draft of this book I was sent this prayer by Rev Robert Duerden who in turn had been sent it by his friend in Western Australia. I love how we share God inspired verse. The number of connections within this prayer, written in the first century, with the themes in *Unfrozen*, amazed me, so I had to share it with you, dear Reader.

Lord I will trust you
help me to journey beyond the familiar and into the unknown.
Give me the faith to leave old ways
and break fresh ground with You.

Christ of the mysteries, can I trust you
to be stronger than each storm in me?
Do I still yearn for Your glory to lighten on me?
I will show others the care You have shown me.

I determine amidst all uncertainty always to trust.
I choose to live beyond regret, and let You recreate my life.
I believe You will make a way for me and provide for me,
If only I trust You, and obey.

I will trust in the darkness and know
that my times are still in Your hands.
I will believe You for my future,
chapter by chapter, until all the story is written.

Focus my mind and my heart upon You,
my attention always on You without alteration.
Strengthen me with Your blessing,
and appoint to me the task.

Teach me to live with eternity in view,
Tune my spirit into the music of heaven,
Feed me, and, somehow,
make my obedience count for You.

A little information about Saint Brendan of Clonfert (c 484- c 577). He was an Irishman, regarded as one of the Twelve Apostles of Ireland. He is known for his voyages.

YOUR BUOYANT BONUSES

5. THE TEN COMMANDMENTS

The Commandments

The Ten Commandments were inscribed on tablets of stone by the finger of God. A special box was created to store them, which became known as the Ark of the Covenant and was part of the tabernacle, placed in the Holy of Holies behind a curtain. Servants had to be very careful when transporting the Ark of the covenant from place to place and if they made a mistake it would cost them their lives. This is what happened to Uzzah (2 Samuel 6:7).

Moses recorded the Ten Commandments in Exodus 20:2-17 and Deuteronomy 5:6-21. Most people know the shorter version, which comprises of one sentence for each commandment.

1. You shall have no other gods before Me.
2. You shall not make idols.
3. You shall not take the name of the LORD your God in vain.
4. Remember the Sabbath day, to keep it holy.
5. Honour your father and your mother.
6. You shall not murder.
7. You shall not commit adultery.
8. You shall not steal.
9. You shall not bear false witness against your neighbour.
10. You shall not covet.

The Apostle Matthew records Jesus response regarding the Commandments:

'Hearing that Jesus had silenced the Sadducees, the Pharisees got together. One of them, an expert in the law, tested him with this question: "Teacher, which is the greatest commandment in the Law?" Jesus replied: "Love the Lord your God with all your heart and with all your soul and with all your mind. This is the first and greatest commandment. And the second is like it: Love your neighbour as yourself. All the Law and the Prophets hang on these two commandments"' (Matthew 22:34-40).

APPENDIX A

HIERARCHIES OF NEED

Comparisons

God's Hierarchy of Need—you may have a different list and it is a great exercise to see what you would add or subtract.

See the next page to compare the two structures.

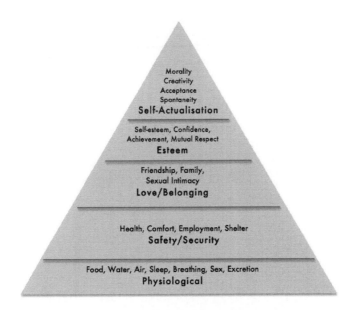

Morality
Creativity
Acceptance
Spontaneity
Self-Actualisation

Self-esteem, Confidence,
Achievement, Mutual Respect
Esteem

Friendship, Family,
Sexual Intimacy
Love/Belonging

Health, Comfort, Employment, Shelter
Safety/Security

Food, Water, Air, Sleep, Breathing, Sex, Excretion
Physiological

Maslow's Hierarchy of Need

Forgiveness
Blessings
Joy, Self-control
Love & Peace
Love thy Neighbour

Wisdom, Understanding,
Counsel, Knowledge
Gifts & Fruits

Baptism, Fasting,
Meditation, Devotion, Favour
Passion for the Bible

Discussion, Communication, Prayer, Hope, Deliverance,
Identity, Purpose and Meaning
Relationship with God

Awe, Reverance, Worship, Praise, Salvation, Faith
Fear of the Lord

God's Hierarchy of Need

APPENDIX B

BECOMING UNFROZEN QUADRANT

Do you want to:

- Overcome the 3Ds in your life?
- Discover your Unique Spirit-filled Personality?
- Move from Victim to Victor?
- Find ways to stop being a 'People Pleaser' and work from your authentic self?
- Step into His Warming Light?

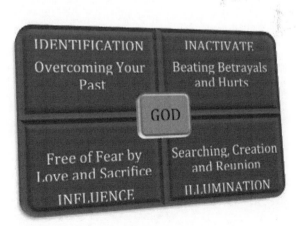

Never again be stuck in your Past.
Learn how to let go and make workable Plans for your life.
Visit Ladeyadey.com

APPENDIX C

BECOMING UNFROZEN BOOTCAMP

Confidence comes from discipline and training.
ROBERT KIYOSAKI

Congratulations!

You've invested in yourself and been brave to explore your 3Ds that life has sent you and know that God can give you the fourth dimension, deliverance from them.

Our website begins a deeper journey to rid yourself of the frozen wastelands of the lies of disappointment, disillusionment or discouragement. Are you stuck in the Past, surrounded by Betrayal, focussing on your Fear or in a continued Search for Him? We would love you to join our growing tribe interested in their spiritual self-discovery by becoming Unfrozen (Ladeyadey.com). We will save you a spot. It's a great way to stay connected, challenged and encouraged.

If you would like additional help planning to break the ice and melt your heart—I'M IN.

We have an experience that's perfect for you and your situation. We call it Becoming Unfrozen.

The purpose is simple—melt your heart by opening the door and stepping into God's warming light. Becoming Unfrozen Bootcamp helps you to customise your P.L.A.N.S.—finding your and God's plans for your life, discover your Unique Spirit-Filled Personality and put on your armour of protection and much more.

Our Becoming Unfrozen Bootcamp range from an online course to an in-person experience of a three-day programme.

This one-of-a-kind experience allows you to process your own situation by letting go of your past and melting into His love for you. I serve as your transforming coach and spend time personally coaching each attendee. Together, we'll craft your Unfrozen Plan of Action and expose the lies of the 3Ds in your live moving to a hopeful and hope filled future leaving the past in the past. Prepare for a life-changing experience.

If you are interested in taking your next step, we have a Becoming Unfrozen Bootcamp perfect for you and your budget. Come and check us out: Ladeyadey.com

BECOMING UNFROZEN BOOTCAMP

ACKNOWLEDGEMENTS

Knowledge is in the end based on acknowledgement.
LUDWIG WITTGENSTEIN

Thank You

It might take a village to raise a child but it takes a team of dedicated supporters to birth a book. Thank you all and let us pray that Unfrozen has a long life, that it is read by many and supports people to fight their 3Ds and know God.

1. *The Holies*
   God
   Jesus
   Holy Spirit who was beside me at each touch of the keyboard and loved an early morning start!
2. *The Family*
   Doris Shaw (my Mum)
   Denis Peter
   Abbirose
   Candice Alicia
3. *The Editors, Proofreaders and Professionals*
   Kary Oberbrunner,
   Rev Robert Duerden, Pat (P.J.) Jacobs and Wendy Oldershaw.
   Keith Loven, Kevin Pouter.

4. *Courageous Characters*

>To the people who were brave enough to have their real names revealed and their stories or opinions put in print. It has given life the chapters, taking dry 'case-studies' into personalised stories. A special thanks to my family, who had no choice but to have their stories retold via my memory.

>Canon Rev Chris Bowater, Rev. Dr. Clifford Hill, Donna Drouin (Poem), Frances Marchant, Glyn and Jane Davies,

>Rev Geoff Larcombe and Dee Larcombe, Kary Oberbrunner, Katharine Welby-Roberts, Kikusaburo (Kiku) Horinouchi, Moira Howes, Nicola Watson, Pauline Dobson, Penel Duerden, and Ted Banks.

>Many thanks to everyone else whose stories or circumstances I have used to illustrated real life happenings and given a pseudonym.

5. *Cheer Leaders or the Leaders of the Cheers*

>Aimee Holland, Carol Radford, Ibolya Read, Lynn Robinson, Manjeet Sidhu, Rosemary Young, and The Igniting Soul Tribe (especially David Branderhorst and Emily Myers)

6. *Inspirational well-know names from the Past and Present*

>Abraham Harold Maslow, Ahmed Osman, Albert Einsteen, Alhazen, Alphonsus Liguori, Professor Amit Sood, Archimedes of Syracuse, Aristotle the Stagirite, Saint Augustine of Hippo, Bear Grylls, Bill William, Bruce Wydick, C S Lewis, Carl Jung, Charles Dickens, Cheryl Ford, Cortez, Craig and Charlie Reid, Dr David Prezant, Donald Miller, Dorothy Parker, Sir Edmund Hillary, Dr Gary Chapman, Geoffrey Chaucer, George MacDonald, George Orwell, Giovanni Porta, Goldsworthy Gurney, Dr Harry Harlow, Harold Ramis, Heinrich Hertze, Herman Sprengle, Hippocrates, HRH King George III, HRH Prince Charles, Dr Hunter Doherty 'Patch' Adams, Idina Menzel, Sir Isaac Newton, Ivan Petrovich Pavlov, Jacques Yves Cousteau, James Goll, Rev Jarrod Cooper, Jason Vale, Javier

Sotomayor, Joanna Chu, Johann Wilhelm Ritter, John Lee Hancock, John Lennon, John Steinbeck, John Walker, Johnny Cash, Kerry Kirkwood, Kristen Anderson-Lopez, Lady Mary Heath, Laine Rutledge, Loretta Young, Ludwig Wittgenstein, Mahatma Gandhi, Martin Luther King Jr, Dr Martin Seligman, Martin Sheen, Metropolitan John of Pergamon, Michael Oher, Mother Teresa, Sir Nicholas Winton, Olaf Romer, Oskar Schindler, Phil Keaggy, Pope Gregory (6th Century), Pope John Paul II, Pythagoras, Rev Dr Rowan Williams, Robert d'Isigny, Robert Laurence Binyon, Robert Lopez, Robin Williams, Roger Bacon, Rose Kennedy, S J Tuohy, Samuel P Langley, Shelia Burnford, Sidney Sheldon, Rev Steve Holmes, Steven Pressfield, Terence, Thomas Aquinas, Thomas Drummond, Thomas Edison, Todd Albertson, Tony Hancock, Victor Hugo, Dr Viktor Emil Frankl, Walt Disney, Walter Bradford Cannon, William Herschel, William Holman Hunt, William Shakespeare, and William the Conqueror.

Inspirational Organisations or Places

Christian Artists Together, Christian Dental Fellowship, Keble College Oxford, Lawyers Christian Fellowship, Manchester Art Gallery, Parachute Regiment, Pharos of Alexandria, Royal Marines, SS Canberra, St Paul's Cathedral, The Armed Forces Christian Union, Transform Work UK, and Worship Academy.

7. *Church Family*

Dr Adrian and Heather Holdsworthy, Annie Munro, Betty and Dave Jeal, Bob Oldershaw, Caroline Simm, Frank Cliff, Keith and Diane Maltby, Kate Bunn, Kay and John Pratchard, Laura Tattershall, Richard and Charlotte Thorneycroft, Sarah & Guy Salmon, Sue and Ted Banks, Sue Tuck, Val Dowle. Members of New Life Church Ministries (Sleaford).

8. *Musketeers*

It is amazing that we have transformed from a staff team to friends. Ten years after moving on, we still meet regularly, tracking each other's lives and celebrating the highs and supporting each other in the lows.

Angela Bassett, Ruth Brown, Carolyn Cliff, Tish Cook and Nicola Watson.

9. *Social Media Matters*

The Tribes which boast me in my author journey.

Dan Harrison, Derek Halpern, Grant Baldwin, Loral Langemeier, Joanna Martin, Joanna Penn, Joe Bunting, Joyce Meyer, Shawn Coyne, and Veronica Pullen.

10. *Finally*

Thanks to—YOU—Dear Reader

REFERENCES

*There are dozens of references to God in the
Scriptures for every one to the figure of Satan.
This reflects a sometimes forgotten theological truth
that the devil is by no means God's counterpart.
He is a creature, not the Creator.*
JOHN ORTBERG

Bible Translations:

New International Version (NIV): HOLY BIBLE, NEW INTERNATIONAL VERSION. Copyright © 1973, 1978, 1984 by International Bible Society. Used by permission and THE HOLY BIBLE, NEW INTERNATIONAL VERSION®, NIV® Copyright © 1973, 1978, 1984, 2011 by Biblica®.

New Living Translation (NLT): The *Holy Bible*, New Living Translation, copyright ©1996, 2004, 2007. Used by permission of Tyndale House Publishers, Inc., Carol Stream, Illinois 60188.

New King James Version (NKJV): New King James Version®. Copyright © 1982 by Thomas Nelson. Used by permission. All rights reserved.

The Message: Copyright © 1993, 1994, 1995, 1996, 2000, 2001, 2002 by Eugene H. Peterson

TPT: are taken form The Psalms: Poetry on Fire, The Passion Translation®, copyright © 2014. Used by permission of BroadStreet Publishing Group, LLC, Racine, Wisconsin, USA. All rights reserved.

Front Matter

Keller Helen, *Brainy Quote Helen Keller,* September 2015, (BrainyQuote. com, Xplore Inc), http://www.brainyquote.com/quotes/quotes/h/helenkelle109209.html.

The Faith Mission Bible College, 1986, http://www.fmbc.ac.

The Order of St Leonard, 2009, http://www.orderofstleonard.org.

Breaking the Ice

Hillary Edmund, BBC Home, July 2015, http://news.bbc.co.uk/onthisday/hi/dates/stories/january/4/newsid_4051000/4051107.stm.

Sheldon Sidney, Search Quotes, July 2015, http://www.searchquotes.com/quotation/%27%27A_blank_piece_of_paper_is_Gods_way_of_telling_us_how_hard_it_to_be_God.%27%27_/695904.

Scriptures

New International Version (NIV): 1 Samuel 16:7, Psalm 139:13, Proverb 4:23, Jeremiah 1:5, Philippians 1:6.

Research

Disney Enterprises Inc, adapted by Sarah Nathan and Sela Roman, From the Movie Disney *Frozen Book of the Film* (Paragon Books Ltd), 2013.

Disney Walt, *Frozen,* DVD, Directed by Chris Buck and Jennifer Lee, (Walt Disney Studios Home Entertainment (UK & Ireland), a division of The Walt Disney Company Ltd) Burbank CA, 2014

Oberbrunner Kary, *Day Job to Dream Job: Practical Steps for Turning your Passion into a Full-Time Gig,* (Baker Books), 2014.

Pinsky Mark I, *Disney's Frozen might be the most Christian Movie Lately,* (Theguardian.com), 25 January 2014, http://www.theguardian.com/commentisfree/2014/jan/25/disney-frozen-religious-allegory

Robinson Belinda, Mail Online: Girls' name 'Elsa' makes the list of 500 most popular names in the United States for the first time in over 100 years—thanks to Disney movie Frozen, 5 July 2015, (Daily Mail), http://www.dailymail.co.uk/news/article-3150136.

Tsiaras Alexander, *The Invision Guide to a Healthy Heart*, (HarperCollins Publishers), 2005.

Wartick J W, *Disney's "Frozen"- A Christian Reflection*, (Blog: J.W. Wartick - "Always have a Reason"), 3 February 2014, http://jwwartick.com/2014/02/03/disneys-frozen.

1. Your Persuasive PAST

Binyon Robert Laurence, *For the Fallen, and Other Poems*, (Leopold Classic Library), 2015.

Cash Johnny, Johnny Cash. BrainyQuote.com, Xplore Inc, 2015, http://www.brainyquote.com/quotes/quotes/j/johnnycash188009.html.

Dickens Charles, *Great Expectations* (Wordsworth Editions) 1992.

Martindale Wayne & Root Jerry, *The Quotable Lewis - An encyclopaedic selection of quotes from the complete published works of C S Lewis* (Tyndale House Publishers, Inc) 1989.

Oberbrunner Kary, Kary Oberbrunner Igniting Souls, http://www.karyoberbrunner.com.

Orwell George, *1984,* (Penguin, New Ed edition), 1998.

Wikipedia Contributors, *Carl Jung*, September 2015, (Wikipedia, The Free Encyclopedia), https://en.wikipedia.org/w/index.php?title=Carl_Jung&oldid=682194885

Wikipedia contributors, *Disappointment Island*, (Wikipedia, The Free Encyclopaedia), August 2015, https://en.wikipedia.org/w/index.php?title=Disappointment_Island&oldid=677508077.

Discography
Lopez Robert, Anderson-Lopez Kirsten, Emanuel Kiriakou, Menzel Idina, *Let it Go,* Walt Disney, Wonderland Music Company, CD, 2013.

Scriptures
New International Version (NIV): Deuteronomy 32:7, Psalm 23, Proverbs 23:7, Ecclesiastes 3:1, Daniel 2:21, Joel 1:3, 2:28, Acts 2:17, 2 Peter 3:8.
New King James Version (NKJV): Proverbs 29:18.

New Living Translation (NLT): Isaiah 55:8.

The Message: Ecclesiastes 11:7-8, Ephesians 1:4.

Research

Carthey Caroline, *BLOG: What to do when Church Leaders disappoint You*, July 2015, http://vanderbloemen.com/insights/what-to-do-when-church-leaders-disappoint-you.

Kushner Harold S, *When Bad Things Happen to Good People*, (Avons Books), 1981.

Wikipedia Contributors, *Let It Go (Disney Song)*, September 2015, (Wikipedia, The Free Encyclopedia), http://en.wikipedia.org/wiki/Let_It_Go_(Disney_song)#Charts.

2. Your Huggable HOPE

Andersen Hans Christian, Pedersen, Vilhelm (Illustrator) Paull, H B (Translator), *The Snow Queen*, (Hythloday Press), 2013.

Dante Alighieri, *The Devine Comedy*, (Acheron Press), 2012.

Davies Glyn, Davies Jane, *Education for Life*, 1999 http://www.educationforlife.net.

Fort Alice B, Kates, Herbert S, *Minute History of the Drama* (Grosset & Dunlap, New York), 1935.

Frankl Viktor E, *Man's Search for Meaning. An Introduction to Logotherapy*, (Beacon Press, Boston), 1963-2007.

Frankl Viktor, *The Official Website of the Viktor Frankl Institute Vienna*, June 2015, http://www.viktorfrankl.org/e/chronology.html.

Grylls Bear, *Mud, Sweat and Tears - The Autobiography*, (Channel 4), 2012.

Grylls Bear, *True Grit, The Epic True Stories of Heroism and Survival that have Shaped my Life*, (Bantam Press), 2013.

Hancock Tony, *Tony Hancock Famous Last Words* at The Phrase Finder, June 2015, http://www.phrases.org.uk/quotes/last-words/suicide-notes.html.

Highfield Roger, Science Editor, *DNA Survey finds all humans are 99.9% the same*, The Telegraph 10 December 2002 (Telegraph Media Group

Limited), http://www.telegraph.co.uk/news/worldnews/northamerica/ usa/1416706/DNA-survey-finds-all-humans-are-99.9pc-the-same.html.

King Jr Martin Luther, Brainy Quote, (BrainyQuote.com, Xplore Inc), August 2015, http://www.brainyquote.com/quotes/quotes/m/martinluth297522.html.

Maslow Abraham H M, *A Theory of Human Motivation* (Wilder Publications), 2013.

Pope Alexander, *Essay on Man* (Pitt Press Series), 1913.

ten Boom Corrie and Betsie, *Ten Boom Museum*, September 2015, http:// tenboom.org.

Terence (Publius Terentius Afer), Theatre Database, 2002, (TheatreDatabase. com) http://www.theatredatabase.com/ancient/terence_001.html.

Unknown, *Mind for Better Mental Health: Cognitive Behavioural Therapy (CBT)*, September 2015, (Mind), http://www.mind.org.uk/information-support/drugs-and-treatments/cognitive-behavioural-therapy-cbt/#. VfO1ep1VhBc.

Wikipedia Contributors, *Hope*, June 2015 (Wikipedia, The Free Encyclopaedia) https://en.wikipedia.org/w/index.php?title=Special: CiteThisPage&page=Hope&id=678957151

Wikipedia Contributors, *The Snow Queen*, September 2015 (Wikipedia, The Free Encyclopaedia), https://en.wikipedia. org/w/index.php?title=Special:CiteThisPage&page=The_Snow_ Queen&id=678768274.

Williams Robin, Variety, *Police: Robin Williams' Death Due to Hanging*, Wilco.com, September 2015 (Verity Media, LLC a subsidiary of Penske Business Media LLC), http://variety.com/2014/film/news/ robin-williams-death-due-to-hanging-1201281095.

Wydick Bruce, Glewwe Paul, Rutledge Laine, *Does International Child Sponsorship Work? A Six-Country Study of Impacts on Adult Life outcomes*, (Journal of Political Economy), April 2013.

Discography

Keaggy Phil, Albertson Todd, *Thank You for Today*, Strobie Records, Phil Keaggy, CD, 2006, Album: *Dream Again*.

Research

Disney Walt, *Frozen*, DVD Directed by Chris Buck and Jennifer Lee, (Walt Disney Studios Home Entertainment (UK & Ireland), a division of The Walt Disney Company Ltd), Burbank CA 2015.

Scriptures

New International Version (NIV): Psalm 139:14, Proverbs 23:18, 24:14, Matthew 17:20, Acts 20:35, Romans 8:24-25, Hebrews 11:1.
New King James Version (NKJV): Proverb 23:7.
New Living Translation (NLT): Daniel 9:23.
The Message: Proverb 24:26, Isaiah 40:11.

Research

Carpenter Ed, *Research Shows Dramatic Benefits to International Child Sponsorship* September 2013, (University of San Francisco), https://www.usfca.edu/news/research-shows-dramatic-benefits-international-child-sponsorship, , University of San Francisco.

3. Your PLANS

Liguori Alphonsus, Brainy Quote, BrainyQuote.com, September 2015, (Xplore Inc), http://www.brainyquote.com/quotes/quotes/a/alphonsusl358220.html.
Rostron Hilda Isabel, (Editor), *The Lord's Prayer and other prayers for children*, (Ladybird Books Ltd), 1961.
Solomon Charles, *Art of Frozen*, (Chronicle Books), 2013.

Scriptures

New International Version (NIV): Genesis 50:20, Judges 6:36-38, Psalms 20:4, 138:8, Proverbs, 3:5-6, 16:3, Jeremiah, 1:5, 29:11, Matthew 14:22-34, 19:26, 20:1-16, 25:12, Mark 1:17, John 4:6-42,14:16-17, 14:26, 17:11, romans 2:11 Ephesians 4:14, 4:18, Revelation 22:17.
New King James Version (NKJV): Matthew 4:19.
New Living Translation (NLT): Matthew 16:18, 1 Peter 4:10.
The Message: Matthew 5:5, 2 Peter 1:10-11.

Research

Adey Ladey, God's Gifts: What are the Gifts and Fruits of the Holy Spirit and Where to find them in the Bible, (Pink Parties Events Ltd), 2013.

Ramis Harold, Rubin Danny, *Groundhog Day*, DVD, Directed by Harold Ramis, (Columbia Pictures Corporation), Illinois, USA, 1993.

Williams Rowan (Most Revd), Facebook, June 2015, https://www.facebook.com/pages/Most-Revd-Rowan-Williams/9599364033.

4. Your BETRAYAL, Beaten!

Scriptures

New International Version (NIV): Psalm 55, Proverb 18:21, Zechariah 11:12, Matthew 24:10, 26:35, 26:75, Mark 14:10, 14:72, Luke 22:48, John 13:21, 18:10, Romans 1:29-32, Ephesians 6:12.

New King James Version (NKJV): Luke 1:37.

New Living Translation (NLT): Psalms 41:9, 56:8, Matthew 24:12, 26:38-45, Romans 3:13, 2 Corinthians 7:10.

5. Your HEALING: Self-help and God-help

Adams Hunter Doherty "Patch" Dr., Sept 2015, http://www.patchadams.org.

Adams Patch M.D., Mylander Maureen, *Gesundheit! Bringing Good Health to you, the Medical System and Society through Physician Service, Complementary Therapies, Humor, and Joy*, (Healing Arts Press), 1996.

Edelman David, Zabell Elizabeth, *Diabetes Daily*, June 2015, http://www.diabetesdaily.com.

Kennedy Rose, *Brainy Quote*, BrainyQuote.com, September 2015, (Xplore Inc), http://www.brainyquote.com/quotes/quotes/r/rosekenned597699.html.

Kirkwood Kerry, *The Power of Blessing* (Destiny Image® Publishers, Inc), 2010.

Mayer Robinson Kara, reviewed by Smith Michael W, *10 Surprising Health Benefits of Sex*, 2005-2015, (WebMD LLC), http://www.webmd.com/sex-relationships/guide/sex-and-health.

Rosman Paul Dr, Edelman David, *Thriving with Diabetes: Learn how to take charge of your body to balance your Sugars and improve your lifelong Health - featuring a 4-step plan for long-lasting success,* (Fair Winds Press) October 2015.

Steinbeck John, *Travels with Charley,* (Penguin Classics, New Ed edition), 2001.

Vale Jason, *Turbo-charge Your Life in 14 Days,* (Thorsons) 2014.

Wikipedia Contributors, *Hippocrates,* September 2015, (Wikipedia, The Free Encyclopaedia) https://en.wikipedia.org/w/index.php?title=Special:CiteThisPage&page=Hippocrates&id=679804414.

Young Loretta, Brainy Quote, BrainyQuote.com, September 2015, (Xplore Inc) www.brainyquote.com/quotes/quotes/l/lorettayou195832.html.

Scriptures

New International Version (NIV): Genesis 4:24, Exodus 17:8-15, 17:12, Numbers 6:24-26, Deuteronomy 32:35, 1 Chronicles 4:10, 2 Chronicles 20, Psalms 31:5, 37:8, Proverb 19:5, Ecclesiastes 4:12, Ezekiel 36:26, Matthew 6:9-18, Mark 16:19, Luke 11:2-4, 23:34, 23:46, 6:28, John 8:12, Acts 7:55-56, Romans 8:1-2, 8:31, 8:34, 12:20, Galatians 5:22-23, Ephesians 6:10-18, Philippians 4:6, 2 Timothy 4:16, 1 Peter 4:7-11.

The Message: Matthew 18:21-22.

Discography

Lopez Robert, Anderson-Lopez Kirsten, Emanuel Kiriakou, Menzel Idina, *Let it Go,* Walt Disney Wonderland Music Company, CD, 2013.

Reid Craig, Reid Charlie George MacKay, Kevin Guthrie, Antonia Thomas, Freya Mavor, Gale Telfour Steven, *Over and Done With,* Neapolitan Music, Sunshine on Leith CD, 2013.

Research

Godwin Roy, *Ffald-y-Brenin,* 2015, (The Ffald-y-Brenin Trust Ltd), http://www.ffald-y-brenin.org.

Unknown, *NHS Choices; Benefits of love and sex*, September 2015, (Gov UK), http://www.nhs.uk/Livewell/Goodsex/Pages/ValentinesDay.aspx.

Uvnas-Moberg Kerstin, The Oxytocin Factor: Tapping the Hormone of Calm, Love and Healing, Pinter & Martin Ltd; (2nd edition), 2011.

6. Your Heart under His PROTECTION

Cousteau Jacques Yves, Brainy Quote, BrainyQuote.com, September 2015, (Xplore Inc), http://www.brainyquote.com/quotes/quotes/j/jacquesyve204394.html.

D'Ambrosio Marcellino Dr, *The Crossroads Initiative*, September 2015, http://www.crossroadsinitiative.com/library_author/13/st._gregory_the_great.html.

Gandhi Mahatma, *History The Creators of World of Tanks Biographies Mahatma Gandhi*, 2014, (AETN UK), http://www.history.co.uk/biographies/mahatma-gandhi.

Grylls Bear, *Bear Grylls*, August 2015, http://www.beargrylls.com.

Guinness Book of Records, *Best Selling Book of non-fiction*, *The Bible*, 2015, (Guinness World Records), http://www.guinnessworldrecords.com/world-records/best-selling-book-of-non-fiction.

Kastenbaum Robert, Encyclopedia.com, *Seven Deadly Sins* Macmillan Encyclopaedia of Death & Dying, 2002, (The Gale Group Inc), http://www.encyclopedia.com/topic/Seven_deadly_sins.aspx.

Lewis Michael, *The Blind Side: Evolution of a Game*, (W W Norton & Company), 2007.

Mother Teresa, *Mother Teresa of Calcutta Centre Official Site*, 2015, http://www.motherteresa.org/layout.html.

Pope Gregory, Demacopoulos George E (Translator), *The Book of Pastoral Rule*, (St Vladimir's Seminary Press, US), 2007.

Tuohy Leigh Anne, *Leigh Anne*, June 2015, http://www.leighannetuohy.com.

Tupper Frederick, *Chaucer and the Seven Deadly Sins*, (Nabu Press), 2010.

Wellman Jack, *What Christians Want to Know*, 2010-2015, (Telling Ministries LLC), http://www.whatchristianswanttoknow.com/what-are-the-seven-deadly-sins-and-their-meanings.

Wikipedia Contributors, *Seven Deadly Sins*, September 2015, (Wikipedia, The Free Encyclopaedia), https://en.wikipedia.org/w/index. php?title=Seven_deadly_sins&oldid=679884770.

Scriptures
New International Version (NIV): Genesis 28:15, 2 Samuel 11:27, Job 42:7-17, Psalms 34:17, 51:11, 91:1, 91:4, 91:11, 121:2, Isaiah 33:6, 59:2, Jeremiah 31:3, Habbakkuk 1:3, Malachi 3:6, Matthew 4:11, 6:19-18, 10:30, 27:46, Luke 11:2-4, 12:7, 21:18, John 10:10, 14:1-32, 21:25, Romans 8:31, 1 Corinthians 12:7, Ephesians 2:8, 6:11-18, Hebrews 4:12, 11:8, 13:8, 1 Peter 1:3-7.

Discography
Redman Matt, *10,000 Reasons (Bless the Lord)* (Kingsway) CD 2011 Album: 10,000 Reasons.

Research
Bond Anthony, ISIS release video showing 30 Ethiopian Christians being Beheaded.   Vid shows 15 men being beheaded and another group being shot in their heads, 20 April 2015, (SEARCH Society to Explore and Record Christian History), http://www. thechristians.com/?q=content/isis-release-video-showing -30-ethiopian-christians-being-beheaded.

Christians in Crisis, 21 Egypt Christians Praised God Before Beheadings, Source: BosNewsLife, 18 February 2015, (Christians in Crisis International Ministry), http://www.christiansincrisis.net/latest-news/ 3754-21-egypt-christians-praised-christ-before-beheadings.html.

Hancock John Lee, *The Blind Side*, DVD, Directed by John Lee Hancock, (Warner Bros Pictures Summit Entertainment), Universal City, California, 2009.

7. Your Enemy? FEAR is not Your Enemy

365 Fear Nots, *Biblical Truths on Fear and Worry*, September 2015, (365fearnots.com), http://365fearnots.com.

Breazeale Ron, *Catastrophic Thinking—Catastrophic Thinking is ruminating about irrational worst-case outcomes,* March 2011, (Psychology Today - Sussex Publishers, LLC), https://www.psychologytoday.com/blog/in-the-face-adversity/201103/catastrophic-thinking.

Breazeale Ron, Duct Tape Isn't Enough: Survival Skills for the 21st Century, (Bounce Back USA), 2009.

Bülow Louis, *Oscar Schindler His List of Life,* 2015-17, http://www.oskarschindler.com.

Busey Gary, Good Reads, *(Goodreads Inc),* http://www.goodreads.com/author/quotes/3335268.

Cannon Walter Bradford, *Bodily Changes in Pain, Hunger, Fear, and Rage: An Account of Recent Researches Into the Function of Emotional Excitement,* (Appleton-Century-Crofts), 1929.

Fear Factor, *Fear Factor, Best Friends aired Sept 27 2004 on NBC,* NBC 2001-2006, 2011-, (A Division of NBCUniversal), http://www.tv.com/shows/fear-factor/best-friends-364833.

Gardner David, Passengers' terror as flight attendant screams 'We're going to crash!' and rants about 9/11 before being wrestled to the ground by colleagues, 09 March 2012, (Daily Mail), http://www.dailymail.co.uk/news/article-2112819/Flight-attendant-screams-going-crash-rants-9-11-wrestled-ground.html.

Grylls Bear, *Brainy Quote,* BrainyQuote.com, August 2015, (Xplore Inc), http://www.brainyquote.com/quotes/quotes/b/beargrylls512993.html.

Heath Mary, *The History of flight - Aviation Quotes,* September 2015, http://www.456fis.org/THE_HISTORY_OF_FLIGHT_-_AVIATION_QUOTES.htm.

Holmes Steve, *Alabaster Jar - Stories of Female Leaders from Church History,* August 2015, http://alabasterjar.org.uk.

Jake Kanter, Broadcast Now, March 2015, (Media Business Insight Ltd), http://www.broadcastnow.co.uk/news/bbc-acquires-female-aviator-film/5083969.article.

Jamieson Jeremy P, *Public Speaking and Stress Responses,* 15 June 2013, (Psychology Today), https://www.psychologytoday.com/blog/the-many-sides-stress/201306/public-speaking-and-stress-responses.

311

Seligman Martin E O, *Learned Optimism: How to Change Your Mind and Your Life*, (Vintage: Reprint Edition), 2006.

Seligman Martin E O, *Master Resilience Training Programme*, 2015, Penn (University of Pennsylvania), Positive Psychology Centre, http://www.ppc.sas.upenn.edu and http://www.positivepsychology.org/services/resilience-training-army.

Sood Amit, *Journal of General Internal Medicine, Stress management and resilience training among Department of Medicine faculty: a pilot randomized clinical trial*, (Society of General Internal Medicine), 2011.

Sood Amit, *Train Your Brain, Engage Your Heart, Transform Your Life*, (Morning Dew Publication), 2010.

Sotomayor Javier, *Guinness World Records*, 2015, http://www.guinnessworldrecords.com/world-records/highest-high-jump-(male).

The Scout Association, *Scouts Association*, July 2015, *(The Scouts Association)*, http://scouts.org.uk/about-us/organisational-information/chief-scout/?gclid=CMT0p-ab6ccCFUFmGwoduesKKg.

Welby-Roberts Katharine, *Blog: A conglomerate of yodeling hippopotami*, 2015, http://katharinewelby.com/2015/04/13/fear.

Wikipedia Contributors, *Fight-or-flight response*, Wikipedia Contributors, August 2015, (Wikipedia, The Free Encyclopaedia), http://en.wikipedia.org/wiki/Fight-or-flight_response.

Wikipedia Contributors, *Mary Lady Heath*, July 2015, (Wikipedia, The Free Encyclopaedia), https://en.wikipedia.org/wiki/Mary%2C_Lady_Heath.

Wikipedia Contributors, *RMS Titanic*, August 2015, (Wikipedia, The Free Encyclopaedia), https://en.wikipedia.org/w/index.php?title=RMS_Titanic&oldid=678477390.

Winton Nicholas Sir, *Sir Nicholas Winton*, 2015, http://www.nicholaswinton.com.

Scriptures

New International Version (NIV): Exodus 20:3-17, Deuteronomy 5:6-21, 10:12, 31:8, 31:12-13, Joshua 4:24, 24:15, 1 Samuel 12:24, 23:5, 2 Samuel 23:2-5, 2 Chronicles 19:7, 26:5, Job 28:28, Psalms 19:8, 25:14, 34:9, 128:1,

Proverbs 1:7, 9:10, 10:27, 14:27, Ecclesiastes 12:13, Isaiah 11:3, 30:27, 48:17, Daniel 6:1-28, 10:7-8, Matthew 4:11, 6:14, 7:11, 10:1, 10:28, 26:7, Mark 12:31, 14:3, Luke 7:37, 11:2-4, 11:13, John 3:16, 12:3, 13:34-35, 14:1, 14:6, 14:12-14, 14:27, 15:12, 18:36, 20:22, Acts 9:31, Ephesians 6:12, Galatians 5:1, Ephesians 1:5, 2 Timothy 1:7, James 1:17, 1 Peter 5:7, 1 John 4:18.
New King James Version (NKJV): 1 Corinthians 9:26.
The Message: Nahum 1:2-3.

Research

Bamber Paul, *Gestalt in Action,* 2015, http://www.gestaltinaction.com/library/essays/fear.

Brace Robin A, *Yes, the Heart Really can "Think" and have Emotions!,* 2006, http://www.ukapologetics.net/biblicalheart.htm.

Dr Jeremy, *Medic Guide, What's the difference between adrenaline (epinephrine) and noradrenaline (norepinephrine)?* July 2008, , http://medicguide.blogspot.co.uk/2008/07/whats-difference-between-adrenaline.html.

Good Therapy, *Helping People find therapists. Advocating for ethical therapy. Fear,* 2007-2015, (GoodTherapy.org), http://www.goodtherapy.org/therapy-for-fear.html.

Jeffers Susan, Feel the Fear and Do it Anyway: How to turn your Fear and Indecision into Confidence and Action, (Vermilion), 2007.

Klein Sarah, *Adrenaline, Cortisol, Norepinephrine: The Three Major Stress Hormones, Explained,* 2013, (Huffington Post), http://www.huffingtonpost.com/2013/04/19/adrenaline-cortisol-stress-hormones_n_3112800.html.

Lightie Kimberly, *All about Icebergs,* 2011, (The Ohio State University, College of Education and Human Ecology), http://beyondpenguins.ehe.osu.edu/issue/icebergs-and-glaciers/all-about-icebergs.

Mills Samuel, *Trusting in Jesus ... is living your life with Hope,* September 2015, http://www.trusting-in-jesus.com/Commandments-of-Jesus.html.

Unknown, *Institute in Basic Life Principles: What are the commands of Christ? 49 Commands of Christ,* September 2015, (Institute in Basic Life Principles), http://iblp.org/questions/what-are-commands-christ.

Unknown, *Psalm 30:5 - Joy Comes in the Morning,* 2004, (aBible.com), http://www.abible.com/devotions/2004/20040527-0940.html.

8. Your LOVE will find a Way

Blum Deborah, *The Monkey Wars,* (Oxford University Press), 1994.

Ford Cheryl V, The Pilgrim's Progress Devotional: A Daily Journey Through The Christian Life, (Crossway Books), 1998.

Harlow Harry F, Interview, (Pittsburgh Press-Roto, 1974.

Harlow Harry F, The Nature of Love, (American Psychologist, vol 13, 573-585), 1958.

Hugo Victor, *Les Misérables,* (Penguin Classics - Reprint edition), 1982.

Solomon Charles, Art of Frozen, (Chronicle Books), December 2013.

Webb David, All About Psychology, Jun-05, http://www.all-about-psychology.com.

Scriptures

New International Version (NIV): Psalm 23:4, Proverb 17:17, Song of Solomon 8:6, John 15:12-13, Acts 9:4-6, 9:7-19, 13:6-12, 26:11-12, 1 Corinthians 13:1-8, Titus 3:1-2, 1 John 4:16, 4:19-20, 1 Peter 4:8.

Research

Bible Questions Answered, *Why did Paul change his Name from Saul to Paul,* September 2015, http://bibleq.net/answer/1923.

Chapman Gary, *The 5 Love Languages,* September 2015, www.5lovelanguages.com.

Fact Slides, *Your Heart,* September 2015, http://www.factslides.com/s-Your-Heart.

Hugo Victor, *Les Misérables,* (Penguin Classics - Reprint edition), 1982.

Kreeft Peter, *Perfect Fear Casts out all 'luv',* 2015, www.peterkreeft.com.

Reckart Cohen G, *The Cross is a Symbol of Jewish Intolerance and Hate against Jesus and Messianic Believers*, 2015, http://jesus-messiah.com/apologetics/jewish/cross-hate.html.

Sanskrit Dictionary for Spoken Sanskrit, *Spoken Sanskrit.de Dictionary*, September 2015, http://www.spokensanskrit.de/index.php?tinput=love.

Unknown, *Bakers Evangelical Dictionary of Biblical Theology - Heart*, September 2015, (Bible Study Tools), http://www.biblestudytools.com/dictionary/heart.

9. Your SACRIFICE

Frankl Viktor, *Philosophical and Psychological Foundations of Education*, September 2015, http://www.uky.edu/~eushe2/quotations/frankl.html.

Kasperkevic Jana, *The Guardian: Two Teachers in Louisiana Movie Theater Shooting Hailed as Heroes*, 24 July 2015, *(Guardian News and Media Ltd)*, http://www.theguardian.com/us-news/2015/jul/24/louisiana-movie-theater-shooting-heroes-teachers-lafayette.

Lomax Eric, *The Railway Man*, (Vintage), 2014.

Pressfield Steven, *Brainy quote Steven Pressfield*, September 2015, (BrainyQuote.com, Xplore Inc), http://www.brainyquote.com/quotes/quotes/s/stevenpres679154.html

Pressfield, Steven, Coyne Shawn (Editor), *The War of Art: Break through the Blocks and Win your Inner Creative Battles*, (Black Irish Entertainment LLC), 2012

ten Boom Corrie, Buckingham Jamie, *Tramp for the Lord: The Years after 'The Hiding Place'*, (Hodder & Stoughton), 2005.

ten Boom Corrie, Shrill Elizabeth, Sherrill John, *The Hiding Place*, (Hodder & Stoughton), 2004.

Scriptures

New International Version (NIV): Isaiah 53, Romans 12:1-2, 1 Corinthians 13:5-6, 15:58, 2 Corinthians 10:5, 1 John 2:2, 3:16, 4:10.

Research

Far East Prisoner of War Community (FEPOW) Community, September 2015, http://www.fepow-community.org.uk.

Pressfield Steven, *Steven Pressfield Online*, July 2015, http://www.stevenpressfield.com.

10. Your SEARCHING Heart

Adams, Douglas, *The Hitch Hikers Guide to the Galaxy*, (William Heinemann), 1995.

Clouston Eriend and Boseley Sarah, *From the archive, 14 March 1996*, September 2015, (theguardian), http://www.theguardian.com/theguardian/2013/mar/14/dunblane-massacre-scotland-killing.

Drouin Donna, *The Spirit was there* April 2012

Gumbel Nicky, *Alpha*, September 2015, (Holy Trinity Brompton Church), http://www.alpha.org.

Keble College, Oxford, *Holman Hunt painting at Keble College, Oxford*, August 2015, (Keble College, Oxford), http://www.keble.ox.ac.uk/about/chapel/chapel-history-and-treasures.

Lewis C S, *Mere Christianity*, (William Collins), 2012.

Manchester Art Gallery, *Pre Raphaelite Tour*, August 2015, (Manchester Art Gallery), http://manchesterartgallery.org.

Miller Donald, Brainy Quote, August 2015, (Xplore Inc), http://www.brainyquote.com/quotes/quotes/d/donaldmill523588.html.

Samples Kenneth R, *Reasons to Believe, Augustine of Hippo (part 1of 2); from Pagan, To Cultist, To Skeptic to Christian Sage*, September 2015, (Reasons to Believe), http://www.reasons.org/articles/augustine-of-hippo-part-1-of-2-from-pagan-to-cultist-to-skeptic-to-christian-sage.

Sheen Martin, *Hear it First*, August 2015, http://www.hearitfirst.com/blog/9-famous-christian-actors.

St Augustine, Benignus O'Rourke Fr (Translator), *Confessions*, (Darton, Longman and Todd Ltd), 2013.

St Paul's Cathedral, *Holman Hunt painting at St Paul's Cathedral*, August 2015, (The Chapter of St Paul's Cathedral), https://www.stpauls.

co.uk/history-collections/the-collections/collections-highlights/the-light-of-the-world.

Wikipedia Contributors, *Dunblane School Massacre*, September 2015, (Wikipedia, The Free Encyclopedia), https://en.wikipedia.org/w/index.php?title=Dunblane_school_massacre&oldid=677960077.

Wikipedia Contributors, *The Light of the World (painting)*, September 2015, (Wikipedia, The Free Encyclopaedia), https://en.wikipedia.org/w/index.php?title=The_Light_of_the_World_(painting)&oldid=661972567

Wikipedia Contributors, *William Holman Hunt*, September 2015, (Wikipedia, The Free Encyclopaedia), https://en.wikipedia.org/w/index.php?title=William_Holman_Hunt&oldid=673630685.

Scriptures

New International Version (NIV): 1 Kings 19:13, Psalm 139, Proverb 8:17, Ezekiel 34:11, Micah 1:3-4, Matthew 7:8, 17:20, 19:24, Mark 10:25, Luke 15:4-31, 18:25, 1 Corinthians 6:12, Hebrews 11:6, 1 John 4:2, 4:19, Revelation 3:20.

New King James Version (NKJV): 1 Kings 19:12, Matthew 16:26.

New Living Translation (NLT): James 4:8.

The Message: Ephesians 3:17.

The Passion Translation (TPT): Psalm 139:7-12.

Research

Deo Gloria Trust, *What is Contact for Christ?* September 2015, (Contact for Christ), http://deo-gloria.co.uk/cfc.php.

Got Questions, *What does it mean that God speaks in a still small voice?* September 2015, (Got Questions Ministries), http://www.gotquestions.org/still-small-voice.html.

11. Your Heart, His CREATION

Bowater Chris, Townsend Stuart, *Worship Academy,* 2015, (Worship Academy), http://www.worship-academy.com.

Christian Dental Fellowship, 2015, http://www.cdf-uk.org.

Drouin Donna, Gibson Glenda, *Christian Artists Together,* 2007, http://www. christianartiststogether.co.uk.

Edwards Sharon, *When Walt Disney came to Lincolnshire,* 27-Dec-12, *(BBC),* http://www.bbc.co.uk/programmes/p01349c2.

Goodreads, *George MacDonald,* 01 July 2015, (Goodreads Inc), http://www.goodreads.com/quotes/499420-i-would-rather-be-what-god-chose-to-make-me.

Lawyers' Christian Fellowship, 2015, (Lawyers' Christian Fellowship), https://lawcf.org.

Milmo Cahal, *Death of an Asylum Seeker: the tragic story of the eritrean teenager killed just as he made it to Britain,* 09 December 2014, (The Independent), http://www.independent.co.uk/news/uk/home-news/death-of-an-asylum-seeker-the-tragic-story-of-the-eritrean-teenager-killed-just-as-he-made-it-into-britain-9913284.html.

Prezant David J, *Faculty Profile: David J Prezant M.D.,* September 2015, (Albert Einstein College of Medicine), http://www.einstein.yu.edu/faculty/2422/david-prezant.

Saint Augustine, *Brainy Quote,* BrainyQuote.com, August 2015, (Xplore Inc), http://www.brainyquote.com/quotes/quotes/s/saintaugus384153.html.

The Armed Forces Christian Union, September 2015, (AFCU), http://www.afcu.org.uk.

Transform Work UK, 2003, http://www.transformworkuk.org.

Unknown, *What does the Bible say about the Second Coming of Jesus?* September 2015, (Christian Bible Reference Site), http://www.christianbiblereference.org/faq_secondcoming.htm.

Wikipedia Contributors, *Norton Disney,* September 2015, (Wikipedia, The Free Encyclopaedia), https://en.wikipedia.org/w/index.php?title=Norton_Disney&oldid=678392709.

Zamosky Lisa, *A legacy of illnesses from 9/11,* 05 September 2011, (Los Angeles Times), http://articles.latimes.com/2011/sep/05/health/la-he-911-wtc-cough-20110905.

Scriptures
New International Version (NIV): Genesis Chapters 1 & 2, Exodus 2:25, Deuteronomy 8:19, Proverb 16:18, Isaiah Chapter 53, Hosea 13:6, Zechariah 12:10, Mark 13:32-33, Luke 2:1-7, John 14:3, 2 Corinthians 9:7, Galatians 4:4.
The Passion Translation (TPT): Psalm 139:1-6.

Research
Ayad Daniel, Blog: Why did God send Jesus when He did?, September 2015, https://danielayad.wordpress.com/2012/06/21/why-did-god-send-jesus-when-he-did.

Farias Bert, The Sign of Christ's Coming: A Vision given to Oral Roberts, (Charismanews), http://www.charismanews.com/opinion/the-flaming-herald/51037-the-sign-of-christ-s-coming-a-vision-given-to-oral-roberts.

Got Questions, What does it mean that God sent Jesus in the "fullness of time"? Why did God send Jesus when He Did?, September 2015, (Got Questions Ministries), http://www.gotquestions.org/fullness-of-time.html.

Livability, Choices for Disabled People, September 2015, (Livability), http://www.livability.org.uk.

New Shopper, Asylum Seekers cling to bottom of Coach from France, September 2015, (A Gannett Company), http://www.newsshopper.co.uk/news/10688443.Asylum_seekers_cling_to_bottom_of_coach_from_France.

Ryle J.C., Jesus Came at the Perfect Time? September 2015, http://www.jesus.org/birth-of-jesus/roman-world/jesus-came-at-the-perfect-time.html.

Ryle, J.C., The Gospel of Luke, (CreateSpace Independent Publishing Platform), 2014.

Silas, Christ's Crucifixion, July 2015, http://www.answering-islam.org/Silas/crucified.htm.

unknown, Christianity in Britain: Constantine and Augustine, 27 April 2011, http://www.bbc.co.uk/religion/religions/christianity/history/uk_1.shtml.

12. Your Heart's REUNION

Burnford Shelia, *The Incredible Journey*, (Vintage Children's Classics), 2013.

Goll James W, *Praying for Israel's Destiny - Effective Intercession for God's Purposes in the Middle East*, (Sovereign World Ltd), 2005.

HRH Prince of Wales, The Official Website of The British Monarchy, September 2015, (The Royal Household - Crown), http://www.royal.gov.uk/thecurrentroyalfamily/theprinceofwales/theprinceofwales.aspx.

Lewis C S, *The Pilgrim's Regress*, (Fount), 1977.

Parker Dorothy, *The Collected Dorothy Parker*, (Penguin Classics, (New Ed), 2001.

Pope John Paul II, *UT UNUN SINT On Commitment to Ecumenism*, May 1995, (Libreria Editrice Vaticana), http://w2.vatican.va/content/john-paul-ii/en/encyclicals/documents/hf_jp-ii_enc_25051995_ut-unum-sint.html.

Royal Marines, September 2015, (Royal Navy MOD), http://www.royalnavy.mod.uk/our-organisation/the-fighting-arms/royal-marines.

SS Canberra, *SS Canberra The Return, July 11,1982*, (You Tube), https://www.youtube.com/watch?v=LTdfIQLT07U.

The Parachute Regiment, September 2015, (Crown), http://www.army.mod.uk/infantry/regiments/23304.aspx.

Unknown, Death has lost its Sting, Go Song, August 2015, (Gosong.net), http://gosong.net/death_has_lost_its_sting.html.

Wikipedia Contributors, *Augustine of Hippo*, September 2015, (Wikiquote), https://en.wikiquote.org/w/index.php?title=Augustine_of_Hippo&oldid=2002433.

Wikipedia Contributors, *Chesterton G K*, September 2015, *(Wikipedia, The Free Encyclopaedia)*, https://en.wikipedia.org/wiki/G._K._Chesterton.

Williams, Bill, *The history of Light and Lighting*, 1999, http://www.mts.net/~william5/history/hol.htm.

Scriptures

New International Version (NIV): Genesis 1:3, 17:7, 25:9, Exodus Chapters 7-12, 10:21-23, Esther 9:19, Job 29:2, Psalms 27:1, 150:1-6, Proverbs

16:9, 30:18-19, Isaiah 11:2, 25:8, 43:1, 49:16, Daniel 2:22-23, Hosea 13:14, Joel 2:28, Nahum 1:7-10, Malachi 3:7, Matthew 3:16-17, 5:16, 6:6, 10:33, 18:2-6, 18:20, 19:6, 24:36, 26:29, Mark 1:35, 9:36-37, 10:13-16, 13:32, 16:16, Luke 10:20, 15:6-7, 22:18, John 3:3-5, 8:12, 9:31, 10:28-30, 14:18, 14:2-3, Acts 1:7, 2:17, 2:38, 2:42, Romans 6:4, 14:12, 1 Corinthians 15:54, 2 Corinthians 3:17, Ephesians 5:8, 1 Timothy 2:8, Titus 2:12-13, Hebrews 6:4-6, 13:4, James 1:5, 5:16, 1 John 1:3, 3:15, 4:20, Revelation 21:4, 21:8, 22:13, 2:17.

New Living Translation (NLT): Matthew 18:6.

The Message: Ephesians 3:20.

Research

Chapman Gary, The 5 Love Languages: The Secret to Love that lasts, (Moody Press), 2015.

Frost Robert, The Road Not Taken, Dover Publications Inc.; Rep Una edition, 2002.

Got Questions, *Why is God going to give us a white stone with a new name?* September 2015, (Got Questions Ministries), http://www.gotquestions. org/white-stone-new-name.html.

Lee Nicky & Sila, *The Marriage Course*, 2015, (Holy Trinity Brompton), http:// www.relationshipcentral.org.

Servan-Schreiber David, Healing Without Freud or Prozac. Natural approaches to curing Stress, Anxiety and Depression, (Rodale International Ltd), 2005.

Unknown, *Rejoicing in Heaven*, 18 February 2012, (Grace Thru Faith), https:// gracethrufaith.com/ask-a-bible-teacher/rejoicing-in-heaven.

Full Circle

Elizabethan Era, *Hernando Cortes*, September 2015, http://www.elizabethan-era.org.uk/hernando-cortes.htm.

Frankl Viktor E, *Man's Search for Meaning. An Introduction to Logotherapy*, (Beacon Press, Boston), 1963-2007.

Shakespeare, William, *As you like it*, (Wordsworth Editions), 1993.

Scriptures
New International Version (NIV):   Exodus 3:14, 14:14, Deuteronomy 33:27, 1 Samuel 15:29, 2 Kings 19:14-35, Matthew 4:1-11, John 8:44, Romans 14:16, Ephesians 6:10-18, Hebrews 6:18, 1 Timothy 6:20, Titus 1:1-2, 1 Peter 2:1.

Research
Southon Mike, *Biblical Theology in Action: Every Battle in the Bible*, September 2015, (Constantly Reforming), https://constantlyreforming.wordpress.com/every-battle-in-the-bible.

Your Buoyant Bonus

2. The Lord's Prayer

Scriptures
New International Version (NIV): Matthew 6:9-18, Luke 11:2-4

3. The Sinners Prayer or Your Salvation Prayer
The UCB Word for Today, United Christian Broadcasters, Operations Centre, Westport Road, Stoke-on-Trent, ST6 4JF or www.ucb.co.uk free issues of the daily devotional are available for the UK and Republic of Ireland, http://www.ucb.co.uk/word-for-today.html, 2015.

4. Prayer of Saint Brendan
Ewing Phil, *Blog: Blue Eyed Ennis: St Brendan The Navigator,* September 2015, http://blueeyedennis-siempre.blogspot.co.uk/2012/05/st-brendan-navigator.html.
Wikipedia Contributors, *Brendan,* September 2015, (Wikipedia, The Free Encyclopaedia), https://en.wikipedia.org/w/index.php?title=Brendan&oldid=681044419.

5. The Ten Commandments

Bennett, *Life, Hope & Truth: 10 Commandments List*, September 2015, (Church of God, a Worldwide Association Inc), https://lifehopeandtruth.com/bible/10-commandments/the-ten-commandments/10-commandments-list.

Scriptures

New International Version (NIV): Exodus 20:2-17, Deuteronomy 5:6-21, 2 Samuel 6:7, Matthew 22:34-40.

Appendices

Kiyosaki Robert, *Brainy Quote Robert Kiyosaki*, September 2015, (BrainyQuote.com, Xplore Inc), http://www.brainyquote.com/quotes/quotes/r/robertkiyo450847.html.

Acknowledgements

Wittgenstein Ludwig, *Brainy Quote Ludwig Wittgenstein*, September 2015, (BrainyQuote.com, Xplore Inc), http://www.brainyquote.com/quotes/quotes/l/ludwigwitt165051.html

General Research and Interesting Websites

365 Promises, September 2015, (Father Heart Communications), www.365promises.com.

BBC Radio Lincolnshire, *Nicola Gilroy Show - The Lunch Bunch,* September 2015, (BBC), http://www.bbc.co.uk/radiolincolnshire

BBC Radio Lincolnshire, *Radio Station Facebook Page,* September 2015, (BBC), https://www.facebook.com/bbclincolnshire

Bunting Joe, *Great Creative Writers are Serious about their Writing. Are you?* 1999, (The Write Practice), http://thewritepractice.com.

Gill John, Exposition on the Bible, April—September 2015, (Biblos.com), http://www.biblehub.com.

Mansel Martin H, Bible Quotation Collection, (Lion Publishing plc), 1999.

Minter Kelly, Wherever the River Runs: How a forgotten people renewed my hope in the Gospel, (David C Cook), 2014.

Shakespeare, William, *As you like it,* (Wordsworth Editions), 1993.

Swindoll Chuck, Hope Again: When Life Hurts and Dreams Fade, (Thomas Nelson), 1997.

Thesaurus.com, *Roget's 21st Century Thesaurus, Third Edition,* 2009, (Philip Lief Group), http://www.thesaurus.com.

Unknown, *Bible Versions and Translations,* 2014, http://www.biblestudytools. com.

Unknown, *Open Bible info,* 2001, (Crossway Bibles, publishing ministry of Good News Publishers), http://www.openbible.info.

ABOUT THE AUTHOR

Writing a Book is an adventure in itself—life-changing
LADEY ADEY

Short Biography

Ladey is someone who has battled with personal and professional disappointments, disillusionments and discouragements and found the door which opened to HIS warming light. This has been achieved through spiritual healing based on forgiveness and blessings on those who, unintentionally, (in the main) hurt her and others.

This book is about her and others' journey who have been hurt by life's disappointments, disillusionment and discouragements which translate into life's challenges and life's stuff. She believes you need to be the true YOU in everything that God intended.

Interwoven is her passion for God, her love for modern culture and music. Often it will be a phrase from songs or writings that jumps out and makes her write. She is known for thinking 'outside the box'. One colleague joked,

"The problem with Ladey is she doesn't even see the box, let alone work outside it!" and other said,
"When most people think about their lives and plan for new roads, usually starting small, Ladey has already planned a motorway or a freeway!"

What is one person's problem is another's solution and advantage, and Ladey believes it is important not to let other people's opinions define You.

Ladey is an accomplished Author, Speaker, Trainer and Passionpreneur. She is a regular on local radio, BBC Lincolnshire's "lunch bunch". She is an avid conference speaker and workshop leader with a unique style ensuring that people's life stories are heard. Determined to support people in their journey to move forward and heal from their life's 3Ds. She has empathy with hurting people. A believer in tough love she can be quite blunt in her quest to move people on from 'victim' status to 'victor' status enabling them to embrace HIS healing power and warming light.

Ladey lives in Lincolnshire, UK and is married to her darling, Denis – they met in their teens and have seen married life in the Military, were baptized on the same day and have had many God adventures together. They have two adult daughters, Abbirose and Candice, who have contributed to this book. They share their mother and father's humour, love of music, dancing, card and board games plus a passion for life.

Previous Writings:
God's Gifts—An Introduction what are the Gifts and Fruits of the Holy Spirit and Where to find them in the Bible (Kindle Edition) on Amazon

Contact me
Twitter: ladey_adey
Facebook: www.facebook.com/becomingunfrozen
Ladeyadey.com

Printed in Great Britain
by Amazon.co.uk, Ltd.,
Marston Gate.